# Praise for
# *A Different Way*

"*A Different Way* is a genuine treasure and superb work in spiritual formation. I kept turning the pages and discovering sparkling gems of wisdom. Mining deep into Christian history, Hall brings insights into living in the way of Jesus that are exceedingly relevant to our times. I highly recommend it."

—Richard J. Foster, author of *Celebration of Discipline*
and *Learning Humility*

"Too often, we can become lost, distracted, and confused, drawn down unhelpful paths, forgetting the way forward. In this helpful and practical guide, Hall returns us to the path of Jesus, showing how to stay the course through well-worn spiritual disciplines, which ultimately inspire love."

—Bishop Robert Barron, founder of Word on Fire and
bishop of the Diocese of Winona-Rochester

"Hall has a vast knowledge of spiritual formation, practical theology, desert spirituality, and life. This is a transparent, praxis-filled book that draws from the wisdom of a well-lived life."

—Gary W. Moon, MDiv, PhD, founding executive director
of the Martin Institute and Dallas Willard Center at
Westmont College and author of *Apprenticeship with
Jesus* and *Becoming Dallas Willard*

"Hall is one of the wisest, most grounded Christians I know. He dares us to live as if Jesus meant the stuff he said."

—Shane Claiborne, author of *The Irresistible Revolution* and
*Rethinking Life*

"I hope this wonderful book touches many hearts like it has touched mine!"

—Richard J. Mouw, PhD, president emeritus of
Fuller Theological Seminary

"This book is a warm welcome letter inviting all readers into a life with Jesus. Hall offers a winsome way in for the curious nonbeliever and a refreshingly honest voice for those who already believe. Drawing on the spiritual practices of Christians throughout history, Hall shows us with beautiful realism what a Christ-shaped life can be like."

—Rebecca Konyndyk DeYoung, Calvin University,
author of *Glittering Vices*

"A gift and a revelation. Hall is searingly honest and has known deep wounds in life. It is because of this and his great learning that he is able to help us find the deep way of Jesus. I cannot imagine anyone not being helped by this guide."

—John Ortberg, author of *Water-Walking* and
*The Life You've Always Wanted*

"You have in your hands a rare treasure! Hall describes vividly for us the vision of 'a graced life of faithfulness to Jesus, and love for God and neighbor' in a way that evokes within us a passionate desire to reach out for it."

—Trevor Hudson, author of *Seeking God*

"A close friend of Jesus and seasoned traveler on the good way, Hall offers readers glimpses of stunning vistas and wise counsel on how best to navigate the journey into an ever-deepening friendship with Jesus. Standing as we are at a crossroads, Hall provides desperately needed guidance for our times."

—Miriam Dixon, coauthor of
*Meditations on the Birth of Jesus*

"If you are searching for God and looking for an expert guide to an encounter with Jesus that resists our caricatures and understands our struggles, I highly recommend engaging *A Different Way*."

—Rev. Joel Elowsky, PhD, director of the Center for the
Study of Early Christian Texts, Concordia Seminary

"Deeply moving, authentic, helpful, edifying, and transformative, full of grace and truth. This is must reading for truly following Jesus in a different way, with love and joy."

—Siang-Yang Tan, senior professor of clinical psychology at
Fuller Theological Seminary, senior pastor emeritus of First
Evangelical Church Glendale, and author of *Counseling and
Psychotherapy: A Christian Perspective*

"*A Different Way* is ultimately a presentation of what authentic conversion to Jesus Christ looks like in our day. I am grateful to Hall for giving us this treasure that I intend to share with many."

—Bishop Edward J. Weisenburger,
Diocese of Tucson, Arizona

"Both timely and critical: calls us back to the very roots of following the way of Jesus Christ. Hall himself is that rarest of writers: with a razor-sharp mind and a soft and tender heart. I commend him and his message to you without reservation."

—Pete Greig, founder of 24–7 Prayer International and author of *Red Moon Rising* and *Dirty Glory*

"If you long to learn how to walk in step with Jesus, I can think of no better guide."

—Carolyn Arends, recording artist, author, and director of education at Renovaré

"If you are looking for a signpost that points you back to or further along the Jesus way, truth, and life, you might expect it to look a bit unlike what you've seen before. It'll point to *A Different Way*."

—Steve L. Porter, executive director of the Martin Institute for Christianity and Culture at Westmont College, professor of spiritual formation and theology at Biola University, and editor of the *Journal of Spiritual Formation & Soul Care*

"With humor, transparency, scholarly insight, the gifts of a winsome storyteller, and a heart lovingly opened to the kingdom of God, Hall invites us to cast off our distorted views of God. You will laugh and cry and meander a bit too. It is the equivalent of an annual checkup for the soul!"

—Juanita Campbell Rasmus, speaker and author of *Learning to Be*

"What a marvelous summary of the Christian faith! What a compelling invitation into the Christian life! Following Hall's recommendation, I read, I paused, and I reflected. I am a better Christian as a result."

—Evan B. Howard, professor of Christian spirituality at Fuller Theological Seminary and author of *Praying the Scriptures*

"Hall's new book is a breath of fresh air in the spiritual formation literature, for it grounds its direct and practical wisdom in the fundamentals of Christian theology in a way that few other books do."

—Steven D. Boyer, professor of theology at Eastern University and coauthor of *The Mystery of God*

"What Hall shares here is gold passed through the fire of cruciform faithfulness into the shape of our human God."

—Cherith Fee Nordling, PhD, associate professor at the Robert E. Webber Institute for Worship Studies and Regent College

# A Different Way

—

## Recentering the Christian Life Around Following Jesus

—

# Christopher A. Hall

HarperOne
An Imprint of HarperCollinsPublishers

FIRST EDITION

Library of Congress Cataloging-in-Publication Data is available upon request.

ISBN 978-0-06-320754-7

23 24 25 26 27  LBC  5 4 3 2 1

To the Renovaré staff: Carolyn Arends, Justine Olawsky, Nathan Foster, Brian Morykon, Melanie Gillgrist, Monty Harrington, Kim Lownes, Melody Leeper, and Grace Pouch. Valued colleagues, but much more importantly, my pals.

# Contents

# A Different Way

# Introduction

What it means to be a Christian today can get confusing. We read of declining church numbers and multiple scandals, or that the fastest growing religious affiliation today is "none." Christians are better known for what they are against or for whom they dislike or hate, rather than for what they are for or do. It is easy to get the idea that Christians are those desperately holding on to outdated beliefs and practices, who are afraid of the future and wish things would go back to "the way things used to be."

But all those impressions would miss what should be the main point of what it means to be a Christian. I understand why this is confusing. For those seeking an explanation for how we got into this situation, this is not that book. Instead, this book is my invitation to readers, whether Christian or not, whether church attenders or not, to recenter how we understand what it means to be a Christian in the way it was originally meant. My hope is not merely to provide a Catholic or Protestant or Orthodox interpretation, but one most Christians through the centuries would affirm.

Jesus offers us the ability to live a different way. This is not different just to stand out, but different in a way that fills us with longing, a sense of goodness and joy with a deep resonance within us that this is how things were meant to be. Following this way should be the foundation for what it means to be a Christian.

This book is for those who haven't foreclosed on God's existence, even though they may be skeptical that reliable knowledge of God is possible. Or for folks who have not left the Christian faith behind but sense that their lives with Jesus are misaligned or decentered. I'm offering these seekers an opportunity to recenter their journey with Jesus.

But it is also for Christian folks who sense a gap between their words about Jesus and the reality of their lives. As one mentor expressed to me, the gold of our lives too often fails to support the currency of our words. These believers long for greater congruence between their words and actions. They long for their lives to ring true, not tinny. They desire to become better people and are eager to learn how. The want to walk more faithfully in Jesus's footsteps. They want to get back on track. So this book may serve as a reminder of why we do what we do and what we should be about.

Considering a different way with Jesus may involve significant changes in how we act or understand God, ourselves, or the world. Recentering may make us uncomfortable as the terrain of our world shifts. Yet taking a new journey, walking a new path, can also be exhilarating. The quest to discover new lands has motivated, indeed driven, human explorers across thousands of years. Interior landscapes offer themselves for our exploration and can generate that same exhilaration.

So, in *A Different Way* I invite you to navigate your life with Jesus as your guide, a way I have found meaningful and compelling over the multiple decades I have been traveling this path. My hope is to provide a road map for you to take such a journey.

This book offers you something worth considering. What's the worst thing that could happen? You spend a few hours with Jesus—the greatest teacher in human history—your knowledge of his teaching and life deepens, and you continue on your way.

Perhaps, though, by spending time with Jesus a different way will open for you. Picture a door swinging open that you had imagined forever locked, a portal into a more fulfilling, flourishing life. This book may provide the key. Why foreclose on that possibility?

The vast panoply of human tragedy sometimes overwhelms us; we struggle to reconcile our pain and sadness with the possibility of God's goodness, power, and love. Yet isn't one last pondering of Jesus's life and teaching worth the effort? So much hangs in the balance.

## Reflection Questions

*A Different Way* ponders the issues, longings, and questions we often address, experience, or raise in our search for a good life, a life lived well with God. This is not a mere intellectual exercise, as if thinking correctly is all we need to master. Living a different way involves the whole being: thoughts, words, deeds, and so on. That is why I have included "Pause and Reflect" sections in each chapter to stimulate your own pondering and questioning. Some are prayers; some are questions for journaling. These exercises will be found in the "Pause and Reflection" boxes. These reflection questions are my invitation to slow down and to consider deeply the issues being discussed so they seep into your life and consciousness.

They are rest areas for you to pause and catch your breath. As you rest with Jesus, you may sense an opportunity for a conversation, much like the Samaritan woman who talked with Jesus at the well in John 4. She never expected to encounter a Jewish teacher willing to speak with her; an unexpected discussion and exploration of her life's story ensued.

She met Jesus at Jacob's well in Sychar, a Samaritan town. She often drew water in the heat of the day, hoping to avoid women who knew of her checkered history. Jesus saw her. He talked with her. He asked her questions. And he received her questions with great interest, just as he's interested in your questions—and your life.

So, as you read *A Different Way*, go slow. Walk through the book at the pace of Jesus, a man who had so much to do yet never seemed hurried or frantic. When I pose a reflection question, take time to consider it. Chew on the question like a cow chews on its cud. It may be a question you've been asking yourself for a long time or a question you've wanted to pose to God but didn't dare ask.

Jesus loves questions. I'm sure he has some he wants to ask you. And he is more than willing to receive the ones you want to ask him. Our questions—and those of Jesus—illuminate key road signs for us as we travel a different way with Jesus. So if you sense road signs like STOP AND LISTEN, YIELD, STEEP GRADE, SHARP CURVE AHEAD, FOLLOW THIS WAY, CROSSROAD, or SAFE TO PASS, please pay attention. I recommend keeping a journal as you read to document these moments so you can return to them and consider more deeply all the steps along the way.

## A Thematic Road Map

Here's the thematic road map of *A Different Way*. Roughly the first half of the book maps the lay of the land as we recenter our path with the different way of Jesus. We'll learn to reorient ourselves by asking a series of key questions:

- What's God like?
- What does it mean to be God's precious image-bearer?

- Why did God create us with bodies?
- What does it mean to be an embodied self or soul?
- Does God love us?
- If so, why is life so difficult, and sometimes profoundly tragic?
- What does God desire for us as we live through our gift of years?
- What is God offering us?
- What is God asking of us?
- How might a clearer understanding of time and the time we inhabit in human history help us navigate our journey with Jesus?
- What opposition can we expect to encounter as we travel with Jesus toward our true home?

The second half of the book looks at specific *practices* of Jesus and how these practices informed and shaped how he lived his different way and nurtured his relationship with the one he called Father. This is the deeply practical side of the book, though the first half is far from abstract. You'll find chapters on learning to read the Bible into your heart; on the mystery of prayer; on slowing, solitude, and silence; on learning how to live toward a life of simplicity; and on learning to be honest with God about the darkness that can inhabit our hearts.

The final chapter focuses on what I call "misery markers" and "beacon lights" in our spiritual lives and hopefully brings our journey together to a wise and helpful conclusion.

Throughout *A Different Way* I encourage you to practice walking in step with Jesus, at a pace neither faster than his nor slower than he desires. He wants to walk through our lives with us. We are his fellow pilgrims, traveling light, heading toward home. If we learn to walk in Jesus's footsteps, as demanding and occasionally painful as the road may be, by God's grace we'll reach the end of our journey smiling and in good shape.

Wise travel with Jesus, though, requires willing attentiveness to him as our trustworthy guide and companion. Sometimes the winds on our journey will blow hard, thunder will erupt, and clouds will descend. Occasionally we'll be tempted to yell, "Lord, this can't possibly be the right direction." Yet, if we trust in our own personal GPS, sooner or later it will lead us into trouble. We'll swerve off course and predictably run into roadside misery markers. They hurt. I write about these markers quite a bit in the last chapter.

Jesus offers us his faithful companionship and direction on a different way from that followed by the crowd, and he lovingly provides us with beacon lights to keep us on course. In a moment, I'll share with you one beacon light whose radiance dispelled darkness that had enveloped me as a young man.

And so, in this book I offer you Jesus's different way. I have been traveling with him for many years and found him trustworthy and wise. He has been a good, reliable friend. He offers his footsteps to you to walk alongside him. "Come travel with me," I hear him calling to us all. "My path is for you, too."

As we welcome Jesus's offer of a different way, as we learn to trace his footsteps, to slip into his shoes, healing will slowly seep into our wounded feet. We may walk with a limp, but we'll be walking strong and true. I see him reaching out his hand to you. Grasp it firmly. He wants to walk with you on *a different way*.

## Uncle Bob: A Beacon Light

I thought it might be helpful for you to hear how I first discovered this different way. A troubling and sad aspect of my early life's story was my attraction to violence and the dark side of life. This pull toward darkness began when I was around six. I recall my mom's concern as she watched me draw airplanes. Most had swastikas on the vertical stabilizer. "Oh, honey, you don't want to draw those." But I did. For some reason I still can't fully explain, the evil represented by the swastika resonated in my very young heart.

As I grew older, the lure of darkness strengthened. Sometimes I did violent things. My actions were shameful. The memory of them still hurts. In my teens, I was increasingly drawn to violent movies. Horror films were especially appealing.

My uncle Bob played a special role in my life during these troubling years. When I was with him, the draw to darkness receded, and I felt more peaceful. I still have the New Testament he gave me as I entered UCLA at the age of eighteen. He could see I was a searching, frustrated, angry young man. God seemed distant, inaccessible, incomprehensible. Old, ingrained habits constantly snapped at my heels. It was a discouraging, perplexing time for me.

Many weekends I'd drive up the coast from LA to Uncle Bob and Aunt Ern's house in Portola Valley, sometimes showing up unexpectedly. They always had a spare room for me. I'd hunker down with earphones clamped to my head, shutting out the world, listening to the Doors for hours on end. I'd show up for meals and sometimes disrupted the peace by voicing my displeasure with God, Christians, and the world in general. "If Christians really believed what they say is true, surely they'd be living differently! Jesus's life and teaching may be true. The lives of those who claim to follow him don't look like his."

I pointed my finger at others, but in the recesses of my heart, I knew my life was out of kilter, off balance, twisted, curved in on itself. In my more honest moments, I sensed that the cracks I so eagerly condemned in others' lives were more than matched by the crevasses in my own soul.

Uncle Bob listened patiently to my rants. He took my questions seriously. He was willing to argue with me, but in such a way that I never felt attacked, demeaned, or condemned.

I wonder if my uncle knew how closely I was watching him. Uncle Bob was far from perfect, yet his life was attractive and compelling, even beautiful. As I pondered how he lived, Uncle Bob's beacon light beamed in Jesus's direction. My uncle's generosity, love, and acceptance created in me a deep desire to find a different way. From that push I eventually discovered that goodness and light were more appealing than evil and darkness, but it was a journey, not an instant change. That is why following Jesus is called a way and not just a destination. And the first step is deciding to embark on the way Jesus is inviting us to follow.

Recently I ran across the acronym VUCA, whose four letters stand for *volatile, uncertain, complex,* and *ambiguous.*[1] These four words characterize the world we now inhabit. In our globalized world, we are standing in three feet of gasoline, terrified that someone will drop a match. Is it possible to live a loving, stable, centered life after the pattern of Jesus in our volatile, unsteady, complex world? I argue yes. Through the wisdom and power of Christ, we learn to recenter our lives on Jesus's life and teaching through transformative practice. Jesus models in his humanity and divinity what he has created us to be: little Christs through the power of his Spirit.

## Pause and Reflect

Here are some reflection questions to start you on this journey.

How would you describe the way you have been living your life? What has defined or shaped your goals, your decisions and choices, how you spend your time and resources? Was this way based on things you consciously decided or based on things you unconsciously inherited from others?

Has the way you've chosen to live produced peace or pain, flourishing or failure, delight or disillusionment, beauty or ugliness? Is your current way in sync with how you think you should live?

Why have you chosen to continue to live this way? Are other alternatives available that you haven't considered adequately?

How has God been nudging you to consider a different way?

What is the outcome of the path you are on? Are you unwittingly traveling on a dead-end street?

# CHAPTER ONE

# Reject Distorted Views of God

The more one is in one's right mind . . . the more one
is unfettered by distorting misperceptions, deranged
passions, and the encumbrances of past mistakes—
the more inevitable is one's surrender to God.

—David Bentley Hart, *That All Shall Be Saved*

A s I said, being a Christian involves learning to live our lives
in a different way, learning to walk in Jesus's footsteps. Jesus
invites us to be his friends, companions, and disciples as we
learn to walk together. That entails trust. We have to trust that Jesus
knows who he is and where he's going. To trust is ultimately to surrender, and as Hart mentions, surrender to God involves breaking
free from "distorting misperceptions" of what God and what we are
like.[1]

And when it comes to all the things we have learned about God so
far in our lives, many of us have a lot of baggage to sort through.

Have you ever been to a carnival? Carnivals are less common than
they used to be, but you may have had a chance to visit one and had lots
of fun on the rides, stuffing yourself with funnel cake, fresh fudge, or
candy apples, and perhaps visiting the fun house.

As a boy, I loved the fun house; I enjoyed standing in front of the curved mirrors usually located near the entrance or the exit. These mirrors, large sheets of curved glass, are purposely designed to distort our appearance. A tall person appears short and squat. A thin person may look wide and chubby. I recall giggling as I changed expressions or body positions, and funny images appeared in the mirror.

Fun house mirrors deliberately distort reality and do their job well. They're fun because we know what we're seeing in the mirror isn't real. "It's only a distorted image," we remind ourselves.

Unfortunately, it's possible to have fun house mirror images of God and of ourselves that we mistake for the real thing. These false images distort our perceptions. What I perceive in the mirror is not a true reflection of the real God or the real me. Yet it seems so real.

The question then becomes, "How can we clarify our vision of God and of ourselves?"

If your picture of God is distorted, it is time to smash the fun house mirror. *Distorted and dysfunctional ideas about God* foment immense human misery. Always.

Trevor Hudson shares honestly his past struggles with distorted views of God. His mentor, a wise and gentle guide, raised these harmful ideas to Trevor's consciousness by simply asking, "Trevor, what is your picture of God?"

Trevor writes, "For the first time in my life, I stopped to think about my image of God. Yes, I did feel that I needed to earn God's grace. Yes, I did believe I had to achieve his affirmation. Yes, I did sense that God would withdraw his blessings if I did not measure up. Gradually it dawned on me that I had come to view God as a somewhat passive spectator, sitting in the balcony of my life, whose applause would only come in response to satisfactory performance. A dysfunctional picture of God, I was discovering, had expressed itself in a dysfunctional way of living."[2]

## Pause and Reflect

"What's God like?" is the most important question a human being will ever ask. Our answer to this question significantly influences how we live through the gift of years God gives us. Ponder what you really think God is like. You might consider writing on a pad your description of God. You can be honest and open. Know that the Lord is pleased with your desire to see him clearly. He won't be shocked by anything you write. Get your view of God out of your mind—things can be foggy there—and onto a piece of paper. This is the image of God we need to work with. Don't be afraid or shocked by what you read. All God's image-bearers occasionally struggle with a fun house mirror view of God. Thankfully, our vision of God can be clarified.

To embrace and live a different way requires the purposeful rejection of a fun house mirror God for one who looks like Jesus. Ponder the following questions. Particularly focus on those you find especially relevant.

- Is my picture of God drawing me closer to God or pushing me away? Do I really want to spend time with this God?
- How has my view of God been formed?
- What words have shaped my understanding of God?
- Who are the people that taught me about God?
- What life experiences have significantly influenced how I think about God?

## Distorted Views of God

I was a professor and administrator at Eastern University for twenty-four years. I regularly taught a course titled Foundations of Christian

Spirituality.³ As I taught Foundations over the years, we often began with the same theme: distorted views of God people were raised with. If we wish to walk daily with Jesus, we need to trust the God who leads us, and we had better be sure we are following the right God.

One common distorted view students struggled with was God as a *distant, demanding parent*, with a whiny voice that sounds like this: "You know I love you, honey. But I don't understand why you're not doing better. Look at how much I've given you. When I read your grade report, I see only Bs and Cs. There are even some Fs! Why aren't you doing better? I've given you so much, and this is the best you can do? I want As, not Bs and Cs, and surely not Fs! You know I love you, honey."

What do we do with a God who sounds like that? We repeatedly attempt to meet the demands of that whiny, demanding, dissatisfied voice. Often, exhausted and discouraged, we try to turn it off. We cover our ears. Or, if things get really bad, we kill that distant, demanding voice. We stop believing. We kiss faith in God good-bye.

I'm reminded of Norman Bates in Alfred Hitchcock's film *Psycho*. Even after Norman had murdered his mother, he couldn't escape her nagging, accusing, disappointed, abusive voice. There she sat, mummified in Norman's basement but still alive in Norman's mind. His mother's voice, her distressing, poisonous words, still tormented Norman. He began to dress like her. Talk like her. Act like her. She drove Norman insane. A Norman Bates god does no one any good.

Quite a few students pictured God as a *drill instructor, a divine DI*. Have you ever served in the armed forces? If you have, you know what the tough, frightening voice of a military drill instructor sounds like. It's loud. It's demanding. It's unrelenting. Now turn it into the voice of God.

"Yeah, I love you! But we've got a lot of work to do around here.

You need to get in shape. You are weak, a failure! Can you hear me? No one gets tired around here. Try harder! Do more! You are pathetic. Wake up! When I talk to you, you will address me as 'sir.' Do you understand me?"

Some students struggled with a third troubling view, God as a *cosmic monster.* Students saw the evil and sin constantly occurring in the world—sometimes experiencing it very directly—and struggled to reconcile the enormity of the world's evil and suffering with the reality of a loving God. They thought this evil and suffering must be God's will because he is sovereign over everything.

I remember a nighttime talk with my oldest son, Nathan, when he was around eighteen. I was watching the 76ers, and the game was almost over. Nathan had spent most of the evening upstairs, catching up on schoolwork.

He ambled quietly down the stairs as the 76ers game ended, walked over, and sat next to me on the couch. It was around ten in the evening. I noticed his eyes were red. *Had he been crying? What was up?*

On the edge of tears, Nate asked me quietly, his voice choking, "Dad, where was God at Auschwitz?"

Nate had been upstairs reading about the Holocaust for his history class, and much of what he was learning was new, horrifying, and very difficult for his maturing mind to process. He believed God was loving, good, and powerful. So why did God allow such evil to happen? God loved all human beings. God was good. And God surely had the power to intervene. Yet thousands of people were murdered every day in the gas chambers of that terrible place.

How does one reconcile the existence of a good, loving, powerful God with the fact that seventeen thousand people went up in smoke and ash each day at Auschwitz?

We talked about evil, free will, the story of the Jews, and the wickedness of anti-Semitism. I tried to create a conceptual framework Nate could use to process all the issues involved in answering such a significant, difficult question.

"What's God like, Dad? What's God like?"

What a fair question. What an important question. It's one all human beings ask. I identified with Nate's sad, tear-filled ponderings. For I, too, have struggled with the goodness of God. You probably have, too. It all comes down to the same bottom-line question: Can we trust God?

## Can God Be Trusted?

My tussle with these questions ignited in 1971, though it had been smoldering from around age thirteen. What happened? On Christmas day, I think in 1970, my dad and mom separated.

Christmas day was always very special for the Hall family. It was the one day of the year when my dad especially demonstrated his love for our family in a very concrete way.

Dad belonged to "the Greatest Generation" so eloquently described by Tom Brokaw. During the last year of the war against the Japanese, Dad flew dive bombers—the Dauntless and the Helldiver—as a nineteen-year-old pilot. If you ever tour the aircraft carrier *Yorktown*, now permanently docked in Charleston, South Carolina, you can spot Dad's face on the back wall of the briefing room. He's being briefed for an upcoming mission with other young pilots. No one looks happy, though many look quite determined.

Thankfully Dad survived the war and married my mom, and they began to raise a family together. As the years passed, they slowly drifted apart. There's no need for me to dwell on the details of the divorce. Each played a role in the breakup of the family. How God's precious image-bearers struggle to love one another!

On Christmas day, 1970, I was home in Virginia from UCLA for Christmas break. Fond memories and lively expectations filled my heart as I headed down the stairs Christmas morning.

I expected to find Christmas stockings stuffed, presents under the tree, and a warm, inviting breakfast before we began the official festivity of unwrapping each gift one by one. Instead, things were shockingly quiet. "What's going on?" I asked myself. "Where is everyone?"

Then I saw them. My older brother and Dad were standing outside talking, and neither looked happy. I turned away from the living room window, walked into the dining room, and found my mother sitting at the dinner table crying. I had never seen her cry before. "Mom, what's going on?" I asked, dreading her answer.

"Your dad's leaving me," she whispered.

"No, he's not," I said to myself.

For the next ten months I did everything in my power to keep my parents together. I wanted more Christmases. More Thanksgivings. More birthday celebrations with the family whole.

It was not to be.

Where was God in all this family horror? My faith in God was just beginning to bud in college. How would it survive a breakup between Mom and Dad?

Hope soared back in LA as I discovered a Bible verse stating that God hated divorce (Mal. 2:16). I naively coupled this verse with Jesus's promise that he would do anything I asked for in his name (John 14:13). What could be more in line with God's will than a family staying together, whole and happy?

I prayed and expected reconciliation. As the months passed, I prayed my heart out. "God, keep our family together." After all, I reasoned,

God hates divorce. God has promised to hear my prayer. I prayed fervently, expectantly, longingly. "God doesn't break his promises," I said to myself. I had read the same thing in the Bible. That was good enough for me.

Then the letter arrived. I recall the envelope looked official, formal, perhaps with the words *Official Document* stamped on it. I opened it slowly. I believe my hands were shaking. It contained the news no child, whatever age, wants to receive. The divorce had been finalized. My parents were no longer married.

As I stared at the courtroom document, I felt utter dismay. It quickly shifted into anger. Hot, sorrowful words spilled out of my mouth, fiery coals of disillusionment and disappointment with God. "You liar," I muttered. "You promised. You promised! I hate you."

The person I thought was my friend had purposely, sadistically tossed a hand grenade into my family circle. I had trusted God with childlike faith, had willingly placed my tender heart in God's hands, and he had crushed it. Perhaps you have felt the same way when life doesn't make sense.

My disappointment with God deepened over the next few months. What was I to do with the ache in my heart and the confusion in my mind? What do you do when trust has been violated, betrayed, shattered? I had trusted Dad. I had trusted Mom. And I had trusted God. I decided the trusting would stop, a decision that, frankly, got me nowhere.

How so? I was not going to stop loving my parents. How could I? They were embedded in my heart. And what was I going to do with God? An ember of trust in God still flickered beneath the ashes of disappointment. A knowing beyond knowing, a tiny spark of faith still glowed, but for a long stretch I did my best to snuff it out.

My UCLA friends increasingly worried about me. To be honest, they didn't know much more about God than I did. Many of us came to faith at the same time. They simply loved me and hung with me as I started to drink and recklessly act out my disillusionment with God and life in general.

Finally, one Saturday morning my pals—new believers like me and knuckleheads to boot—intervened directly; they sensed that if I continued to follow my foolish, self-destructive path, more tragedy lay ahead.

A group of us played basketball every Saturday morning at Pali High in Pacific Palisades. Three or four guys picked me up—I think I was hung over—and I rested in the backseat, tired, sad, and looking forward to just running up and down the court for an hour or two.

Two of them, one on each side, leaned into me. I could barely move, and that's exactly what they wanted. The drive to the Palisades is about twenty minutes from UCLA, west on Sunset Boulevard. Instead, I noticed we were following a different route, first west down Wilshire, then south on the 405, the San Diego freeway.

"Where are we going?" I mumbled.

"To Culver City. There's a guy there we have to pick up who wants to play ball with us," one of them lied.

*Whatever,* I thought to myself, and dozed off.

Fifteen minutes later we pulled up to an apartment building. "Come on up," somebody said. "Looks like he's not ready yet." I lumbered out of the car, climbed lazily up a set of stairs, and walked into the living room of an apartment I didn't recognize.

To my surprise and dismay, I faced a larger group of my friends, male and female. Why were they here? I felt confused, then angry. A brief, uncomfortable moment passed.

Then someone courageously asked, "Chris, what's wrong? We're worried."

"What's wrong?" I snapped. "I'll tell you what's wrong." For the next hour and a half my long-suffering, gutsy friends gave me a precious gift: the gift of silence. They just sat and listened to the angry, profane monologue of a heartbroken image-bearer, one so tempted to disbelieve and so longing to trust but terrified to do so.

I remember at one point someone said, "That must be so hard."

"You're damn right it's hard," I spit out. The rest of the group stayed silent, patiently absorbing my angry disillusionment, much like God had done since I learned of the divorce.

Finally, I ran out of words. I had nothing left to say or, it seemed, to hope. Boxing with God was exhausting. My arms were too short. "I'm tired," I said. "I don't want to play ball. I want to go back to school."

No one argued with me. Indeed, no one really said much at all. Someone loaned me a car, and I began the drive back to campus. I didn't want to be with anyone else. I just wanted to sleep. "A lot of good that did," I inwardly moaned.

And then it happened. I was headed north on the 405, just past San Vicente Boulevard, when I felt a weight suddenly, inexplicably lift off my chest. It hurt. I gasped in pain.

Simultaneously, I sensed someone in the car, a gentle, kind, tangible presence behind me, gazing at me as I drove. I know it sounds crazy, but I'm not lying. In the midst of my disbelief, disappointment, and disillusionment, God showed up.

Have you read C. S. Lewis's *The Chronicles of Narnia*? As I recall and ponder those three minutes that changed the direction of my life, I remember it felt like Aslan (the Jesus-like lion in the books) was curled up on the backseat. And then he spoke. This is what I heard in my mind and heart: "My dear boy, you're going to have to trust me. I could try to explain to you all that's involved with your parents' divorce, all that occurred between your mom and dad as their years together passed. I choose not to do so. It is too complex for you to comprehend. You must leave these things with me. You must trust me. I am what you hoped me to be. I haven't changed. Trust me, my dear one. Trust me."

Even now, as I write these words fifty years later, tears fill my eyes.

"I can't. I can't. I want my family back. I want more Christmases. I want things to be the way they were." As I drove north, I began to weep deeply, tears of sadness, tears of farewell to what would never be again, tears flowing from a crushed heart. I had no desire to say good-bye to what had been so good, to what I loved so deeply. Yet Aslan—I do believe it was Jesus—was nudging me toward a new beginning. As I reached the Wilshire Boulevard exit, he was still with me in the backseat, gazing at me, waiting, waiting, waiting.

To this day, I have no rational explanation for what occurred that morning on the 405. When I left Culver City and headed north, I was deeply disappointed and disillusioned with God. When I pulled off the 405 onto Wilshire, about five miles later, my young faith, as shredded as it was, began to knit together. Pure grace visited me in the backseat of that car.

There was no happy resolution to the divorce. The family circle was never restored. That devastating Christmas was the last I ever experienced with my family together. Pain remains. I feel it in my chest and in my throat as I recall that horrible time. Yet, inexplicably, my life with God—as immature as it was—had been revived.

My experiences and perplexities, though, are not unique. Many of you have had similar ones. We cry out, "Lord, what's going on? Why is the world the way it is?" And behind our questions lurk even deeper, more troubling ones: "Lord, are you good? Can you be trusted? *What are you like?*"

These are not easy questions to resolve. And sometimes, as in my case, resolving them does not mean that I discovered the right answers. But I learned enough to trust and move forward. We'll continue to ponder the question of God's goodness, love, and power in *A Different Way*. Whatever conclusions we reach, at least from a Christian perspective, must correspond with what Jesus teaches about his Father, and about himself.

## An Indulgent Grandfather?

The last distorted view of God mentioned by Eastern students was picturing God as an *indulgent grandfather* whose "highest hope at the end of the day" is, as C. S. Lewis writes, "that everyone had a good time." In this view, Trevor Hudson comments, we picture God as "a divine candy machine (just say a prayer and you get what you want)."[4] God as a divine bellhop comes to mind.

"Oh, they do get into mischief!" we hear this God chuckling. "What am I going to do with them?"

God's not all that concerned about my sin, we presume, so why should I be?

Have you ever found yourself thinking and behaving this way? I surely did in my younger days.

Of course, there are many more fun house mirror views of God that confuse us and blur our vision. There may well be hundreds. Here are a few more mentioned by Trevor Hudson:

- God as an impersonal force
- God as a heavenly tyrant
- God as a scrupulous bookkeeper.[5]

Fun house mirror views of God often lurk below the surface of our consciousness; they invade our dreams, incubating nightmares of what God is like. Distorted views of God, though, inevitably leak into our conscious thinking and living, warping our ability to live and love in line with the truth of who God actually is. Trusting in the wrong idea of God will lead us off the path we wish to follow.

## Pause and Reflect

**What distorted views of God do you struggle with? How did they develop? How can you—with God's help—change them?**

## The God Who Seeks the Lost

Of course, Jesus knew about our hesitations and distortions and so gave us teachings about the God we should trust in. We find three parables or stories in Luke 15, all told by Jesus to help his precious image-bearers understand what God is like. Each story makes the same point: *God longs for those who are lost.* First we see that God is like a shepherd who searches for the one lost sheep out of ninety-nine (Luke 15:7). Next Jesus says God is like a woman who loses a coin and is frantic to find it (Luke 15:8–10). Finally, God is like a father who longs for his wayward son to come home (Luke 15:11–32).

What does Jesus long for us to grasp? God searches for those who have lost their way. God rejoices over people who admit that they've sinned, change their minds about the direction of their lives, and confess honestly what has gone wrong. All three stories emphasize the joy that occurs in heaven when a cracked image-bearer finally says, "I've sinned. I'm sorry. I'm lost. I want to come home."

When the lost sheep is found, the shepherd "calls his friends and neighbors together and says, 'Rejoice with me; I have found my lost sheep.' I tell you that in the same way there will be more rejoicing in heaven over one sinner who repents than over ninety-nine righteous persons who do not need to repent" (Luke 15:6–7).[6] The woman who finds her lost coin responds in the same way: "And when she finds it, she calls her friends and neighbors together and says, 'Rejoice with me; I have found my lost coin.' In the same way, I tell you, there is rejoicing in the presence of the angels of God over one sinner who repents" (Luke 15:9–10).

The third parable is the best known of the three. Almost all of us have heard the story of the prodigal son. Actually, I'm worried that we've heard it so many times we've become anesthetized to its rich texture and beauty. I think Philip Yancey was concerned about the same thing, so he rewrote the story of the prodigal son about a lost girl. I think he got it just right. Yancey writes:

A young girl grows up on a cherry orchard just above Traverse City, Michigan. Her parents, a bit old-fashioned, tend to over-react to her nose ring, the music she listens to, and the length of her skirts. They ground her a few times, and she seethes inside. "I hate you!" she screams at her father when he knocks on the door of her room after an argument, and that night she acts on a plan she has mentally rehearsed scores of times. She runs away.

She has visited Detroit only once before, on a bus trip with her church group to watch the Tigers play. Because newspapers in Traverse City report in lurid detail the gangs, the drugs, and the violence in downtown Detroit, she concluded that is probably the last place her parents will look for her. California, maybe, or Florida, but not Detroit.

Her second day there she meets a man who drives the biggest car she's ever seen. He offers her a ride, buys her lunch, arranges a place for her to stay. He gives her some pills that make her feel better than she's ever felt before. She was right all along, she decides: her parents were keeping her from all the fun.

The good life continues for a month, two months, a year. The man with the big car—she calls him "Boss"—teaches her a few things that men like. Since she's underage, men pay a premium for her. She lives in a penthouse, and orders room service whenever she wants. Occasionally she thinks about the folks back home, but their lives now seem so boring and provincial that she can hardly believe she grew up there.

She has a brief scare when she sees her picture on the back of a milk carton with the headline "have you seen this child?" But by now she has blond hair, and with all the makeup and body-piercing jewelry she wears, nobody would mistake her for a child. Besides, most of her friends are runaways, and nobody squeals in Detroit.

After a year the first sallow signs of illness appear, and it amazes her how fast the boss turns mean. "These days, we can't mess around," he growls, and before she knows it, she's out on the street without a penny to her name. She still turns a couple of tricks a night, but they don't pay much, and all the money goes to support her habit. When winter blows in she finds herself sleeping on metal grates outside the big department stores. "Sleeping" is the wrong word—a teenage girl at night in downtown Detroit can never relax her guard. Dark bands circle her eyes. Her cough worsens.

One night as she lies awake listening for footsteps, all of a sudden everything about her life looks different. She no longer feels like a woman of the world. She feels like a little girl, lost in a cold and frightening city. She begins to whimper. Her pockets are empty and she's hungry. She needs a fix. She pulls her legs tight underneath her and shivers under the newspapers she's piled atop her coat. Something jolts a synapse of memory and a single image fills her mind: of May in Traverse City, when a million cherry trees bloom at once, with her golden retriever dashing through the rows and rows of blossomy trees in chase of a tennis ball.

*God, why did I leave,* she says to herself, and pain stabs at her heart. *My dog back home eats better than I do now.* She's sobbing, and she knows in a flash that more than anything in the world she wants to go home.

Three straight phone calls, three straight connections with the answering machine. She hangs up without leaving a message the first two times, but the third time she says, "Dad, Mom, it's me. I was wondering about maybe coming home. I'm catching a bus up your way, and it'll get there about midnight tomorrow. If you're not there, well, I guess I'll just stay on the bus until it hits Canada."

When the bus finally rolls into the station, its air brakes hissing in protest, the driver announces in a crackly voice over the microphone, "Fifteen minutes, folks. That's all we have here." Fifteen minutes to decide her life. She checks herself in a compact mirror, smooths her hair, and licks the lipstick off her teeth. She looks at the tobacco stains on her fingertips, and wonders if her parents will notice. If they're there.

She walks into the terminal not knowing what to expect. Not one of the thousand scenes that have played out in her mind prepare her for what she sees. There, in the concrete-walls-and-plastic-chairs bus terminal in Traverse City, Michigan, stands a group of forty brothers and sisters and great-aunts and cousins and a grandmother and great-grandmother to boot. They're all wearing goofy party hats and blowing noise-makers, and taped across the entire wall of the terminal is a computer-generated banner that reads "Welcome home!"

Out of the crowd of well-wishers breaks her dad. She stares out through the tears quivering in her eyes like hot mercury and begins the memorized speech, "Dad, I'm sorry. I know . . ."

He interrupts her. "Hush child. We've got no time for that. No time for apologies. You'll be late for the party. A banquet's waiting for you at home."[7]

Jesus is saying, God is like that father. Can you trust that God?

## A Last, Long Conversation

If we are confused about the questions of God and what God is like or what God will do, we are in good company. The apostle John records for us a last, long conversation Jesus had with his disciples. In this final talk before his death, Jesus emphasizes truths about God and himself he wants to embed in the disciples' minds, for these are the apostles who will be Jesus's chief representatives on earth after his ascension into heaven. It is the apostles who will speak and write on Jesus's behalf, bearing witness to who he is, what he has accomplished, and what he is still doing in the world through the Holy Spirit.

This conversation wasn't easy for the disciples. How so? Well, among other things, Jesus starts the discussion by announcing he is leaving, and nobody is happy about this.

"Do not let your hearts be troubled. You believe in God; believe also in me. My Father's house has many rooms; if that were not so, would I have told you that I am going there to prepare a place for you? And if I go and prepare a place for you, I will come back and take you to be with me that you also may be where I am. You know the way to the place where I am going." (John 14:1–4)

For many of us these are comforting words, words of encouragement, words that keep us going during times of testing, loneliness, illness, or grief. Not so with the disciples. Jesus's teaching about leaving and coming back made little biblical or theological sense to them. Why?

From their perspective—and that of Israel as a whole—God's promised Messiah wasn't supposed to come and then leave. The Messiah was supposed to stay, to announce and establish God's kingdom. God's Anointed One was supposed to come to reign, to end Israel's exile and domination under foreign rule, to heal, to defeat Satan, to conquer death.

For Thomas, Peter, Philip, and the rest of the apostolic band gathered that last evening with Jesus in the upper room, their messianic expectations were grounded on the promise of the prophets that Israel's Messiah would come and rule in Jerusalem (cf. Isa. 2:1–5). All the nations would stream to God's Anointed on Zion. This present evil age would end. The age to come would begin under the leadership of the anointed king of Israel, the promised Messiah.

The disciples had no desire for a coming-then-leaving messiah; they believed Jesus was the Anointed One of God, and they wanted him to stay. Jesus had fulfilled their messianic expectations up to this point. Why now this talk about leaving? Why was he going away? Where was he going?

We perceive the disciples' confusion in the question Thomas poses to Jesus. "Lord, we don't know where you are going, so how can we know the way?" (John 14:5). Thomas is puzzled, confused, frustrated. "Lord," he seems to be saying, "you're not being helpful. Why are you leaving? Where are you going? Messiahs don't leave. They stay."

Jesus's response to Thomas probably left him confused, though it is a saying well loved by Christians. "I am the way and the truth and the life. No one comes to the Father except through me. If you really know me, you will know my Father as well. From now on, you do know him and have seen him" (John 14:6–7).

Philip responds on behalf of the entire group: "Lord, show us the Father and that will be enough for us" (John 14:8).

As Jesus replies to Philip, we sense a hint of impatience in his voice, toward Philip and all the apostles. They should understand by now. "Jesus answered: 'Don't you know me, Philip, even after I have been among you such a long time? Anyone who has seen me has seen the Father. How can you say, "Show us the Father"?'" (John 14:9).

Could Jesus be clearer? *When we look at Jesus, we see the Father.*

What's God like? God is like Jesus. Jesus invites us to replace our fun house mirror view of God with Jesus as God's incarnate Son. If we look at Jesus and immerse ourselves in his words and life, we'll find God. Like the apostles before us, we don't need to have all the answers before we decide to simply trust that Jesus will be there as we start walking with him.

I have met very few people who have nasty things to say about Jesus. Most of the problems people have with the Christian faith *concern us.*

If we've been deformed into the image of a fun house God, the picture of God we present to the world will be warped and twisted. No wonder people often say, "I don't have a hard time with Jesus. It's Christians I can't stand."

For some of us, our first big step toward spiritual healing, spiritual wholeness, and spiritual sanity needs to be a big step toward Jesus. I often suggest that people take the next three to five years and just read the Gospels—Matthew, Mark, Luke, and John—over and over again. There is no need to rush.

As you read and ponder, hidden icebergs of ingrained, false patterns of thinking will slowly crack and melt. Christ's healing light will shine into the unseen nooks of our personality. Darkness will recede. Fun house mirror reflections of God will fade. A new picture of God will slowly set in and stabilize.

I repeat again. *What's God like? God is like Jesus.*

This first step toward Jesus will be hard for some of us, for we've been hurt in the past. We've been wounded by what people taught us about God. We've been injured by what people said about Jesus.

Jesus never tires of saying to each precious image-bearer, "I want to embrace you and make you like me."

Jesus's invitation is for everyone. No one is left out. Hear Jesus saying to you, "You are my beloved. My dear, dear girl, my dear, dear boy. Come to me. You've been laden too long with burdens too heavy for you to carry. Give them to me. Trust me. You are loved. You are safe. I will not harm you. It is time to release your life into my light and love. Come home. There is a fire waiting and a banquet prepared."

Jesus has prepared a holy feast for us—his precious body and blood—that nourishes, enlivens, and gladdens heart, mind, soul, and body. It's a meal to be enjoyed for all eternity, one that will never sate our appetites. In the age to come, we will feast forever in the company of Jesus.

# CHAPTER TWO

# Learn to Live in an In-Between Time

One dare not think they can properly interpret the
Gospels without a clear understanding of the concept
of the kingdom of God in the ministry of Jesus.

—Gordon Fee and Douglas Stuart,
*How to Read the Bible for All It's Worth*

What many people don't fully appreciate is that Jesus has
reconfigured time.[1] At first glance, the idea of time reconfigured and rearranged is startling and unexpected. How
can time change?

Time's readjustment relates to key issues and concerns of our life
with Christ and our process of becoming more like him. If we fail to
understand the new nature of time, the course and challenges of our
spiritual development will be puzzling, frustrating, and discouraging.

Here's what I mean: Do you ever feel like a strange mixture of old
and new? I'm now, for example, living in my eighth decade, and the
evidence of aging is plastered all over my face. Creases surround my
eyes. My hair has changed from black to white. My vision is blurred;
if I didn't have a good pair of glasses, I'd be in real trouble. Not only
have I grown old physically, but timeworn emotions and habits can un-

predictably raise their heads. Impatience suddenly ripples to the surface. When 3 p.m. arrives, the hour when fatigue settles in, my assistant warns everyone else, "Beware, the filter is down."

Simultaneously, though, I sense I'm growing younger. In baptism, I experienced a new birth. Jesus's words to Nicodemus prove true: "Very truly I tell you, no one can see the kingdom of God unless they are born again" (John 3:3). Though my physical eyes are weak and tired, my spiritual vision continues to sharpen. I am being renewed.

Peter, the great apostle, echoes Jesus's words to Nicodemus. "Praise be to the God and Father of our Lord Jesus Christ! In his great mercy he has given us *new birth* into a living hope through the resurrection of Jesus Christ from the dead, and into an inheritance that can never perish, spoil or fade" (1 Pet. 1:3–4).

Though old habits remain, their strength is weakening. New habits are forming. I'm not the same person I once was, though the ancient me lurks in the shadows. I'm gradually experiencing the transformation Jesus offers all who follow him as we learn to walk in his shoes.

In concrete ways, I am growing old according to regular time, but I am also being made new through my journey with Jesus. This is the first sense of how time has been reconfigured.

## The New You

The apostles love to talk and write about "new" life, "new" people, and "new" things. Think of Peter. Luke tells us the story of Peter's arrest and imprisonment by the same people who condemned Jesus before Pilate. Peter sits in chains in prison, perhaps convinced that his life and ministry have reached their conclusion. Suddenly an angel appears: "'Go, stand in the temple courts,' he said, 'and tell the people all about *this new life'"* (Acts 5:20). New life. New beginnings. A new time has arrived for Peter and for us.

Paul frequently writes in his letters about the "new." He, like the angel that appeared to Peter, reminds Roman Christians that "just as Christ was raised from the dead through the glory of the Father, we, too, may live *a new life*" (Rom. 6:4).

God in Christ, Paul explains, is offering us a *new way*, the way of the Spirit. "But *now*, by dying to what once bound us, we have been released from the law so that we serve *in the new way of the Spirit*, and not in the old way of the written code" (Rom. 7:6).

Paul exhorts the Corinthians to be new, unleavened bread, not dough filled with old yeast. "Get rid of the old yeast, so that you may be *a new unleavened batch*—as you really are" (1 Cor. 5:7).

The cup of wine Christians share in the Eucharist, Paul teaches, is "*the new covenant*" in Christ's blood (1 Cor. 11:25). Christians—the Corinthians in this case—are "ministers of *a new covenant*—not of the letter but of the Spirit" (2 Cor. 3:6).

If "anyone is in Christ," Paul writes joyfully, "*the new creation* has come: The old has gone, *the new is here*" (2 Cor. 5:17). "Neither circumcision nor uncircumcision means anything; *what counts is the new creation*" (Gal. 6:15).

Paul rejoices that God is creating a *new humanity* out of Gentiles and Jews. "His purpose was to create in himself *one new humanity* out of the two, thus making peace" (Eph. 2:15).

Not only so, but in Christ, God offers us a "*new self*" and the possibility of thinking and living in a different way from old patterns. "You were taught, with regard to your former way of life, to put off your old self, which is being corrupted by its deceitful desires; *to be made new* in the attitude of your minds; and *to put on the new self*, created to be like God in true righteousness and holiness" (Eph. 4:22–24).

"Do not lie to each other, since you have taken off your old self with its practices *and have put on the new self*, which is being renewed in knowledge in the image of its Creator" (Col. 3:9–10).

Other New Testament writers also speak of many new things. In the letter to the Hebrews, we read: "The days are coming, declares the Lord, when I will make *a new covenant* with the people of Israel and with the people of Judah" (Heb. 8:8). "Christ is the mediator of a *new covenant*" (Heb. 9:15).

"You have come to God, the Judge of all, to the spirits of the righteous made perfect, to Jesus the mediator of *a new covenant*, and to the sprinkled blood that speaks a better word than the blood of Abel" (Heb. 12:23–24).

A "*new order*" has arrived (Heb. 9:10); "*a new and living way*" has been opened into the holiest part of the Temple "by the blood of Jesus . . . that is, his body" (Heb. 10:19–20).

Peter, in his second letter, speaks of a "*new heaven and a new earth, where righteousness dwells*" (2 Pet. 3:13).

John, in Revelation, hears a "*new* song" (Rev. 14:3). Like Peter, John celebrates "'a *new* heaven and a *new* earth,' for the first heaven and the first earth had passed away, and there was no longer any sea" (Rev. 21:1).

As the prophecy of Revelation closes, John sees "*the new Jerusalem*" descending from heaven, "as a bride beautifully dressed for her husband" (Rev. 21:2). And there he is, Jesus, seated on the throne and loudly declaring, "I am making everything *new*!" (Rev. 21:5). New. New. New.

Ponder these new things with me, all brought to us by the incarnate Son, Jesus: new life, the new way of the Spirit, new unleavened bread, new covenant, new creation, new humanity, new self, new order, new song, new heaven, new earth, new Jerusalem. Don't these new wonders make you smile? Don't they renew your hopes for the future? Don't they open up new, unexpected possibilities? They do for me.

## Pause and Reflect

**Pray with me:**

Lord, you are making all things new. How glad we are new beginnings are possible, that you love to make things new. For we have grown old before our time, Lord. Here we are, old, cracked image-bearers, sensing new things beginning in us. Make us new, Lord. Make us young again in you. We offer ourselves to you. We offer all that is old in us to you. Do with it what you must. Gently kill what needs to die. Less old, Lord. More new. Amen.

What came to mind as you prayed this prayer? What is something new emerging in you now?

## "The Time Has Come"

Let's explore more thoroughly the old time in which we live—this present evil age (Gal. 1:3–5)—and the new time Christ offers us: the age to come. Where to begin? We'll first examine Jesus's teaching on the kingdom of God. Christ's kingdom teaching reveals to us the nature of the time in which we live. One age is ending. Another is beginning. Yet, until Jesus returns, the ages unexpectedly overlap.

How many sermons have you heard about the kingdom of God? In all likelihood, not many. Yet, as Gordon Fee and Douglas Stuart explain, one "dare not think they can properly interpret the Gospels without a clear understanding of the concept of the kingdom of God in the ministry of Jesus."[2] I think they're right.

Fee and Stuart insist that the theological spine of the New Testament is eschatological. What do they mean? Consider the common Greek word *eschatos*. Its ancient, commonplace meaning is quite simple. *Eschatos* means "last." Picture a row of dominos falling as one strikes another. The last domino to fall is the *eschatos*. The last person standing in a line to buy a movie ticket is the *eschatos*.

Now transfer this everyday meaning of *last* to the Bible. Scholars use the word *eschatology* to refer to "last things" or "the last time" or "end time." "Eschatology has to do with the end, when God brings *this age* to its close."[3] Note carefully the reference to "this age."

For the moment, simply remember there will be an end when this present age stops, a time characterized by sin and evil.

The teaching of Jesus's cousin—John the Baptist—points to the new time, the new age that is breaking into the midst of this present evil age. "I baptize you with water," John announces. "But one who is more powerful than I will come, the straps of whose sandals I am not worthy to untie. He will baptize you with the Holy Spirit and fire" (Luke 3:16).

John's role is to prepare the way for the Messiah, the Anointed One of Israel. His prophetic message is "good news" for Israel (Luke 3:18). From John's perspective, what is the good news? The Messiah and the Messiah's kingdom are at hand.

With Jesus's baptism by John and John's subsequent arrest and imprisonment, Jesus's public ministry begins. What are the first words out of Jesus's mouth? "*The time has come. . . . The kingdom of God has come near.* Repent and believe *the good news!*" (Mark 1:15). The kingdom of God is breaking into the midst of this present evil age.

Consider carefully what Jesus is saying. Jesus's announcement of the good news—a message that broadens as his ministry continues—initially does not mention the forgiveness of sins. Nor does Jesus refer to his death on the cross or his resurrection from the dead.

Jesus's definition of the "good news" at the beginning of Mark's

Gospel is quite focused. What is the good news? *"The time has come. . . . The kingdom of God has come near"* (Mark 1:15).

How would Jesus's Jewish audience have understood his words? What hopes, what expectations, what questions, what dreams would Jesus's announcement have raised in their minds?

Most "Jews in Jesus's day were eschatological in their thinking." There's that word *eschatological* again. "That is, they thought they lived at the very brink of time, when God would step into history and bring an end to *this age* and usher in *the age to come*."[4] In a word, faithful Jews believed that when the Messiah appeared, one age ("this present evil age") would end and another begin ("the age to come").

## Expectations Modified

Over the next three years of Jesus's ministry, people seem confused by Jesus's teaching and actions. After his imprisonment, John the Baptist sends messengers to Jesus who ask, "'Are you the one who is to come, or should we expect someone else?' Jesus replied, 'Go back and report to John what you hear and see: The blind receive sight, the lame walk, those who have leprosy are cleansed, the deaf hear, the dead are raised, and the good news is proclaimed to the poor. Blessed is anyone who does not stumble on account of me'" (Matt. 11:3–6).

Jesus directs John's attention to specific actions. Jesus is healing sicknesses. He's exorcising demons. He's confronting the devil. He's railing against injustice. He's caring for the poor and oppressed. He's even raising the dead!

Now ponder this question carefully: *Why* did Jesus do these particular things? He, as Israel's Messiah, is waging war against key characteristics of this present evil age: sin, sickness, the demonic, evil people triumphing, injustice, the continuing exile of Israel, and death. As the promised Messiah, Jesus must confront each of these features of evil—and he does. Mark's Gospel makes this clear.

Jesus proclaims the "good news" and announces the "time has come" and "the kingdom of God has come near" (Mark 1:14–15). Should we be surprised that demons immediately resist the kingdom's arrival? As Jesus teaches in the synagogue in Capernaum, a demon-possessed man cries out, "What do you want with us, Jesus of Nazareth? Have you come to destroy us? I know who you are—the Holy One of God" (Mark 1:24).

Jesus responds immediately to this demonic challenge, commanding the demon to shut up and exit the tormented man. Note that this power encounter is no contest between equal powers and authorities. The impure spirit quickly submits to Christ's command, convulses the man, and comes out with a shriek (Mark 1:26). Quite a scene!

What's the message in this powerful deliverance from the devils? In Jesus—Israel's promised Messiah—*the age to come* is breaking into the midst of *this present evil age*. The reign of God—God's kingdom—has arrived in the person and work of Jesus. A key sign of the kingdom's in-breaking is the exorcism in the synagogue at Capernaum and the other exorcisms Jesus performs.

A similar dynamic is evident in Jesus's healings. How so? Sickness characterizes this present evil age. It is one of its fundamental, sad markers. Thus the Messiah must exercise power to heal to demonstrate that the messianic kingdom is at hand, ruled by King Jesus. Mark front-loads healings in his Gospel to make this very point. For instance, Jesus heals Simon's mother-in-law of a fever in Mark 1:30–31. Her healing signifies that *the kingdom of God is invading this present evil age*.

Mark describes the arrival of the kingdom in his summary of Jesus's early ministry: "That evening after sunset the people brought to Jesus all the sick and demon-possessed. The whole town gathered at the door, and Jesus healed many who had various diseases. He also drove out many demons, but he would not let the demons speak because they knew who he was" (Mark 1:32–34). Jesus gags the demons. He doesn't want these inveterate liars' testimony, for they would surely twist his message.

Healings. Exorcisms. Other miracles. Good news preached to the poor and oppressed. Injustice challenged. In a wonderful messianic fashion, the age to come is breaking into the midst of this present evil age. Israel's king, the descendant of great King David, has arrived.

Jesus's teaching and actions were "signs that the end had begun (e.g., Matt. 11:2–6; Luke 11:20, 14:21, 15:1–2). Everyone kept watching him to see if he really *was* the Coming One."[5]

## The Hinge Pin

In Mark 8, we reach the hinge pin of Mark's Gospel. The focus of Jesus's teaching dramatically changes. From this time forward, in both his public and private ministry, Jesus teaches that Israel's expectations must change, and *so must the expectations of those who choose to follow him*, down to our present day. If we are to walk in Jesus's footsteps, we must heed Jesus's message.

First, at Caesarea Philippi, Jesus asks his disciples a crucial messianic question. "Who do people say I am?" (Mark 8:27). The disciples respond with a Whitman's Sampler of common Jewish messianic expectations. Perhaps Jesus is John the Baptist raised from the dead; others believe he is Elijah, a common Jewish expectation. Others think he is one of the prophets. Then Jesus asks his disciples the key question: "But what about you? Who do you say I am?"

### Pause and Reflect

Take a moment and ask yourself the question Jesus asked his disciples: "Who do you say I am?" How would you respond? Is the pattern demonstrated in your daily life—your concrete behaviors—congruent with your testimony about Jesus?

Peter responds immediately that Jesus is the Messiah, the Anointed One of Israel (Mark 8:29). What are Peter's expectations as he identifies Jesus as the Messiah? Should we be surprised that Peter's beliefs still largely correlate with those of Israel as a whole? He is, after all, a Jew.

Peter believes that as Israel's Messiah, Jesus will reign as Israel's king. Israel's long exile under foreign domination will end. Sickness, injustice, Satan and the devils, evil, sin, and death will all be overcome in the victory the Messiah accomplishes.

Soon, Peter believes, this present evil age will draw to a close and the age to come be fully manifest with Jesus reigning as Israel's rightful king. I can see the other disciples nodding their heads in agreement.

Why, then, does Jesus warn Peter and the disciples in Mark 8:30 not to tell anyone who he is? Not tell anyone? How strange. For in the first seven chapters of Mark's Gospel, Jesus and his apostles have publicly declared in word and action that he is the Messiah. And now he wants the disciples to keep this a secret? Why?

*If the disciples preach about Jesus based on their current understanding, Israel will fail to comprehend who Jesus is or what he has come to accomplish. The disciples still don't grasp the kind of messiah Jesus is.*

The apostles, along with all Israel, believe the Messiah—the "Anointed One"—will bring this present evil age to an end; Jerusalem will soon be raised up, all the nations will stream into Zion and acknowledge God's glorious reign, and Israel's long exile under foreign domination will finally end. God's kingdom will be established on earth as the Messiah reigns in Jerusalem (cf. Isa. 2:1–5). Indeed, soon there will be a new heaven and a new earth.

So, because the apostles don't yet clearly perceive the meaning of Jesus or Jesus's kingdom, mum's the word (Mark 8:30). The disciples have lots to learn about themselves, the Messiah, the kingdom of God, the nature of discipleship, and the necessity of the cross and resurrection.

In the rest of Mark 8, Jesus predicts his rejection by the elders of Israel, and his suffering and death and resurrection; these things must happen. He "must suffer many things and be rejected by the elders, the chief priests and the teachers of the law, and . . . he must be killed and after three days rise again" (Mark 8:31).

These predictions hardly excite or encourage the apostles. How would you feel if you were one of them? You had been expecting to reign with Jesus, and Jesus starts talking about crosses! Jesus's teaching about a cross for himself, and for those who would follow him, was confusing—indeed, horrifying. Why would the God of Israel allow Israel's Messiah to die on a Roman cross? Among other things, wouldn't such a death indicate God's cursing rather than blessing?

The disciples knew their Bible. Moses, for instance, clearly taught that the body of a criminal convicted and executed for a capital offense must be hung on a pole or tree as a sign of God's curse resting upon him. Yet the exposed body must be buried before nightfall. "Be sure to bury it that same day, because *anyone who is hung on a pole is under God's curse*" (Deut. 21:23).

Moses's instruction sheds light on the disciples' struggle with Jesus's teaching about crosses, suffering, and death. *How could the cursed of God be the blessed of God*, Israel's anointed king and deliverer from exile?

Should we be surprised, then, that Peter takes Jesus aside and rebukes him? We would have done the same thing. Peter's motive seems praiseworthy. He has no desire to see Jesus harmed or killed. But these possibilities are not Peter's principal difficulty. Peter's objections are biblical and theological. Plain and simple, on the basis of Moses's teaching, the cursed of God cannot be the blessed of God. A cursed and executed messiah cannot deliver Israel from exile.

## The Disciples in Shock

Jesus's reply to Peter shocked and hurt him. "'Get behind me, Satan!' he said. 'You do not have in mind the concerns of God, but merely human concerns'" (Mark 8:33).

Jesus is insistent and unapologetic in his prediction of suffering and death as God's will for him as Israel's king. The same is true, Jesus teaches, for those who follow him. In this present evil age, Jesus's disciples must expect crosses not thrones, persecution not acceptance and welcome. As Tom Wright puts it, "What the four gospels are eager to tell us, then, is that the messianic kingdom that Jesus is bringing will come through his suffering and indeed the suffering of his followers."[6]

Jesus couldn't be clearer: "Whoever wants to be my disciple must deny themselves and take up their cross and follow me. For whoever wants to save their life will lose it, but whoever loses their life for me and for the gospel will save it" (Mark 8:34–35). Stanley Hauerwas comments, "The new David is not one whose purple is immediately evident, but rather his power can be found only in his crucifixion. It will take new eyes and ears to see and hear the truth proclaimed through the cross."[7]

To learn to walk in Jesus's shoes is to join hands with him on a path that leads to a cross. A different way entails new eyes and ears.

### Pause and Reflect

Pray with me:

Lord, I don't like talk of suffering, trials, and crosses. This frightens me. Haven't you asked enough of me already? Yet, Lord, I want to be faithful. Help me to wrap my mind, heart, and body around this new demanding teaching. Move me through the power of your Spirit to a new place of courage, perseverance, and acceptance. I trust you, Lord. Do what you must. Amen.

What came to mind as you prayed this prayer?

## More Uncomfortable Predictions

Twice in Mark 9, Jesus again predicts his rejection, death, and resurrection. And twice the disciples fail to understand. "They left that place and passed through Galilee. Jesus did not want anyone to know where they were, because he was teaching his disciples. He said to them, 'The Son of Man is going to be delivered into the hands of men. They will kill him, and after three days he will rise.' *But they did not understand what he meant and were afraid to ask him about it*" (Mark 9:30–32).

The disciples' previous messianic expectations are set in cement. The apostles remain fixated on glory. Only at the foot of Jesus's cross will their expectations finally be shattered and their understanding of genuine glory gradually begin to change. It is Jesus's cross and subsequent resurrection that will radically, irreversibly transform their understanding. This transformation has surely not yet occurred.

As this little band of Christ followers continues their last sad pilgrimage to Jerusalem with Jesus, questions of status, glory, and honor still preoccupy them. Shockingly, they argue about who is the greatest (Mark 9:33–34). They fail to perceive the cruciform pattern of status in Jesus's kingdom. Jesus demonstrates tremendous patience, a patience he still exercises toward us, his image-bearers, for we, too, are slow to see, hear, and understand.

## The Journey to Jerusalem Continues

The dismaying and discouraging journey continues in Mark 10. Jesus once again predicts his rejection, suffering, death, and resurrection. "They were on their way up to Jerusalem, with Jesus leading the way, and the disciples were astonished, while those who followed *were afraid*. Again, he took the Twelve aside and told them what was going to happen to him. 'We are going up to Jerusalem,' he said, 'and the Son of Man will be delivered over to the chief priests and the teachers of the law. They will condemn him to death and will hand him over to the Gentiles [the Romans], who will mock him and spit on him, flog him and kill him. Three days later he will rise'" (Mark 10:32–34).

The disciples remain confused and afraid. Their minds linger on thrones and glory. In fact, even though Jesus repeatedly warns them as to what awaits in Jerusalem, James and John still see fit to ask Jesus for the privilege to sit at his right and left hand in his kingdom (Mark 10:35–40). When the other disciples overhear this devious and selfish request, they are "indignant with James and John" (Mark 10:41). The apostolic band is splintering under the pressure of Jesus's teaching. Their false hopes, fueled by pride and ambition, will prove too weak to sustain them in the days to come.

Do you think Jesus ever asked himself the question "Maybe I should start all over again with a different group?" Would we, though, have acted any better if we were walking in the disciples' shoes? I think not. Would we have wanted to change our shoes for those of Jesus? We, too, are slow to learn and slow to change. We don't enjoy having pet ideas or behaviors challenged. I am quite apt to take the easier way. Are you?

### Pause and Reflect

**Where might you be tempted to take the easier way? Can you identify specific instances in your life with Jesus when he offered a difficult path and you opted for an easier way?**

Jesus calls the disciples together for another surprising teaching session; his words remain relevant for us. Jesus redefines *greatness* and in doing so inverts the disciples' value system. Jesus gives *greatness* a new meaning.

A Roman procurator such as Pontius Pilate represented the Roman power structure in Jerusalem. His troops—professional killers—flaunted their authority and power: recognize the glory of Rome or there will be grave consequences. Jesus described them well: "You know that those who are regarded as rulers of the Gentiles lord it over them, and their high officials exercise authority over them" (Mark 10:42).

Jesus unreservedly rejects this model of greatness. He considers it a lie. "Not so with you," he teaches the apostles. Those great in the eyes of God are servants, not bosses; unrecognized, not celebrities; doorkeepers, not power brokers. Could Jesus's teaching be clearer? "Instead, whoever wants to become great among you must be your servant, and whoever wants to be first must be slave of all" (Mark 10:43–44).

Jesus's teaching shaped the consciousness and behavior of future Christians such as Bernard of Clairvaux. Notice how Bernard's words to his monastic brothers echo those of Jesus: "Learn the lesson that, if you are to do the work of a prophet, what you need is not a scepter but a hoe."[8] Richard J. Foster comments, "[Jesus] totally and completely rejected the pecking-order systems of his day. . . . Therefore the spiritual authority of Jesus is an authority not found in a position or a title, but in a towel."[9]

With this new teaching ringing in their ears, one so foreign to Roman and Jewish perspectives, the disciples continue on their journey to Jerusalem with Jesus leading the way.

We know how events unfold. Jesus's predictions prove true. Betrayal by Judas, trial before Israel's religious authorities, crucifixion by the Romans. As Jesus dies on the cross, seemingly cursed of God, he cries out, "My God, my God, why have you forsaken me?" (Mark 15:34).

Yet cursing, desolation, and death are not the end of Jesus's journey with the apostles. After three days, Jesus rises from the dead. Tragedy morphs into triumph. The apostles' journey with Jesus continues, with a new map and a new destination. Yet the way remains cruciform.

What happens immediately after the resurrection? Luke lets us know. Jesus continues to teach the disciples, and the content of his teaching is very specific. "After his suffering," Luke writes, "he presented himself to them and gave many convincing proofs that he was alive. He appeared to them over a period of forty days and spoke about the kingdom of God" (Acts 1:3).

Jesus invests forty post-resurrection days in his chosen apostles. Jesus calls the disciples to be witnesses, but they must get the message right and the road map straight. They still don't understand what the future holds in store. "Then they gathered around him and asked him, 'Lord, are you at this time going to restore the kingdom to Israel?'" (Acts 1:6).

From the apostles' perspective, what's left to be fulfilled? Isn't the time right for this present evil age to end and God's kingdom to be fully restored to Israel? Surely, the apostles think, all things have now been accomplished. Isn't it now time for Jesus to reign as God's Anointed in Jerusalem, for Israel's long exile to end and Jerusalem to be lifted up above the nations?

Rather than reigning in Jerusalem, though, Jesus leaves! He ascends into heaven, and a cloud hides him from the disciples' sight (Acts 1:9). Jesus promises to return, but in the meantime, in the midst of this present evil age, Jesus charges the disciples with a specific task. They are to be his witnesses "in Jerusalem, and in all Judea and Samaria, and to the ends of the earth" (Acts 1:8). This apostolic witness will entail martyrdom, not majesty.

Unexpectedly, at least for the apostles, their witness will be proclaimed in the midst of this present evil age with all its nastiness: sin, injustice, sickness, exile, demonic resistance, and death. The apostles' testimony that "the time" is at hand occurs during an unexpected overlap of the ages. Yes, the age to come has arrived, but its consummation will have to wait. And yes, we still await its consummation.

## D-Day and V-E Day

Christ's followers live simultaneously in two ages: this evil age and the age to come. An *unexpected overlap* between the ages has occurred. Until Jesus returns, Christ's disciples *live between the times*. We live in Christ's kingdom. And we live in this present evil age. Fee and Stuart helpfully comment, "Here is where problems show up for the early church and for us. Jesus announced the coming kingdom as having arrived with his own coming. The Spirit's coming in fullness and power with signs and wonders and the coming of the new covenant were signs that the new age had arrived. Yet the end of *this* age apparently had not taken place. How were they to understand this?"[10] And how are we? *The implications of this unexpected overlap of the ages for our spiritual formation are extremely important.* When we walk in Jesus's shoes, we walk between the times.

In a word, Jesus has introduced *the beginning of the end.* The disciples "came to see that with Jesus's death and resurrection, and with the coming of the Spirit, the blessings and benefits of the future had already come. But in another sense the end had not yet fully come. Thus, it was *already* but *not yet.*"[11] And so are we.

We, too, as Christ's followers and apprentices, are already but not yet. We have experienced God's forgiveness and the transforming power of the Holy Spirit but still wage war with temptation, sin, and evil, in the broader world and in ourselves.

In Christ, death has been conquered. But as long as the ascended Jesus tarries in his return, all human beings experience physical death. Satan has been defeated, yet we still experience demonic attack. We get sick, and at times we are healed, sometimes miraculously. Sometimes our illness remains. Justice for the oppressed springs up like flowers in the desert, yet the poor, the orphan, and the widow too frequently taste the bitterness of injustice.

Think of D-Day, the invasion of France on June 6, 1944, by the Allied forces at the end of the Second World War. As the Allies established a beachhead on the sands of Normandy, the Germans' hopes for victory in the war were dashed. *Yet the fiercest fighting lay ahead.* The Germans fought with fanatic intensity over every foot of occupied territory for the next eleven months. Finally, after great bloodshed, the war in Europe ended on May 8, 1945.

A similar pattern is true for Christ followers. The beachhead is taken by Jesus at Golgotha and three days later with the wonder and glory of his resurrection. But fierce struggle and fighting remain for those who proclaim their allegiance to Jesus from the day of his ascension to this very day.

The dynamic of "already but not yet" helps explain the spiritual tension we experience as we live in this in-between time, the time between Christ's first and second coming. "Precisely because the kingdom, the time of God's rule, has been inaugurated with Jesus's own coming, we are called to *life* in the kingdom, which means life under his lordship, freely adopted and forgiven but committed to the ethics of the new era and to seeing them worked out in our own lives and world in this present age."[12]

We long for Christ's return. We long to see his kingdom consummated. But until that day arrives, "by the Spirit we are to live out the life and values of the 'age to come' that has already been set in motion through the resurrection."[13] We walk in Jesus's shoes in the midst of this present evil age.

Living well in the overlap of the ages is something we *learn* how to do. It is a skill we learn, much like apprentices master their craft under the watchful eye and discipline of their master.

If the language of "this present evil age" or "the age to come" is new for you, consider Paul's teaching. In his introductory words to the Galatian churches he writes, "Grace and peace to you from God our Father and the Lord Jesus Christ, who gave himself for our sins *to rescue us from the present evil age*, according to the will of our God and Father, to whom be glory for ever and ever" (Gal. 1:3–5).

Paul writes to the Ephesians that God raised Jesus from the dead and "seated him . . . far above all rule and authority, power and dominion, and every name that is invoked, *not only in the present age but also in the one to come*" (Eph. 1:20–21). At the end of his life, Paul reminds Timothy that godliness "has value for all things, holding promise for *both the present life and the life to come*" (1 Tim. 4:8).

Finally, in one of his last letters, Paul explains to Titus that God's grace "teaches us to say 'No' to ungodliness and worldly passions, and to live self-controlled, upright and godly lives *in this present age*, while we wait for the blessed hope—the appearing of the glory of our great

God and Savior, Jesus Christ, who gave himself for us to redeem us from all wickedness and to purify for himself a people that are his very own, eager to do what is good" (Titus 2:12–14).

What perspectives and practices mark the lives of image-bearers who are learning to live "self-controlled, upright and godly lives *in this present age*"? How do we learn to be more and more new and less and less old? We'll work through these questions in future chapters.

In our next chapter, we examine closely the nature of the opposition we can expect to encounter as Jesus offers us his shoes, his path, and a different way in the midst of this present evil age.

# CHAPTER THREE

# Live Well amid a Cosmic Struggle

There is no neutral ground in the universe. Every square inch, every split second, is claimed by God and counterclaimed by Satan.

—C. S. Lewis, *Christian Reflections*

There can be no neutral people. Every one of us must decide to pick a side. No one gets to be a conscientious objector.

—Lectio 365

Life is often hard. Following Jesus does not mean we escape life's difficulties, but it does mean they take on a different meaning. As we learn to walk in Jesus's shoes, following him on a different way, sometimes our path will be smooth and sometimes rough. Occasionally our pilgrimage will remind us of discovering the green pastures of Psalm 23. At other times we will enter the desert, and the terrain will be stark, dry, and dangerous. Yet, whatever our circumstances, Jesus is always with us as our guide and companion. And it is in our struggles that we often learn the most important lessons of how to live a different way.

"Don't be naive," I hear Jesus saying to us. "You can't travel safely without my guidance. Pay close heed to my footprints. Trace my steps with your own. There are enemies to face. This is to be expected. I have won the great victory. The outcome of the war has been decided. But there will be skirmishes still, and sometimes great battles. One rages within you. Another rages outside of you, though you will not always be aware of the conflict. And of course, there is the Evil One. I have crushed his head, but he still thrashes about. The great peace will one day arrive, but not yet, my child, not yet. Travel with me with your head up, your eyes peeled, and your ears attentive."

Growing spiritually is no easy task. At least I haven't found it easy. We seem to take two steps forward and one step back, if not two. Something within us deeply resists God's work. In this chapter we'll take a look at what's gone wrong with us and how God is working to straighten us out. We'll call this inner resistance the *flesh*, after the manner of the Bible and the church's great tradition.

We ourselves are not the only problem we face. The world we live in has gone bad. Have you noticed? We discussed aspects of what's gone wrong in chapter 2, as we pondered the characteristics of this present evil age and its influence on us. We'll term this second point of resistance the *world*, after Paul's manner of speaking in Romans 12.

The Bible insists that opposition to spiritual change and love's growth within us concerns more than human nature and the world we live in. Jesus fought against evil—supernatural forces fervently opposed to him, his kingdom, and his purposes for the lives of his precious image-bearers of God. The principal name used in the Bible for this personal, supernatural resistance is *Satan*.

Something bad has happened to us, something bad has happened to the world, and something bad has happened to Satan—a warped, evil archangel who resists God's purposes, desires, and love for us, God's precious image-bearers.

## Beginnings

Let's start with the bad news about human beings. No matter what you believe about the story of Adam and Eve, this tale of our origins communicates deep truths about the human condition.

Perhaps the saddest part in the Bible—apart from Christ's passion—is told in Genesis 3. Here, in the story of Adam and Eve's sin in the Garden of Eden and sin's ensuing corruption of them and their descendants, we learn why life is difficult and change so daunting. In our original human parents, we see ourselves and our own story mirrored, and it makes us cringe.

Read Genesis 3 slowly. Did you notice that personal evil is already present in the garden before Adam and Eve sin? Evil lurks in the form of a serpent; this evil is personal, supernatural, and deeply opposed to God's good purposes for this original pair of image-bearers. The writer describes the serpent as "more crafty than any of the wild animals the LORD God had made" (Gen. 3:1).

The serpent is a liar. It hates God. It hates humans. It's in love with death. Enveloped in its scaly skin dwells a malignancy and horror disguised to Eve as a friend and mentor.

There are no specific mentions of evil in the first two chapters of Genesis, though the writer describes the earth as "formless and empty, darkness was over the surface of the deep, and the Spirit of God was hovering over the waters" (Gen. 1:2).

In Genesis 2 we find Adam alone in a garden "in the east, in Eden" (Gen. 2:8). God has given Adam all he needs to flourish. The garden is filled with "all kinds of trees," trees "that were pleasing to the eye and good for food" (Gen. 2:9).

The writer mentions two specific trees, "the tree of life and the tree of the knowledge of good and evil" (Gen. 2:9). As the story progresses, God gives explicit instructions to Adam. "You are *free to eat from any tree in the garden*; but you must not eat from the tree of the knowledge of good and evil, for when you eat from it you will certainly die" (Gen. 2:16–17). Clearly, there is knowledge God does not want Adam to acquire.

Eve has not yet been created when Adam receives this prohibition from God. Later we learn in Genesis 3:2–3 that Eve knows what God has forbidden. Perhaps Adam told her, or maybe she learned this prohibition directly from the Lord.

God's warning is clear: if you eat from this tree, the tree of the knowledge of good and evil, you will die.

The focus of Genesis 2 is much more on gifts and provision than prohibition. God's last beautiful gift to Adam is Eve. "It is not good for the man to be alone," God states. "I will make a helper suitable for him" (Gen. 2:18). And so, God creates Eve from Adam's rib (Gen. 2:21–22).

Adam could not be more pleased. "This is now bone of my bones and flesh of my flesh; she shall be called 'woman,' for she was taken out of man" (Gen. 2:23).

## The Warped Dynamics of Temptation

It is against this background of beauty, abundance, gifts, provision, and warning that the serpent tempts Eve. Ponder the devilish, crafty strategy. "Did God really say," the serpent asks Eve, "'You must not eat from any tree in the garden?'" (Gen. 3:1).

God had said nothing of the kind. A variety of trees flourished in Adam and Eve's garden home, to please both their sight and appetite. The garden is filled with abundance, not scarcity and restriction.

Consider, though, the *dynamics of the serpent's temptation*: the snake portrays God's command—a life-giving, beautiful, protective word—as restrictive, unfair, oppressive, and deceitful.

"Oh, Eve," the serpent hisses. "Can you really trust someone who would treat you like this? Why would God say such a thing? He's keeping something very good from you" (adapted from Gen. 3:1).

Eve initially seems aware that God's command isn't nearly as restrictive as the serpent's question suggests. She and Adam "may eat fruit from the trees in the garden" (Gen. 3:2). God did warn, though, that one tree is off-limits. "You must not eat fruit from the tree that is in the middle of the garden, and you must not touch it, or you will die" (Gen. 3:2).

The serpent immediately *contradicts* what God has said. Eve has never heard such sinister, devilish words. "You will not certainly die" (Gen. 3:4).

The serpent spews falsehoods. God is a liar. God can't be trusted. God doesn't have the best in mind for you. God knows that "when you eat from it your eyes will be opened, and you will be just like God, knowing good and evil" (Gen. 3:5).

The snake's lies are clever; the deception is twisted and perverse. "God is keeping a very good thing from you, Eve. Taste this tree's fruit and untold happiness and fulfillment will be yours. This tree will meet needs and desires you did not know you possess. You'll be just like God, Eve. Oh, Eve, wouldn't that be a good thing, a much better thing than to be hemmed in by an unfair command purposely preventing you from reigning as the queen of the universe, with Adam, your husband, as king?"

With these wicked words the serpent *undermines God's trustworthiness*. How quickly Eve—and then Adam—takes the bait. When they strike the hook, quite literally, all hell breaks loose. "Gotcha," I hear the serpent taunting. This devilish pattern of temptation will reappear for thousands of years to come. *Satan promises much and delivers little.*

When Adam and Eve sin, human nature cracks. It splinters. Imagine Adam and Eve sitting on a garden wall in Eden. They eat fruit from the forbidden tree, lose their balance, fall to the ground, and lie shattered in pieces. They disintegrate. When they choose to trust themselves, they fall apart.

I'm reminded of Humpty Dumpty.

"Humpty Dumpty sat on the wall. Humpty Dumpty had a great fall. And all the king's horses and all the king's men couldn't put Humpty together again."

Yes, we, God's precious image-bearers, are no longer whole. Our human nature lies shattered in fragments on the ground. We have mutated into a corrupt state; a Pandora's box of misery has unlocked in us and been released into the world.

We are not what we were meant to be. Cornelius Plantinga comments, "Along the generations, human nature itself, with its vast and mysterious amalgam of capacities to think, feel, supervise, love, create, respond, and act virtuously—that is, with its vast capacities for imaging God—has become the main carrier and exhibit of corruption. . . . [A]ll serious Christians subscribe to the generic doctrine of corruption, the centerpiece of which is the claim that even when they are good in important ways, human beings are not *sound*."[1]

## Incurvatus in Se

Ponder a vivid metaphor coined by Martin Luther. Luther describes human nature after our ancient parents' sin as *incurvatus in se*, Latin for "curved in on itself." We were created for a nourishing life with God, with God at the center; sin has transformed us into bent creatures, curved in on ourselves.

How does our curved nature manifest itself? Consider God's gift of the Sabbath, one day out of seven, when God offers us rest and renewal. How do we, in our bent state, respond to God's gift of hallowed time—to God's command to slow down and catch our breath?

Ashley Cocksworth observes that bent creatures avoid rest and the solace and strength it provides. In our modern context, curved image-bearers habitually misuse technology to reject the gift of rest the Sabbath offers us. What should serve us instead enslaves us.

Cocksworth comments that the Sabbath invites us to release "the grip of our handheld devices, our false dependency on them, and their gravitational pull downward—which is a peculiarly modern iteration of the *homo incurvatus in se*. . . . To practice a kind of contemplation conceived in the logic of the Sabbath, therefore, involves the reordering of our technological practices on which we are becoming increasingly dependent."[2]

## Pause and Reflect

**How might God be asking you to reorder your technological practices? Is your use of technology disordered rather than ordered, foolish rather than wise? How might you use technology in a saner manner, one that nourishes health and holiness rather than franticness, fear, and addiction?**

## The Flesh: *Sarx*

Paul describes our warped nature as the "flesh." The common Greek word for flesh is *sarx*. It often refers to the stuff that composes our bodies: blood, bone, brain, and so on. Indeed, *sarx* usually has this meaning. *Sarx* in this sense is good, for all that God has created is good.

*Sarx*, though, also has a sadder, more ominous meaning. In this sense, it refers to our bent nature; we are now "flesh," in a sinful condition and subject to sin's power. We are twisted, bent, skewed. We need to get straightened out.

Paul discusses *sarx* in Romans 8:4–13. He describes what's gone wrong in us. Paul teaches that "those who are in *the realm of the flesh* cannot please God" (Rom. 8:8).

I have emphasized *the realm of the flesh* to help us grasp that though the flesh warps each of us, it also has a corporate or group effect. When we combine your flesh with my flesh and my neighbor's flesh, we perceive the world in its negative meaning, what Richard Lovelace describes as "corporate flesh." "Corporate flesh" or "the world" is deeply resistant to God's purpose for our lives.

Consider other verses where Paul mentions the flesh:

Therefore, brothers and sisters, we have an obligation—but it is not to the flesh, to live according to it. For if you live according to the flesh, you will die; but if by the Spirit you put to death the misdeeds of the body, you will live. (Rom. 8:12–13)

Paul's words in Galatians 5 are especially important for our understanding of the flesh. "You, my brothers and sisters, were called to be free. But do not use your freedom to indulge the flesh; rather, serve one another humbly in love" (Gal. 5:13). Clearly, the flesh is not to be indulged; it is to be resisted.

Paul exhorts us to "walk by the Spirit." If we do so, we "will not gratify the desires of the flesh. For the flesh desires what is contrary to the Spirit, and the Spirit what is contrary to the flesh. They are in conflict with each other, so that you are not to do whatever you want" (Gal. 5:16–17).

How does the flesh manifest itself in normal human life? Paul believes the answer to this question is clear. "The acts of the flesh are obvious: sexual immorality, impurity and debauchery; idolatry and witchcraft; hatred, discord, jealousy, fits of rage, selfish ambition, dissensions, factions and envy; drunkenness, orgies, and the like. I warn you, as I did before, that those who live like this will not inherit the kingdom of God" (Gal. 5:19–21).

The flesh is to be resisted, a skill we develop and practice as we mature in Christ.

One caveat. Sometimes people think that *flesh* means our bodies, which they see as being at war with our spirits or souls. That is not what the Bible means by *flesh*, which describes how we are bent or turned in on ourselves, which is a spiritual condition. Our bodies, including their functions and needs, are a gift from God and so should not be treated as an enemy (though it can feel that way when I am on a diet).

### Pause and Reflect

How does your own flesh, your unique bentness, habitually manifest itself? Be as honest as you can in identifying its presence in you, your world, and your life history. Ask those who know you best how your flesh has affected them. If we diagnose the infected wound properly, the medicine we prescribe to fight the infection will be all the more effective.

## The World

Let's now examine the flesh in its corporate aspect, the "world."

Remember that the world as God's good creation is a wondrous, beautiful place (cf. Gen. 1–2). As Psalm 24 declares, "The earth is the

LORD's, and everything in it, the world, and all who live in it; for he founded it on the seas and established it on the waters" (vv. 1–2). "The heavens declare the glory of God; the skies proclaim the work of his hands" (Ps. 19:1).

I recall marveling at photos taken by an electron microscope. They displayed the exquisite complexity and beauty of thousands of colorful crystalline structures completely invisible to the naked eye. *For millennia*, I thought to myself, *the only person who could see these beauties was God.*

God loves to create. God loves stuff. God loves matter. God is very earthy, very worldly, as the creator of all things. All that God has created is good. God loves the world he has created.

*World*, though, also has a darker, more sinister meaning in Scripture. This negative sense doesn't refer to God's good creation, but to a corporate evil force deeply resistant to God's good purposes, a negative force field opposed to God's purposes for creation and Jesus's redemptive work.[3]

Jesus frequently portrays the world as deeply resistant to him, his kingdom, and his followers. Consider the following verses from John's Gospel:

"The world cannot hate you, but it hates me because I testify that its works are evil." (John 7:7)

"You are from below; I am from above. You are of this world; I am not of this world." (John 8:23)

"Now is the time for judgment on this world; now the prince of this world will be driven out." (John 12:31)

"The world cannot accept him [the Spirit of truth], because it neither sees him nor knows him." (John 14:17)

"Peace I leave with you; my peace I give you. I do not give to you as the world gives." (John 14:27)

"If the world hates you, keep in mind that it hated me first. If you belonged to the world, it would love you as its own. As it is, you do not belong to the world, but I have chosen you out of the world." (John 15:18–19)

"I have told you these things, so that in me you may have peace. In this world you will have trouble. But take heart! I have overcome the world." (John 16:33)

"My kingdom is not of this world. If it were, my servants would fight to prevent my arrest by the Jewish leaders. But now my kingdom is from another place." (John 18:36)

Paul reinforces Jesus's teaching about the world:

For since in the wisdom of God the world through its wisdom did not know him, God was pleased . . . to save those who believe. (1 Cor. 1:21)

For our struggle is not against flesh and blood, but against the rulers, against the authorities, against the powers of this dark world and against the spiritual forces of evil in the heavenly realms. (Eph. 6:12)

James forcefully writes, "You adulterous people, don't you know that friendship with the world means enmity against God? Therefore, anyone who chooses to be a friend of the world becomes an enemy of God" (James 4:4).

Finally, in one of his last letters, the apostle John exhorts, "Do not love the world or anything in the world. If anyone loves the world, love for the Father is not in them. For everything in the world—the lust of the flesh, the lust of the eyes, and the pride of life—comes not from the Father but from the world. The world and its desires pass away, but whoever does the will of God lives forever" (1 John 2:15–17).

## A Sad Scenario

Picture the following scenario. It illustrates *who* makes up the world and *how* the world operates. As we've seen, every human is bent. We're all *incurvatus in se*, curved in on ourselves away from God. We're crooked, diseased creatures and serve as host to a variety of vices. Picture them as infectious diseases. We not only host these infections; we spread them to one another, much as COVID-19 is passed from person to person. We are contagious. With regard to the flesh and the world we practice no social distancing.

Review again Paul's words in Galatians 5, where he describes the contagions of the flesh: "Immorality, impurity and debauchery; idolatry and witchcraft; hatred, discord, jealousy, fits of rage, selfish ambition, dissensions, factions and envy; drunkenness, orgies, and the like" (vv. 19–21). We as bent creatures habitually do these kinds of things; it is second nature for us to do so.

Now consider more closely *the social dimension* of these polluted attitudes and actions. Yes, some of them can be performed in private— I can get drunk by myself—but all have social aspects, engagements, and consequences.

Lovelace's term "corporate flesh" is a helpful metaphor that describes the world in its negative dimensions. Think of riots, lynching, racism, genocide, and other group insanities. Entire cultures can lose their minds and descend into corporate evil, madness on a broad scale. The empirical evidence for this insanity is human history.

Lovelace defines *corporate flesh* this way: "When *world* is used in a negative sense in Scripture, what is meant is the total system of corporate flesh operating under satanic control, with all its incentives of reward and restraints of loss, its characteristic patterns of behavior, and its antichristian structures, methods, goals and ideologies."[4]

In Hitler's Nazi Germany, Stalin's Soviet Union, Pol Pot's Cambodia, Hutu power times in Rwanda, and the history of slavery for four hundred years in the United States, a clear pattern of "incentives of reward" and "restraints of loss" is identifiable.

Lovelace writes that corporate flesh manifests itself in many various ways. "Included are dehumanizing social, economic and political systems; business operations and foreign policy based on local interest at the expense of general human welfare; and culturally pervasive institutional sin such as racism. Like the many-headed beast of Revelation 13, the world is secretly compatible with and operative within systems which are antithetical on the surface, such as capitalism and communism."[5]

I think of Germany in the 1930s, when an entire nation embraced the lunacy of National Socialism, with very few people courageous or wise enough to resist the cultural tide. In a horrific inversion of good and evil, Germans embraced horrendous ideas and practices as praiseworthy. The infection rapidly passed from one carrier to another. Soon, an entire culture was diseased. Genuine good was denigrated as weakness or evil. Horrible wickedness was deemed admirable.

Heinrich Himmler, a terribly wicked man, firmly believed that the "Final Solution" was a good thing, for Germany and for the world. In his bent mind and heart, he viewed the Jews as vermin, virulent pests to be exterminated. We possess recorded speeches of Himmler praising SS officers for the courage and strength they daily demonstrated as they feverishly worked to eradicate the Jewish pestilence.

The world regularly manifests its toxic presence in killing of one kind or another. Millions of American slaves and Native Americans died. Consider the German concentration camps, the killing fields of the Khmer Rouge in Cambodia in the late 1970s, the Rwandan genocide in 1994, or the horrors of present-day South Sudan, Yemen, Ukraine. As Helmut Thielicke commented at the end of World War II, "We have seen an increasingly poisonous atmosphere settling down upon our globe and we sense how real and almost tangible are the evil spirits in the air, seeing an invisible hand passing an invisible cup of poison from nation to nation and throwing them into confusion."[6] Thielicke's words are just as applicable in 2023 as they were at the end of World War II.

Francis MacNutt, like Lovelace, writes of the "evil structures and pervasive seductions of our society" and compares them to "energy fields in their own right. These flawed human institutions are also molded and influenced by the demonic world," a truth we will explore under our third category of the cosmic struggle—the devil.[7]

Charles de Foucauld, a saint of the Catholic Church who died early in the twentieth century, comments on what he perceived in his home country of France after a period of solitude in the North African desert: "During nineteen days in France, what struck me most was that all classes of society—above all the least wealthy class and also the Christian families—have increased their tastes for costly and useless things. Carefree, worldly, and frivolous distractions are out of place in such grave times, in times of persecution, and they are not in accord with a Christian life. *The danger lies within ourselves*, and not within our enemies."[8]

What to do? How can we faithfully walk in the steps of Jesus in the midst of the world? Lovelace advises that we "separate ourselves as much as possible from the unholy force field of this planet's corporate flesh; to break our conformity to its characteristic ideologies, methods and motives; and to speak and act prophetically against its injustice and restraint of full human liberation."[9]

J. B. Phillips's translation of Paul's words to the Roman Christians is clear and lively: "Don't let the world around you squeeze you into its mold, but let God re-mold your minds from within" (Rom. 12:2, PHIL- LIPS). The world is "an unholy force field," constantly pulling us away from the values of Christ's kingdom. We have lived within the world's force field all our lives. We breathe its toxic air daily. It affects us all, to one extent or another.

---

### Pause and Reflect

**How might the world's "unholy force field" influence or manifest it- self in the economic or political systems you support? How do you sense it has influenced your perspectives, lifestyle, and ingrained habits? In what practical ways might you begin to break free from its influence?**

---

## Allegiance

Consider the issue of *allegiance*. Ancient Christians sometimes suffered and died as martyrs because they refused to bow to Roman emperors' demand to worship them as gods, a sign of political loyalty from a Ro- man perspective. Early Christians understood, like any martyr of the twentieth or twenty-first century, that their primary allegiance and loy- alty must be to Christ, not to the demands of competing political and religious ideologies.

In the United States the issue of ultimate allegiance always faces the Christian, though often it goes unrecognized. American cultural forces press against us—political, economic, and social. Some American val- ues are praiseworthy. Others are not. The consumerism and materi- alism that mark American culture are apt examples. The question of ultimate allegiance confronted me on a recent vacation visit to San Diego with my wife, Debbie.[10]

One day we visited the USS *Midway*, a huge aircraft carrier now moored in San Diego's harbor. The *Midway* served in a variety of combat settings, including the Gulf War. During our visit I was especially moved as I remembered my dad's experience flying off the USS *Yorktown* as a nineteen-year-old Helldiver and Dauntless pilot in the South Pacific.

So, as Debbie and I walked across the deck of the *Midway* in San Diego, thoughts and emotions rippled through me. Our visit coincided with a moving onboard ceremony celebrating the retirement of a naval officer. A crowd stood silently, indeed reverently, as the officer was "whistled" off the deck from active service. Few eyes remained dry as people stood at attention and a Navy band played "The Star-Spangled Banner." An American flag was folded with care and reverence, soon to be presented to the retiring officer. Shortly before the presentation ended, another officer read a poem with words honoring devotion to the flag and the country it represented.

As I listened to this poem, a testimony to love for country and a remembrance of great sacrifice, a lump formed in my throat. I thought of my dad flying in his Helldiver over vast stretches of the South Pacific, searching for his target and accompanied only by his tail gunner.

Then came the poem's final words, speaking of the American flag itself: "We worship you." I was caught off guard as I faced an unexpected line in the sand I should not—must not—cross. Respect and honor? Yes. Worship? Absolutely not. Ultimate allegiance? No.

Christ's followers will find themselves at prophetic odds with the world as it manifests itself through the corporate flesh of their cultural environment. We should readily applaud, encourage, and support aspects of our culture that align with the values of Christ's kingdom. We should speak and act prophetically against cultural attitudes and behaviors that subtly and occasionally directly oppose the kingdom of God and Christ, its king.

As we ponder the flesh and the world in light of Jesus's call to follow, notice how important it is to slow down, quiet down, think, pray, and thoroughly ponder these key issues. Jesus beckons us to a different way of imagining and understanding ourselves and our world.

## The Devil

As we have seen so far in this chapter, resistance to our spiritual health and growth occurs on three fronts. We cannot effectively move forward in our journey unless we have a clear understanding of who God is, the special nature of the time we are living in (as in, now and not yet), and the nature of the opposition blocking our way. The first front of that opposition—imagine three fronts in a war—concerns *us*. We are bent creatures, *incurvatus in se*. The second front is the world: corporate flesh deeply resistant to the purposes and values of the kingdom of God. The third front, our next focus of attention, is supernatural, personal evil.

The word *supernatural* is related to two Latin words: *super* (above) and *natura* (nature). Supernatural evil, then, is evil active behind the scenes, normally beyond our field of vision.

Paul, an extremely sober theologian, would think modern Christians naive if we suppose our cosmic battle against evil occurs only on the first two fronts: the flesh and the world. No, Paul insists in his letter to the Ephesians: "Put on the full armor of God, so that you can take your stand against the devil's schemes. For our struggle is not against flesh and blood, but against the rulers, against the authorities, against the powers of this dark world and against the spiritual forces of evil in the heavenly realms" (Eph. 6:11–12).

How do we resist Satan and the devils? First, we acknowledge their existence and reject a false sophistication that sounds like this: "The devil? Oh, please. Haven't we grown beyond that? Horns? Tail? Hoofs? Red tights? Grow up. We learned a long time ago that all this nonsense is simply the figment of an immature, overwrought, superstitious imagination."

In the 1980s "sophisticated" people treated the devil—and those who believed in him—with disdain. In 1986 Walter Wink wrote that "angels, spirits, principalities, gods, Satan—these, along with all other spiritual realities, are the unmentionables of our culture."[11]

Things have changed. It's easy to meet folks today who can't stop talking about the devil, who see demons hiding behind every bush, and who seem more interested in the demonic than they are in Jesus.

Perhaps you've read C. S. Lewis's wise counsel concerning the devils in his introduction to *The Screwtape Letters*: "There are two equal and opposite errors into which our race can fall about the devils. One is to disbelieve in their existence. The other is to believe, and to feel an excessive and unhealthy interest in them."[12] So let's avoid both extremes and remain as faithful as possible to the teaching of Jesus and the apostles concerning Satan and his kingdom.

You'll recall from chapter 2 that a key characteristic of this present evil age is demonic opposition to God's purposes. We should not be surprised, then, that as the kingdom of God invades the kingdom of the Evil One, a clash of kingdoms occurs. For instance, as Jesus begins to teach publicly in the synagogue in Capernaum, a man sitting and listening suddenly erupts: "What do you want with us, Jesus of Nazareth? Have you come to destroy us? I know who you are—the Holy One of God!" (Mark 1:24).

Please observe carefully. This is not an encounter between two equal powers. Jesus tells the demon to "shut up," a very strong imperative in Greek (*phimotheti*), and commands the devils to leave the man. The demons obey immediately but remain malevolent. They shriek, shake the man violently, and exit the scene (Mark 1:25–26). Twice Mark describes the demon who speaks to Jesus as "impure" (1:23, 26), a characteristic no doubt true of the entire group.

What does this exorcism—the first recorded in the Gospel of Mark—teach us about Jesus, the kingdom of God, and the kingdom of the devil? Most important, we witness the majestic authority of Jesus as the incarnate Son of God. The clash of kingdoms in Capernaum is not a battle of equal powers. Jesus speaks one word, and the devils obey. Onlookers in the synagogue are amazed at the authority Jesus exercises, both in his teaching and in the exorcism. "What is this? A new teaching—and with authority! He even gives orders to impure spirits and they obey him" (Mark 1:27).

The exorcism in Capernaum is no isolated incident. Instead, Mark views exorcism as a routine aspect of Jesus's ministry and differentiates it from Jesus's healings. "That evening after sunset the people brought to Jesus all the sick and demon-possessed. . . . Jesus healed many who had various diseases. He *also* drove out many demons, but he would not let the demons speak because they knew who he was" (Mark 1:32, 34).

Why doesn't Jesus want the demons to speak about him? Well, as I mentioned in chapter 2, the devils are natural liars. In Jesus's heated debate with Pharisaic opponents in John 8, which concerns the reliability of Jesus's testimony about himself, Jesus argues that his debate opponents refuse to accept his message because they belong to their "father, the devil" and want to carry out their "father's desires. He was a murderer from the beginning, *not holding to the truth, for there is no truth in him. When he lies, he speaks his native language, for he is a liar and the father of lies*" (John 8:44).

The devils—Satan's underlings—are liars; they delight in twisting the truth, a demonic pattern we perceived earlier in the serpent's tempting of Eve in the Garden of Eden (Gen. 3:1–5). Jesus has no need for their witness; any demonic testimony about him or his kingdom would have been entirely unreliable.

Paul deals with the same problem of unwanted demonic testimony when he and Luke encounter a female slave in Philippi. Luke writes that this exploited woman "had a spirit by which she predicted the future. She earned a great deal of money for her owners by fortune-telling. She followed Paul and the rest of us, shouting, 'These men are servants of the Most High God, who are telling you the way to be saved.' She kept this up for many days. Finally Paul became so annoyed that he turned around and said to the spirit, 'In the name of Jesus Christ I command you to come out of her!' At that moment the spirit left her" (Acts 16:16–18).

Happily for the exploited slave woman and sadly for her owners, Jesus through Paul ends the pattern of exploitation and falsehood. Yes, the woman told fortunes, and occasionally they came true, but her reliability was uncertain and her suffering apparent. Paul, on behalf of Jesus, frees her from her torment and tormentors.

Keep three words in mind as we consider the devil and his kingdom, because they are also applicable to our thoughts about the flesh and the world: *resistance*, *dehumanization*, and *authority*.

## Resistance

Knowledge of the lay of the land, the terrain we travel as we walk in Jesus's shoes, is absolutely necessary if we are to avoid danger, disillusionment, discouragement, or despair as we continue our pilgrimage with Christ toward home. Avoid spiritual naïveté. We are presently living in a cosmic war zone and need to think and behave accordingly.

Recall that this resistance appears on three fronts: *We ourselves resist God's work in us.* Our resistance is centered in our flesh. Every precious image-bearer is bent, *incurvatus in se*. Left to us, our natural default position is "me." "Meet my needs," we demand of others, the world, and God. "I may be listening to you, but I'm thinking about me." Ugh.

Thankfully, God is healing us, gracefully and powerfully straightening out his bent creatures. Do you sense, for example, that your inner focus is clarifying, increasingly centered on God, God's kingdom, and not yourself? If so, God is at work. This straightening, though, takes time and requires courage, perseverance, and hope: courage to face what needs to be faced, perseverance to hang in there when things get hard, and hope in Christ that his good work in us will be completed.

As we participate in the wonder of Christ through the power of the Spirit, God delicately and discerningly reweaves the inner warp and woof of our character. God knits carefully and slowly.

On some days, I sense resistance in me to God's weaving. Yet I also sense my resistance is weakening. New character patterns are emerging. Perhaps you are experiencing the same dynamic of resistance, growth, resistance, growth. So let's pray together:

> Lord, weave yourself deep into us. Untie the knots of resistance
> we've woven. Knit the pattern of your character in us. Amen.

The second front of resistance we face in our cosmic war zone is the world, the corporate flesh that surrounds us, pressing us, squeezing us. Surely aspects of our culture are praiseworthy. We should applaud and encourage cultural values that are beautiful and aligned with the values of Jesus's kingdom. However, there are always cultural values that deeply, diabolically resist the purposes of God. It's best to remember that.

The world resists us and we're called to resist the world (cf. Rom. 12:1–2). To resist the world well requires the ability to discern cultural resistances to Christ's kingdom and how we should respond to them.

Let's not be naive or proud, though, in thinking we can eradicate all cultural resistance, for we live amid this present evil age; it will not end until our Lord returns. We are already but not yet. Kingdoms are clashing.

Let's now consider a global cultural resistance to the kingdom of God: dehumanization.

## Dehumanization

Note this well: whenever we see human beings—God's precious image-bearers—dehumanized, the devil is at work in the fields of the world.

Every genocide is birthed from the mouths of great liars spewing falsehoods. The killing always begins with a horrible fabrication about human beings. Hitler, Himmler, Goering, Goebbels—some of the great, malicious liars of the twentieth century—poisoned German culture in the 1920s and 1930s with their great lie: "The Jews are vermin. They aren't human. They're an infection in the pure Aryan bloodstream of the German people. What do we do with vermin? We exterminate them. We eradicate the infection. If we fail to do so, the contagion spreads. It has already infected German culture."

This enormous lie was repeated daily through public speeches, the radio, and print media. It lay at the heart of Nazi propaganda. And the result? The German people succumbed to the weight of this great lie, and millions died.

Lies dehumanize. God's chosen people, the Jews, were grossly dehumanized; the cowards killing them actually believed they were acting courageously. "Only courageous men can stand in a field of ten thousand bodies and do what you have done," Himmler told his SS officers. "The Lord has told me to do this," Hitler lied. Hideous lies and cold-blooded murder. Here we discern the voice of Satan and his murderous work (cf. John 8:44). The mark of the devil is playing fast and loose with the truth. And somebody always ends up dead.

The same pattern is discernible in every genocide. Think of Rwanda in 1994. The horrors committed there between April and July—thousands and thousands of people hacked to death in a country no larger than Vermont—were the rancid fruit of an onslaught of falsehoods building in intensity for over thirty years. As the death toll mounted, Hutu radio stations repeated the great lie: "The Tutsis are cockroaches. Crush them beneath your feet. They're not human. They don't deserve to live."

Lies and murder: the attempt to exterminate Native Americans, the Armenian genocide, the Final Solution in Germany, the killing fields of Cambodia, slavery in the United States. All characterize the devil's work; Satan always seeks to dehumanize. He hates God's precious image-bearers. Whenever we see people demonized—treated as less than fully human—Satan is at work and must be resisted. The strength to resist, though, comes from Christ and the authority Jesus has given to his church—his body on earth—to exercise on his behalf.

## A Clash of Authority

Jesus's authority is unimaginably immense. It is universal in scope. Consider the authority Jesus demonstrates as he delivers the Gerasene demoniac, a precious image-bearer defaced and defeated by the power of the devil. If you want to see what dehumanization looks like, take a long look at this man.

We find the story of the Gerasene demoniac in Mark 5:1–20. Initially we encounter a genuinely horrific scene. Jesus and the disciples have crossed the Sea of Galilee to the Gentile area of Gerasa. As they make landfall,

A man with an impure spirit came from the tombs to meet him. This
man lived in the tombs, and no one could bind him anymore, not even
with a chain. For he had often been chained hand and foot, but he tore
the chains apart and broke the irons on his feet. No one was strong
enough to subdue him. Night and day among the tombs and in the hills,
he would cry out and cut himself with stones. (Mark 5:2–5)

This man is God's precious image-bearer. Mark doesn't tell us how
he ended up in such a horrendous, evil condition and situation. Here he
is, living among the tombs, surrounded by death and seemingly under
the authority of the demons inhabiting him. He now possesses super-
human strength. He cries out day and night, tormented by the devils
who dwell in him and surround him. He is cutting himself, longing to
be delivered from his torment.

Here, indeed, is devilish work. The demons are happily degrading
and debasing this human being; they long for him to die. They are purposely and cruelly wreaking havoc on an image-bearer God has created
and loves. They are malicious. Cruel. Evil. Murderous. And they must
be overcome. Immense authority will soon confront them. Jesus has
arrived on the scene:

When he saw Jesus from a distance, he ran and fell on his knees in
front of him. He shouted at the top of his voice, "What do you want
with me Jesus, Son of the Most High God? In God's name don't torture
me!" For Jesus had said to him, "Come out of this man, you impure
spirit!" (Mark 5:6–8)

Note that when he sees Jesus from a distance, the man runs to Jesus
and falls on his knees in front of him. Yet it is the demons who start
talking. When they start speaking, their fear is evident.

A power encounter has begun, a clash of authority, a confrontation between *drastically unequal powers*. Jesus is the "Son of the Most High God," as the demons themselves confess (Mark 5:7). They are the agents of Satan, acting devilishly on Satan's behalf.

Jesus demands that the demons identify themselves. With horror we learn that more than one devil inhabits this man. "'My name is Legion,' he replied, 'for we are many.' And he begged Jesus again and again not to send them out of the area" (Mark 5:9–10). Thousands of demons. One Jesus. And it's the devils who are terrified.

Be encouraged. The Jesus who strikes terror into the heart of these demonic hordes is the very same Jesus who lives in you. We need not fear anyone or anything.

## Pause and Reflect

Who or what is on your fear list? Satan? An abuser? A memory? The past? The present? The future? Failure? Sickness? Separation from loved ones? Death? The unknown? Lean into Jesus. He is the king of all that is seen and unseen, and his authority is immense, immeasurable, and universal. Reflect on what fear drives you and how it affects you.

The devils beg Jesus for permission to remain in the area (Mark 5:10). It's a foregone conclusion that they will have to leave the man. That is settled.

Recall that this is a Gentile area; we shouldn't be surprised that a herd of unclean animals is feeding nearby, a food source for Gentile communities. "Send us into those pigs," the devils beg. Unclean spirits for unclean animals.

"He gave them permission, and the impure spirits came out and went into the pigs. The herd, about two thousand in number, rushed down the steep bank into the lake and were drowned" (Mark 5:13). They had hoped for finer fare.

Most important, though, is that we recognize the tremendous authority Jesus exercises with a simple word of command. Look closely at all that has happened: a precious image-bearer set free and in his right mind; a legion of demons fleeing from Jesus; two thousand pigs stampeding into the ocean. The authority of Jesus is indeed mind-boggling. "Who is this man?" we ask. He is the eternal Son, the great king, now incarnate on our behalf.

Michael Casey, a Catholic abbot, captures especially well the broader implications of this exorcism for our understanding of Jesus: "If we can hear in our imagination the thundering stampede of the two thousand Gerasene swine as they plunge into the abyss (Mark 5:13), then we will have some idea of the power of holiness which Jesus represents."[13] This is not simply raw, naked power. It is the power of the holy Son of God— the great king of Israel establishing his rights and manifesting his love in Gentile territory—a breathtaking holy authority that terrifies the devils and sends them to flight.

## Baguio City

James exhorts us to submit ourselves to God and resist the devil, and promises he will flee (James 4:7). Peter, too, reminds us to be "alert and of sober mind." Why? "Your enemy the devil prowls around like a roaring lion looking for someone to devour. *Resist him, standing firm in the faith*, because you know that the family of believers throughout the world is undergoing the same kind of sufferings" (1 Pet. 5:8–9).

As we resist the devil and exercise the authority of Christ, we must not act like foolish children incautiously and immaturely poking with sticks at a rattlesnake in the backyard. Likewise, if we see a live wire swinging back and forth in the street, we keep our distance, waiting for trained experts to handle the dangerous situation.

I close this chapter with a story from my own life, hopefully one that illustrates what we have explored in our discussion of the flesh, the world, and the devil. It concerns an experience I had while teaching a group of World Vision workers in Baguio City, a city in Northern Luzon, Philippines.

When I arrived in the Philippines, I knew nothing about Baguio City. Only when my trip was finished did I learn that Baguio City is a well-known center of witchcraft and its associated occult practices.

On arriving in Baguio, I checked in to my hotel, part of a large worldwide chain familiar to me, one I often use in the States. Everything in my room looked and seemed fine. I unpacked, began thinking about the teaching sessions I was to begin the next day, and decided to go for a stroll.

As I walked through open-air markets close to my hotel and glanced in shop windows, I was surprised and somewhat shocked by an abundance of strange wooden carvings, many of them wooden phalluses. Other carvings were of bizarre faces and strange animals I'd never seen in any zoo. *Strange tourist items*, I thought to myself. *What's going on? A fertility cult of some kind?* The carvings were pervasive; my fellow shoppers seemed accustomed to them. *Somebody must be buying them,* I thought. *Why?* Other sexually charged carvings were also for sale.

After an hour or so I returned to my hotel, took a short nap, and had some dinner. When I got into bed for a good night's sleep—my first session was scheduled for the next afternoon—I felt somewhat troubled. I didn't know why. My sleep was fitful and uneasy.

The setting for my teaching sessions was one of the hotel's large ballrooms. Some 250 to 300 World Vision folks had gathered in Baguio City for some rest and relaxation and to hear me teach about spiritual formation.

During my first session, I noticed that the group seemed restless and inattentive, and I taught very poorly. As I spoke, I felt as though I was trudging through mud. None of us were enjoying ourselves. When the session ended, I'm sure folks must have been thinking, *We came to hear him?*

The next day, a Wednesday if I remember correctly, was scheduled to be my last session—or at least I thought it was. Tuesday night, I again slept poorly, restlessly, uneasily. Something about my hotel room made me feel increasingly uncomfortable. And when I taught on Wednesday, I again taught poorly. The World Vision folks continued to look extremely tired and distracted. What was going on? As I finished Wednesday's session, I thought to myself, *Well, sometimes things just go like this.* I looked forward to heading home; I felt lonely, homesick, and disappointed with how things had gone.

While I packed up my notes on the podium, Pastor Joey, the World Vision chaplain in the Philippines, came up to me, smiled, and said, "Chris, we're looking forward very much to what you'll be saying tomorrow. Can you also please give an invitation for people who may not know Jesus to come forward for prayer and counsel?"

I was shocked. I had prepared material for only two sessions. I had nothing prepared for a third. Absolutely nothing. Not only that, but I didn't give "invitations." Billy Graham did stuff like that. I was a teacher, not an evangelist. I had given an invitation once or twice in the past but with little success; at most one or two people came forward. "That's fine," I lied to Joey. "Looking forward to it."

That evening I had dinner and headed back to my room. "What am I going to do?" I asked myself. "I've got nothing to teach, nothing prepared. And I'm supposed to teach a large group of unresponsive, inattentive, distracted people and then give an invitation? What am I going to do?" On top of that problem, my sense of discomfort in my hotel room was increasing. "What's going on? Why do I feel so uncomfortable here?"

Finally, I went to sleep. Around two in the morning I awoke with a weighty presence on top of me. It felt like a body. I know this sounds crazy, but I can only tell you what I experienced. It was a distinct presence, weighty, pressing down on my chest.

Well, what do you do in a situation like that? I pushed hard, and the presence left. But it didn't leave my room. I couldn't see it, but I sensed it across from me in a corner of the room.

Of course, I was frightened, but I was also angry, my modus operandi when I feel threatened. I turned on my bedside lamp, crossed the room, entered the bathroom, and shut the door. I had no experience with this kind of thing. What should I do?

I retrieved a yellow pad from my desk, as I needed to come up with something to say at 8 a.m. to three hundred people in that large hotel ballroom, then returned to the bathroom. The time was 3 a.m. And I had nothing. Not only did I have nothing to say, but there was a distinct evil presence lingering in my bedroom.

"Help me, Lord," I remember praying. "I don't know what to do. There's something outside my bathroom door that's really trying to disrupt things." The hours passed slowly. Four o'clock. Five o'clock. Six o'clock. Seven o'clock. I opened the bathroom door. Finally, bright sunlight was slowly filling the room. I still had written nothing on my yellow notepad. Not a word.

I took a shower, walked uneasily back into my bedroom, and still sensed the presence there. Yes, I know you're thinking: *Why didn't you rebuke it in the name of Jesus?* To be honest, I simply didn't think of that. I was so distracted and uncomfortable that the thought didn't occur to me. And I had very little experience with this sort of devilish nastiness.

I was being bullied, and I didn't know how to respond. My thoughts were centered more on the approaching teaching session, my blank notepad, and Pastor Joey's expectations.

Finally, around 7:40 a.m., I left my room with a sigh of relief and walked to the ballroom. People were slowly entering. A praise band was starting to tune up. A smiling Pastor Joey walked up to me. "We're so looking forward to your message, Chris." I smiled, nodded, and thought to myself, *What message? I got nothing.*

The minutes passed. At about 7:55 a.m., I walked over to the praise band leader. "I'm going to be giving an invitation at the end of my message," I whispered. "Do you think you might play something if there's not much of a response?" I had watched Billy Graham crusades and knew the choir always sang "Just as I Am" after Billy invited people to come forward. I needed all the help I could get, and perhaps a little music might prime the pump for unresponsive folks.

I returned to my seat, gazed at my blank notepad, and glanced at the clock—7:58 a.m. Pastor Joey walked toward the speaker's platform to introduce me—7:59 a.m. Then the Lord spoke. "Tell them what's been happening."

*Well*, I thought to myself. *At least I have something.* Pastor Joey finished his introduction. I took a deep breath, strode to the podium, looked out at the sleepy crowd, and asked, "Can I tell you what's been happening to me over the past few days?" Suddenly, unexpectedly, I had the full attention of my sleepy, inattentive, distracted audience.

As I described what had been going on in my hotel room—admittedly a wild story—people began nodding in agreement. "Has the same thing been happening to you?" I asked. Heads throughout the ballroom nodded. Suddenly I knew what I was supposed to say. It should have dawned on me so much sooner. But we all had been in a deep fog.

I called on the power and authority of Christ, and in his name rebuked the devil for his attempts to bully, distract, and confuse us.

Please know that I had never done anything like this before. I prayed aloud for about six minutes, then sensed the work was done. My audience now sat wide awake and attentive. "Oh," I then remembered. "The invitation."

I took a breath and calmly said, "Perhaps there are some here who would like to come into a relationship with Jesus for the first time. There may be others who long for their relationship with Christ to deepen. I invite you to come forward. I'll be glad to pray for you."

Close to a minute passed. No one responded. I turned toward the praise band leader—perhaps we needed to prime the pump a bit—when two women in the tenth row stood and began to make their way forward. I distinctly recall their chairs scraping and the effort they made as they nudged in front of other people to the end of their row and then walked toward me.

*Well*, I thought to myself, *at least a couple of folks were touched.* Suddenly, though, other folks started to join them from all over the ballroom. I watched in amazement as row after row emptied.

I'm not exaggerating. Soon there was no more room in the front of the podium. People were crowding in the aisles. It looked like the entire room had left their seats and come forward. I smiled, and all these precious image-bearers smiled back. I said a word or two, we prayed together, and finally the meeting ended. It was a wonderful experience. I'll never forget it.

Let's take a step back and analyze what was going on. God wanted to bring life and renewed strength to these dear people, all of whom were engaged in difficult work for World Vision. And for reasons known only to God, he wanted to use a knucklehead like me to help them regain their footing with Jesus.

God's act of revival and renewal occurred in a setting of demonic infestation. As I've mentioned, Baguio City is a gravitational force

field for superstition, demonic activity, witchcraft, and who knows
what else. Christ desired to work in this challenging, resistant environment. He wanted to expand his reign more fully into this con-
taminated territory, much like he did in the land of the Gerasene
demoniac.

I had little experience with spiritual warfare and was poorly prepared for the demonic opposition I encountered so directly. Many
commented that during those first days together they seemed enveloped in a spiritual fog; most shared my struggle with demonic bullying
and intimidation in their own rooms. Here was direct resistance from
the kingdom of the Evil One; initially, the encounter was exhausting,
frightening, and confusing.

The tide turned when we discerned what was happening and *called
on Jesus* to defend us and to exert his authority in the midst of this deep
resistance to him and his kingdom. Jesus gladly and readily responded.

## Three Helpful Questions

Pete Greig poses three helpful questions to ask when we encounter firm
resistance to Christ's kingdom:

1. What's the *diagnosis*? What's going on? As I struggled that last
   night before my 8 a.m. talk, I prayed this prayer continually,
   and the Lord answered at 7:59 a.m.
2. What's the *prognosis*? If we don't deal with this infestation
   in the name of Christ, people will remain distracted and
   discouraged.
3. What's the *prescription*? What should I do? How should I respond? *"Tell them what's been happening to you. Rebuke the
   devil in my name."*[14]

It's time to draw this chapter to a close. Flesh, world, devil. Quite a trio. An unholy trinity of sorts. John Paul II's exhortation comes to mind. "Be not afraid." Now, though, we're prepared to take concrete steps with Jesus to reduce their influence as we live out the gift of years God has graciously given us, however many or few they may be.

## Pause and Reflect

**Pray with me:**

**O God, whose blessed Son came into the world to destroy the works of the devil, redeem us from sin and evil. Grant that, having this hope, we may purify ourselves as he is pure; that, when he comes again with power and great glory, we may increasingly be like him in his eternal and glorious kingdom; where he lives and reigns with you and the Holy Spirit, one God, for ever and ever. Amen.**[15]

**Reflect on what came to mind as you prayed.**

# CHAPTER FOUR

# Work at What You're Not Good At

The surrender of myself to him is inseparable from the
giving up of my body to him in such a way that it can
serve both him and me as a common abode.

—Dallas Willard, *The Spirit of the Disciplines*

As we learn to walk in the footsteps of Jesus, there are important questions we must ask and then ponder carefully. In chapter 1, for instance, we asked the question "What's God like?" and discovered that God is like Jesus. Then we covered the special time frame we need to keep in mind in order to guide our path. Next we addressed what opposes us (flesh, world, devil) as we move forward. In this chapter we'll continue to explore how we can learn from Jesus as we walk this path.

But before we can learn from him properly, we need to understand who Jesus is and why it matters that his nature is both human and divine for our life with him. That will lead to questions concerning who *we* are as human beings created in God's image: Who am I? What does it mean to be an embodied self?

Who am I? How would you answer that question? First we could say, "I am a human being." But as Christians that means we are bearers of

God's image, which shows that we are precious to God. This is the basis for the belief that every human being has value and should be treated with dignity.

According to the Bible, we could also answer the question by saying, "I am an embodied soul." I have a body, a mind, a will, and a soul, which together make me a human being.

Human beings are unique creatures, in significant ways distinct from other forms of animal life. All animals are God's treasured creatures, but they don't inhabit their world in the same way as humans. Consider, for instance, the foxes who regularly scamper through my backyard and occasionally trot across my back porch; they seem to enjoy relating to me but only from a distance.

Foxes don't engage in abstract thinking. An alphabet would be a mystery to them. They can't learn geometric theorems, no matter how long they might spend in a classroom with a mathematics professor. They are not troubled by the problem of evil. When they kill a squirrel or rabbit, or even their own young, they feel no remorse. Foxes are predators. They live their lives by instinct and impulse, drives and reflexes given them as foxes created by God.

Humans are different. We are God's image-bearers (Gen. 1:26). We're capable of abstract thought. Nouns and verbs make sense to us. We can form sentences with complex syntax. We work with numbers and enjoy the math. We can, unlike foxes, ponder geometric theorems or reflect on the problem of evil. The word *evil* has meaning for us, as does the word *good*. We think about God and the question of what God is like, and wonder if God loves us—or doesn't.

I can choose (via my will) to do something (via my body) that I have considered carefully (via my mind). There is a depth within image-bearers (the soul) that other forms of terrestrial life don't possess or experience. All humans—you and me—are embodied selves; we are mind, will, body, and soul.

Yet we are creatures and share common characteristics with other creatures like foxes, trees, and rocks. Note that the word *creature* is related to another word: *creator*. When we describe humans as creatures, we acknowledge and affirm that we have been created by someone else: God. An atheist, to be consistent, would not call humans creatures, for an atheist, by definition, doesn't believe in a creator.

## Bent Creatures

Human beings are God's precious image-bearers, but sadly, something has happened to us, and it's not good. We have inherited from our ancient ancestors—Adam and Eve—a bent nature. We are *incurvatus in se*.

We are not what we were meant to be. We have gone bad, like torn cloth, like rotted meat. Torn cloth slowly unravels, the original hole getting larger and larger. Rotten meat finally disappears: it slowly but surely disintegrates. Unraveled cloth and decomposed meat no longer serve their purpose. Something remains, but it is not the way it was supposed to be. Unraveled thread is no longer whole cloth; decomposed meat is no longer hamburger or steak. The same dynamic is true of human nature; it has unraveled, it is corrupt, and it manifests its corruption as our bodies slowly die.

Recall Luther's descriptive phrase for human nature. Because of our ancient parents' sin, our human nature is now *incurvatus in se*. We are curved in on ourselves. We are warped image-bearers, terribly skewed; we are damaged goods. Dallas Willard puts it this way: "It is this pervasive distortion and disruption of human existence from the top down that the Bible refers to as sin (not sins)—the general posture of fallen humankind. Humans are not only wrong, they are also *wrung*, twisted out of proper shape and proportion."[1]

Does God love us any less in our horrible, unnatural, twisted state?

No. God never stops loving us, for God is love (1 John 4:8). It's not possible for God to act in an unloving manner, though we may experience God's love as extremely painful. God's love is astringent; it can sting like antiseptic dabbed on an open wound.

To use a common phrase, we are "self-centered" creatures; this ingrained, curved stance daily wreaks havoc around the world. The horrors of human history provide empirical evidence that something has gone terribly wrong with us. The question then becomes, What is God doing to make it right?

What is God doing? He is acting to save his precious image-bearers in the remarkably beautiful story and example of Jesus. To walk in the shoes of Jesus, we must understand who he is, how he lived, and what he has done on our behalf to heal our deformed state.

## Fully Human

Jesus was, is, and ever will be fully human. Fully. He is not partly human and partly God. No, Jesus, the incarnate Son of God, is fully human and simultaneously fully God.

Consider with me an important series of questions:

- Did Jesus have a real human mind?
- Did Jesus have a real human soul?
- Did Jesus have a real human will?
- Did Jesus have a real human body?

The ancient church grappled with these questions as it read the Bible and pondered the question, Who is Jesus? Finally, after years of worship, prayer, discussion, and debate, it answered with a resounding yes to all four questions.

*A human mind?* Some ancient Christians believed that Jesus had a human body but a divine mind rather than human mind. No, ancient church leaders responded in council, Jesus had and has a genuine human mind. Luke writes, for example, that Jesus "grew in wisdom and stature" (Luke 2:52). Jesus's knowledge grew as he matured; he first had the conceptual capabilities of a baby boy, then a child, then a teenager, then an adult. His knowledge grew as he grew physically, emotionally, and spiritually.

Simultaneously, though, as the eternal Son of God, Jesus knew all things and never ceased to have this knowledge, for his mind was the mind of God. In the incarnation, Jesus never ceased being God the Son, the second person of the Trinity. He is fully God, fully human—that's who Jesus is and always will be.

Let's continue to explore the nature of Jesus's human mind. Think of his vocation as a carpenter. Jesus learned about the nature of wood from his father, Joseph, though he was the creator of every tree that had ever grown on planet Earth. His skill as a carpenter no doubt developed as his mind and body matured. The very person who created wood now learns about wood, as any human carpenter must. Quite remarkable and incomprehensible!

Jesus learned the Bible just like you and me. He read it. He studied it. He heard it discussed in his family circle. He listened to sermons in synagogue. Yet, as Luke explains, from a very early age Jesus's understanding and interpretation of Scripture caught people's attention. Jesus's parents discovered him at age twelve in the Temple discussing Torah with the teachers of Israel. Who was this child with these profound insights at such an early age? People wondered. And pondered.

The very one who inspired the Scripture now learns the Scripture! How strange. How wonderful. How mysterious. For Jesus was fully human, while never ceasing to exist as the eternal Son, fully divine. As an ancient Christian poet writes, "He who knows all things begins to learn." Jesus has—to this very day—a human mind.

*A human soul?* How about a human soul? Yes, Jesus has a soul, ancient Christian leaders proclaimed. Why? Jesus must be all that we are, *to save all that we are.* Jesus is saving our mind, our soul, our will, and our body. All that we are as humans is *incurvatus in se*, bent and twisted. All that we are needs to be straightened out. So, to save us, the eternal Son of God becomes all that we are apart from sin. Jesus possesses all that characterizes us as humans, including a human soul. Just as we have souls that animate our bodies, so Jesus has a fully human soul, though a sinless one. If Jesus was soulless, he would not be fully human.

*A human will?* Finally, the church read the Scripture and—after significant debate—declared that Jesus has a human will, as we all do. He freely made choices throughout his lifetime. For instance, Jesus chose twelve specific disciples. He chose how he would spend his time, what food he would eat, when and how he would pray and in what places. He never chose wrongly. For Jesus's will was not bent like ours. In his humanity, he never swerved from the will of his Father.

When I think of the choices Jesus freely made, I ask myself how I have exercised my will over the course of my lifetime. I have made good choices, and I've made some hellishly bad ones.

What choices have I made this very day? I arose this morning at 5:30 a.m. and spent time reading, praying, and pondering. I made myself some coffee and popped part of a cinnamon bun in my mouth. Tasted good! Around 7:30 I rumbled into my office, sat down at my desk, and began tapping away at my computer. It's now 8:50. Around nine I plan on making some oatmeal. I didn't have to start my day this way. I chose to do so. All day long I'll be making choices as I exercise my will. So will you. So did Jesus. He has—to this very day—a human will.

If Jesus had been born in the twentieth century in Los Angeles, what

choices would he have made over his lifetime? How would he have nav-
igated the internet or YouTube? How often would he have checked his
cell phone? Would he have had a cell phone? How much TV would he
have watched? What programs would have caught his attention? What
jokes or situations would he have found funny? And what images and
dialogue would have saddened or angered him?

*A human body?* Did Jesus have a real human body? Does he still
have one today? This possibility was very difficult for some ancient
Christians to accept, especially for those from a Greek or Roman background. Greek kids, for example, grew up with Plato as a key teacher
and learned from him that human bodies hinder rather than help spiritual development.

Plato, in fact, referred to the body as a prison that the soul must
escape to make its journey back to God. "*Soma sēma,*" Plato taught.
"The body is a prison." Some Greek Christians, then, viewed the body
as a hindrance to spiritual development and life. Some, known as
Docetists, reflected Plato's skepticism about the goodness of the body.
They argued that Jesus only seemed to have a body.[2]

The ancient church, though, in a decision based on the Bible's teaching, declared in council that Jesus had a *real* body, a body received from
his mother, the Virgin Mary. Jesus had arms, legs, stomach, brain,
blood, tongue, lungs, and male genitals.

Every characteristic of a male human body was true for Jesus's body.
He slept, ate, breathed, had bowel movements, and so on. Jesus has, to
this very day, a resurrected, human body. In his humanity, Jesus is a
resurrected, embodied self. And furthermore, Jesus's body aided him
in his spiritual life and mission as Israel's Messiah.

In his life as an embodied self, Jesus shows his precious image-bearers
that human embodiment is God's created will for us. Embodiment is not
a mistake to be overcome; it is a blessing to be embraced. In a word, God
loves bodies, just as God loves matter in general. God is very earthy, in-

deed much more earthy than we might imagine. We shouldn't be surprised that God uses very earthy means to facilitate our spiritual growth. For instance, what could be more earthy than bread and wine? What could be more earthy—and divine—than the body and blood Christ offers to us in the Eucharist? What could be more earthy than spiritual disciplines such as fasting? In Christ, an earthy God has come to save his people.

If we view our faith simply as an ideational system of some sort—a panoply of abstract ideas—we have profoundly missed the point. Jesus is the *incarnate* Son.

Human mind, human soul, human will, human body—Jesus has them all. He is fully human. Yet not for one instant does he cease being fully divine.

## Fully Human: Why?

We still must go deeper. *Why* did Jesus have to be fully human? What did his humanity enable him to do that could not have occurred apart from the eternal Son's incarnation?

*Every aspect of what it means to be human—all that we are—needs to be saved*, for we are presently fallen and corrupt. Our mind is fallen, our soul is fallen, our will is fallen, our body is fallen. All are infected with sin, all are corrupt, all are dying. To save my mind, Jesus must have a mind. To save my soul, Jesus must have a soul. To save my will, Jesus must have a will. To save my body, Jesus must have a body.

Gregory of Nazianzus, a great ancient theologian, puts it this way: "That which is not assumed is not healed, but that which is united to his Godhead is also saved."[3] That is, if my body is to be saved, Jesus must "assume" or have a human body, along with a human mind, soul, and will, all in union with his divine nature in the incarnation. Jesus

becomes all that I am so that all I am as a human being—God's precious image-bearer—can be healed of the ravages of sin and corruption
in him.

Jesus offers new life to every aspect of our human being. How can he
offer me new life? Jesus is both God and human. In Jesus's humanity,
he becomes all that I am, apart from sin. And through the presence and
power of his divine nature, which is in intimate union with his human
nature, he conquers, indeed, kills, the contamination that is killing me
and you: sin itself.

To repeat: the only aspect of our present human condition that does
not characterize Jesus is sin. Jesus is free from sin's infestation. Not only
is Jesus's human nature uncontaminated, but Jesus never committed an
act of sin, whether in thought, word, or deed. In fact, Jesus invited his
severest opponents and enemies to prove him guilty of sin. In a heated
debate with Jewish leaders the apostle John records for us, Jesus asks a
pointed question: "Can any of you prove me guilty of sin?" (John 8:46).
None of his opponents could.

We may wonder, *Well, if Jesus isn't sinful, is he really human? Does he
genuinely understand my life and my struggles?*

These are fair and important questions. Let's address the first one:
If Jesus isn't sinful, is he really human? Sure. Sin and its awful acts and
effects are not constituent of human nature as created by God. Instead,
sin is a disease, a contamination that infects all humans.

Picture sin and evil like a hole in a piece of cloth that gets wider and
wider, or like rot on a good piece of steak that progressively spoils or
corrupts the entire piece of meat. Or decay in a tooth. The hole is not
the cloth. The rot is not the meat. The decay is not the tooth, but if left
untreated, it would finally destroy the tooth.

Once the hole or rot or decay have accomplished their destructive
work, the cloth has unraveled, the meat disintegrated, and the tooth
fully decayed; what has happened to the hole or rot or decay when their

corrupted work is accomplished? They disappear. Similarly, sin feeds off human nature and, left to itself, destroys it.

Thankfully, the human nature Jesus received from Mary wasn't corrupt like ours. It was not polluted by sin's contamination or infestation. The eternal Son's divine nature, joined to the human nature offered by Mary as she conceived by the Holy Spirit, protected and preserved Jesus's humanity from the contagion of sin.

So, if you want to see what a real human being looks like—one that corresponds to God's original blueprint—*look at Jesus*. Jesus represents what we were created to be: a healthy, whole, sane embodied self. He is the "new" we are all created to be: mind, soul, will, and body. When we look at him, we see the original design for our humanity in its pristine perfection. In Christ, immersed in him in baptism, we are re-created, restored, and renewed. "Therefore, if anyone is in Christ, the new creation has come: The old has gone, the new is here! All this is from God, who reconciled us to himself through Christ . . . not counting people's sins against them" (2 Cor. 5:17–19).

## Jesus Is the Fundamental Pattern for Thinking and Living Well

What pattern does Jesus model for living and thinking well as his image-bearers? How did he live? What were his practices for thinking and living well? How did he nurture his spiritual life, his incarnate life with the Father and the Holy Spirit?

Let's ponder some of his specific practices. Luke tells us that Jesus "often withdrew to lonely places and prayed" (Luke 5:16). He studied the Scripture and discussed biblical texts with the teachers of Israel, even at the age of twelve (Luke 2:46). Before times of temptation and stress, Jesus fasted (Luke 4:1–2). He visited synagogues in towns such as

Nazareth and Capernaum (Luke 4:16; Mark 6:1–2) and regularly traveled to Jerusalem to celebrate Jewish religious festivals such as Passover and Tabernacles (John 2:13; 7:10). He worshiped in the Temple. He prayed and taught his disciples how to pray (Luke 11:1–13).

In his incarnate state, Jesus *learned* how to live life well. As Luke puts it, "He grew in wisdom and stature" (Luke 2:52). A similar dynamic can be replicated in our lives today. We can learn to walk in his steps, to wear his shoes. We grow, and we mature spiritually, mentally, and physically by doing so.

Jesus *learned* to speak. He *learned* to write. He *learned* to read. He *learned* to heed Mary as she called him to dinner. He *learned* to handle a hammer and a saw carefully as he worked with Joseph. He *learned* that it's a good idea to inform his parents if he's going to spend a few days longer in Jerusalem (Luke 2:41–50). He *learned* as he prayed. He *learned* as he studied. He *learned* as he worshiped. He *learned* as he suffered.

In a nutshell, Jesus developed wise dispositions, habits, and behaviors as an embodied self. My point? If Jesus—the preeminent model for us of how to live well—found it necessary to develop and nurture these dispositions and habits—how much more necessary is this for us in our much more troubled condition.[4] *Jesus was not infected with sin, yet he still practiced these disciplines until they became second nature.*

If Jesus prayed, as his precious image-bearer I must learn how to pray. If Jesus studied, I must learn how to study. If Jesus worshiped, I must learn how to worship. If Jesus entered into silence and solitude, the same is necessary for me and you. In Willard's words, "The pervasive practices of our Lord form the core of those very activities that through the centuries have stood as disciplines for the spiritual life. It would seem only logical to emulate his daily actions since he was a great master of the spiritual life. So, isn't it reasonable then to see in those disciplines the specific factors leading to the easy yoke, the light burden, and the abundance of life and power?"[5]

## Obedience and Love

Learning to obey is difficult. For many, the call to obey invokes memories of past and present failures and sins. Who wants to focus on failure? In our most honest moments, we know full well that we have sinned against God and against our neighbor. Ugh. Can't we think about something else?

Plus, we've encountered people who delight in identifying and punishing other peoples' sins. We know what their moral rigorism feels like. They sandpaper our open wounds. We lie prostrate on the ground, weighed down with the failures of our moral history, and they stand on our chests, raising their hands to God in self-exaltation. They delight in beating us with their moral baseball bats. They sound like the Pharisee praying to himself in Jesus's well-known story about the evil of self-righteousness: "God, I thank you that I am not like other people—robbers, evildoers, adulterers—or even like this tax collector. I fast twice a week and give a tenth of all I get" (Luke 18:11–12).

Many of us readily identify with the tax collector, the subject of the self-righteous Pharisee's scorn: "But the tax collector stood at a distance. He would not even look up to heaven, but beat his breast and said, 'God, have mercy on me, a sinner'" (Luke 18:13). The tax collector is thinking clearly and honestly; he's praying in line with the sad truth of his own life.

So, as we explore the nature and dynamics of learning to obey, the safest and wisest place to begin is with the tax collector's prayer. Honesty before God, a broken heart crying out for grace and mercy, is the pathway to healing and restoration. Be encouraged. It is the tax gatherer who walks away justified by God, not the judgmental moralizer: "I tell you that this man, rather than the other, went home justified before God. For all those who exalt themselves will be humbled, and those who humble themselves will be exalted" (Luke 18:14).

As we confess our sin to God—naming it for what it is—we courageously open the door of our moral life to God's merciful, astringent love. We eagerly, expectantly, and yes, somewhat fearfully take a moral inventory of our life's story. What's the present state of affairs in our moral life? In mine? Or yours? What does the moral terrain of our lives resemble? A desert? A well-cultivated field? A lush garden? A frozen wasteland?

Let's ask a very direct question: *What are we not good at when it comes to obedience?* Some of us struggle with lust. We'd like to learn how to live a chaste life. Others battle greed. We'd like to learn how to live more simply, giving rather than grasping. Others struggle with anger. We're walking time bombs, ready to explode at the slightest perceived offense. We long for deeper patience, with others and with ourselves. Some are inflated by pride. We are filled with ourselves, bloated with a deep-rooted sense of superiority.

Have I struck any resonant chords? What's coming to mind as you read these words? What are you not good at?

## Pause and Reflect

**What are the pinch points in your life with God, the points of resistance and failure? The areas where obedience seems well-nigh impossible? What are you not good at? What would you like Jesus to teach you about a different way to live as an embodied self?**

When we tell Christ that we want to learn to love him with our obedience—even if we do so in a whisper—we're giving God a hug.

For genuine, healthy obedience is grounded in love and energized by love. The path of obedience is the path of love, not fear or shame. *We don't obey to gain God's love.* We obey because we are already loved by God and are loving God back. To obey, especially when a broken part of us wants so badly to disobey, is to kiss Jesus on the cheek.

Jesus clearly links love to obedience. "If you love me, keep my commands" (John 14:15). "Whoever has my commands and keeps them is the one who loves me. The one who loves me will be loved by my Father, and I too will love them and show myself to them" (John 14:21). "Anyone who loves me will obey my teaching. My Father will love them, and we will come to them and make our home with them. Anyone who does not love me will not obey my teaching. These words you hear are not my own; they belong to the Father who sent me" (John 14:23–24).

When we listen well to Jesus's words, they serve as a homing beacon for our obedience. I hear Jesus saying, "Stay on this beam, track on this beam, and you'll make it home. The air will be much less turbulent. A smooth landing is ahead. The runway is well lit."

Pray with me:

Lord, teach me to love, teach me to obey, for your mercy is great.

## What Am I Not Good At?

Now we are ready to learn from Jesus. Willard mentions the "pervasive practices" of Jesus. What did Jesus practice? He practiced going to synagogue. He practiced going to his true home, the Temple in Jerusalem. He practiced memorizing Scripture. He practiced silence and solitude. He practiced community. He practiced patience. He practiced perseverance. He practiced worship. He practiced prayer. If we are to keep in step with

Jesus, if we are to follow his footsteps, we will adopt his practices. His practices light the loving path of obedience.

Jesus practiced lots of things. As he did so he formed beautiful habits, habits that consistently channeled Jesus's love to God—his *Abba*—and to his precious image-bearers, his neighbors for the short thirty-three years he lived on earth. Have you noticed how all Jesus's practices directly engaged Jesus's body, along with his mind, soul, and will?

When we practice something, we desire to gain or develop a disposition, habit, or ability. Think of Michael Jordan. I've just finished watching *The Last Dance*, a documentary that follows the championship years of the great Chicago Bulls, a team that included Michael Jordan, Scottie Pippen, Dennis Rodman, and Steve Kerr.

How did Jordan become the greatest player in the history of the NBA? As a high school kid, after a mediocre season as a freshman, Jordan determined to improve his game. He set specific goals. He began to develop the mental skills required to be a great player. He practiced skills his body needed to learn if Jordon was to play at a high level and outperform his competitors.

Yes, it's likely Jordan possessed a special, innate gift that other players didn't have. Still, despite the innate athletic gift, if Jordan hadn't consciously entered a rigorous, strategic program of athletic development, with specific goals in mind, *his innate gift would have remained undeveloped.* Jordan worked hard—harder than the athletes against whom he competed—to reach the goal of winning. He drove himself, and he drove his teammates. The result was an unprecedented series of basketball championships for the city of Chicago.

Initially, probably when Jordan was very young, he started dribbling a basketball. I imagine him at seven or eight, shooting layup after layup in his backyard. Finally, after five hundred or a thousand layups, he didn't need to practice layups anymore. He had trained his mind and body, so that shooting a layup became second nature for his nervous system, mind, and muscles. What originally demanded specific mental and physical focus and effort became effortless.

Jordan continued to practice other more difficult aspects of the game, though he never stopped shooting layups; before a game, he lined up with other Bulls players and ran through layup drills. But the initial hard work had been accomplished. While warming up, Jordan could *concentrate* on other things. He focused on other strategic aspects of the upcoming game, mentally and physically practicing skills he needed to hone and strengthen. *He practiced what he was not good at.*

When I first started to learn to play golf—around the time I was eight—the sport was initially extremely difficult. Who would have thought hitting that little white ball straight would be so challenging? There were far more failures than successes as I topped the ball repeatedly and sometimes whiffed. Occasionally I was tempted to give up. The same was true for baseball and basketball.

Thomas Merton reminds us that beginnings are always hard. The skills I needed to play different sports were initially very difficult to develop. My nervous system and body had to wrap themselves around the athletic skills I desired to develop. In golf, I'd swing at that little white ball, habitually lift my head as I did so, and I would either miss completely or top the ball. "Keep your head down, pal," my dad would coach. "Try it again." And again. And again.

Gradually my brain and nervous system synced, and the golf ball actually started to lift off the ground. Not every time, mind you. My golf ball still travels to strange places today, after I've played this crazy sport for sixty-two years.

But my successful swings are more frequent because of the earlier years of practice. My body and mind have learned to work together. This dynamic shouldn't surprise us. *For we are embodied selves.*

I've never liked to practice, though. This is a weakness in my character. I'd much rather just play the game. Haven't you wished you could *just watch* a major league Hall of Famer like Greg Maddux on TV, then step out on the mound and throw like Maddux? I'm sure we all have.

I think of my beloved nephew Spencer as he was first learning to pitch. I recall attending one of his Little League baseball games—the next step up after T-ball. As his proud uncle, I beamed as Spencer walked out to the mound. He was around seven years old and already a loyal Atlanta Braves fan. It was clear that Spencer had been watching Greg Maddux on TV. He walked like Maddux. He kicked the pitching rubber like Maddux. He shook his glove like Maddux.

Spencer's mannerisms so matched the great pitcher's that the small Little League crowd grew silent in expectation. "Who is this kid? He looks like Greg Maddux out there." Spencer's catcher was wondering the same thing as Spencer bent over and peered in for the sign. Now, seven-year-old catchers and pitchers don't exchange signs in baseball. There's only one pitch to throw, something that looks like a slow lob, and everyone hopes it's going to make it over the plate—from parents to coaches to players. Most of these games for very young Little Leaguers are fairly dull affairs. Lots of walks with an occasional grounder, weak line drive, or shallow fly ball.

Still, there was Spencer, waiting for the sign. And then he did it. He shook off the catcher. For Spencer had seen Greg Maddux shake off his catcher on TV. Not only was Spencer shaking off the catcher. He was holding on first the runner he had inherited from the previous pitcher. Please understand that at this beginning level of Little League, runners can't steal. They must remain on base until the ball is hit or the batter walks.

Yet there was Spencer, glancing over his left shoulder, holding the runner on. I'm convinced the runner wondered, *Why's he looking at me?* Well, Spencer's looking at you because Greg Maddux holds runners on, and Spencer is the new Greg Maddux. Smaller. Younger. But Greg Maddux all the same. The real Maddux would have been proud.

Finally, after a minute or so, just when the home ump was going to intervene in these strange affairs, Spencer went into his windup. His arm reached back and launched the ball—which traveled ten feet or so in a high arc and landed in front of home plate. His catcher breathed a sigh of relief. The ump chuckled. The first base runner relaxed. The folks in the crowd exchanged friendly glances. "Someday he'll get it right," one dad said to another. "It'll just take some time and practice."

Do you remember learning to read and write? I see myself sitting in my first-grade class at Grandview Elementary School in Phoenix, Arizona. The year is 1957. There is my first teacher—I'm afraid I don't remember her name—standing in front of the class; she's pointing to a series of letters she's attached over the chalkboard. "This is an *A*," she pronounces in a friendly manner. "It's a capital *A*. Take a sheet of paper out of your notebook and with your pencil write it on your paper." *Sounds good to me*, I think to myself. *Writing a capital* A *can't be all that hard.* Well, it was.

My young mind was confident. My hand wasn't. There before me on my paper, lying on its side, was my first capital *A*. Gradually, with practice, the *A* managed to right itself, but things continued to prove harder than I had expected. Both my first-grade mind and my first-grade hand would need to practice. Beginnings are hard.

With time and practice, writing the letters of the alphabet became second nature, but I still remember that tough beginning. How was first grade for you? Maybe other difficult beginnings come to mind.

Whether it's sports, gardening, carpentry, plumbing, mechanics, public speaking, writing—or learning to live life well with God— practice of some kind is involved. For we are embodied selves. *The rule of thumb is this: we practice the things we're not good at by watching and imitating someone who does very well what we desire to do.*

We don't learn how to live a different way with God—we don't learn to keep in step with Jesus—by reading abstract principles in an ethics book, though knowing sound ethical principles is surely helpful and necessary for our moral and spiritual development. We learn best by looking closely at Jesus or the lives of great Christians—Catholics call them saints—and then acting in similar ways in our own life context and history.

Imagine you're sitting in your living room on a Saturday afternoon, watching a movie on TV. Unexpectedly, the doorbell rings. You turn off the TV and answer the door. And there stands Jesus! "Hi, friend," he says. "I just thought we'd spend the afternoon together." You invite him in, and for a few minutes you engage in some small talk. Finally, though, Jesus asks, "What can I help you with? What are you not good at? Where could you use some good coaching?"

After a pause—you've been caught a bit off guard—you respond somewhat hesitantly, "Lord, I'm not good at living a chaste life. I struggle with my sexual thoughts and behaviors. I watch the wrong things. Often, I do the wrong things."

In turn, Jesus responds gently and directly. "I know. That's not a surprise to me. I've known that for a long time. So, let's move in a different way together. I'll show you how. I created you as a sexual being, and I know full well what I had in mind. I have no desire for you to be frustrated. Rather, I want you to be fulfilled and at peace. There is a different way I can offer you to live your sexual life. Thanks for naming your sin so openly and honestly. We'll get to a new place together. I'll teach you to walk in my shoes. Let's figure out some new perspectives and practices that can help you change."

There may be other points of struggle for you. Maybe you say to Jesus, "Lord, I'm not good at dealing with money. To be honest, I'm greedy. And I'm envious of what others possess. I think about money all the time. I'm always thinking about what I could buy if only I had a little more cash. I'd like to be rich, not so I'd have more for other people—though that's the lie I tell myself—but so I could buy more stuff for myself. Jesus, that's the true state of affairs when it comes to me and money. I'd like to change, but I don't know how."

"Thanks for recognizing that," Jesus quietly responds. "I appreciate that. That wasn't easy to admit. I can teach you how to deal with money in a different way. I promise to help you. The wiser you are with money, the more you'll be able to love others. It'll take some time, but I can help you change. You can become skilled in what you're not good at. I sometimes call that growing in love and holiness."

## Pause and Reflect

Take a moment to list the things you're not good at. Maybe they have to do with sex. Perhaps they have to do with money, anger, envy, greed, or gluttony. Know that you are not unique in your struggles. Ask the Lord to show you where the work needs to be done. Remember that as you exert the effort to change, you're earning nothing from God. Ask for the grace to get to a new place in your relationship with others and with God. The invitation to live a different way is always wide open.

On a piece of paper, draw a line down the center. Create a "sin" column to the left of the line. This is your "I'm not good at this" column. List honestly and openly the sins you struggle with and have confessed lots of times. Next to the "sin" column create a "practice" column. In this column, list a practice or spiritual discipline that can serve as the antibiotic for the infection in the "sin" column. For instance, if you struggle with greed, you might list the discipline of frugality or simplicity next to your sin.

"Yes, this is a problem for me," you honestly admit. "I am a greedy person, even if I'm the only one who really knows how I think and deal with money." Then, rather than running screaming into the night over how greedy you are, list concrete steps toward frugality or simplicity that you can take over the next year, with God's help and through the power of God's Spirit. Try to be as concrete as possible on both the negative and positive sides of the ledger. Remember that Jesus is walking with you, encouraging you all the while.

Dallas Willard, a great coach, writes that when we practice frugality, "we abstain from using money or goods at our disposal in ways that merely gratify our desires or our hunger for status, glamour, or luxury. Practicing frugality means we stay within the bounds of what general good judgment would designate as necessary for the kind of life to which the Lord has led us."[6]

That's good, concrete advice. With the help of Dallas's coaching you might list questions like these next to the word *frugality*, or you may have others of your own:

- What goods or money has God placed at my disposal?
- How do I tend to use money? What habit patterns can I identify in my spending?
- Do I buy things I need or things I want? What's the difference between the two?
- Am I trying to impress people with what I buy?
- Do I have a self-indulgent personality?
- How does my tendency toward self-indulgence manifest itself in how I spend my money?
- Am I a generous person? Does my checkbook support my conclusions?

If I desire to be more generous—a loving disposition for all God's image-bearers to have—how can I cultivate generosity in my life? What concrete steps can I take, however small they may be? Small steps add up. We stumble and fall. We get back up. We stumble and fall. We get back up. Each time we get back up, we're able to walk just a little farther.

On another sheet of paper, list other things you're not good at. Perhaps these dispositions or habits are not sinful, but you recognize they're not helpful. Maybe you're not good at studying. Possibly you need to expand your knowledge of current events or human history or church history. What do you not know that you need to know in these or other areas?

| What I'm Not Good At | What I Can Do to Practice |
| --- | --- |
| I'm not good at church history. | Over the next six months or a year I'm going to expand my understanding of church history by reading _____. (Enjoy compiling a good reading list.) |

It's likely that as we ponder what we're not good at, we'll discern with sharper clarity what we need to stop doing and start doing. Consider a "stop doing" column and a "start doing" column.

For some of us, this exercise may seem intimidating or discouraging. "Chris, I've tried all this before. And I've failed. I'm afraid to try again." I understand. More importantly, Jesus understands. Some changes take a lifetime. And that's fine. Genuine, lasting change takes a long time to occur.

We have much to observe, much to learn, and much to practice. Some may want to learn more about prayer. Such was the case with Jesus's disciples. "One day Jesus was praying in a certain place. When he finished, one of his disciples said to him, 'Lord, teach us to pray, just as John taught his disciples'" (Luke 11:1).

Note the progression. First, the disciples *watched* Jesus praying. And then, without reservation, they asked Jesus to teach them how to pray.

Jesus readily responded, happy the disciples wanted to learn a new skill, a new embodied practice.

## Coaching from Chrysostom

John Chrysostom, a leader of the ancient church in Syria who became archbishop of Constantinople at the end of the fourth century, was an expert on the dynamics of healthy spiritual growth. In a sermon titled "Dead to Sin," John develops an important theme: What is the part we play in our spiritual development?[7]

As Chrysostom ponders this question, he observes that there are some things God has graciously done for us. For instance, we have been baptized into the death of Jesus (Rom. 6:3–4).

Chrysostom accentuates the "demand" Paul "sets before us," one that brings "newness of life by *changing of habits*. For when the fornicator becomes chaste, when the covetous person becomes merciful, when the harsh become subdued, a resurrection has taken place, a prelude to the final resurrection which is to come."[8]

John uses the parable of the prodigal son to illustrate his point. We, like the prodigal son, must *decide* to "leave this strange land of sin" and return to our "home country" and "father." This is a fine starting point for all of us.

### Pause and Reflect

Consider what the "strange land of sin" looks like in your own life. Surround your ponderings with prayer and the grace of God. Honestly explore the geography of this land of exile. Somehow, we ended up far from home. How did we get there? What happened?

Thankfully, by God's grace we have come to our senses. We perceive that the way we've been thinking and living makes no sense. The time has come to leave this strange land and follow a different way. It's time to put on Jesus's shoes and walk in his footsteps.

More decisions—and practices—await us in the future. Plan your journey home; develop your itinerary. Don't be surprised or discouraged if there are hills to climb and deserts to cross. Ask God for grace, insight, and determination—the continual strengthening of your will—to keep placing one foot in front of another. God's grace enables and empowers each footstep.

Chrysostom coaches us to "start back by avoiding vice, going no farther into it, and you have come home." John doesn't say, "Immediately rid yourself of all your vices." Rather, he urges that we not go farther into them. That's surprising, isn't it? Chrysostom explains, "When a person who is sick does not get any worse it is a sign that he's getting better, and so is the case with vice. . . . Go no further and your deeds of wickedness will have an end."[9]

## Pause and Reflect

Identify a particular sin you've confessed lots of times. Write it in block letters in your journal or in a file in your computer. Then say a prayer like this:

Lord, I want to tell you the truth. I've confessed this sin a thousand times to you. I avoid it for a few days, then stumble and fall. The pattern repeats itself, sometimes after a few days, sometimes after a few weeks. There it is. I've named my sin for what it is in block letters. You know it. I know it. And by the power of your Spirit in me, I'm not going to give up. Help me to change and show me how to do so.

## Encouraging Words from Thomas Merton

Let's close this chapter with some encouraging words from Thomas Merton. We've mapped out what we're not good at and devised a plan to change. We may be tempted to think, *If I just get the right technique down, my habits will change automatically.* Merton gently corrects this misconception.

The obstacles we face in our spiritual life, Merton teaches, "have very deep roots in our character, and in fact we may eventually learn that a whole lifetime will barely be sufficient for their removal. For example, many people who have a few natural gifts and a little ingenuity tend to imagine that they can quite easily learn, by their own cleverness, to master the methods—one might say the 'tricks'—of the spiritual life."

Not so, Merton teaches. Don't be misled or deceived. In our "spiritual life there are no tricks and no shortcuts. Those who imagine that they can discover spiritual gimmicks and put them to work for themselves usually ignore God's will and his grace. They are self-confident and even self-complacent."

We will always be beginners. So, accept that we are simply beginners, little children learning to walk. In significant ways, we will always remain so. Jesus offers us his shoes. "Lace them up," he encourages. "Let's walk a different way together."[10]

# CHAPTER FIVE

# Keep in Step with Jesus in Your Gift of Years

God has plenty of time. It is finite humans who run short. In this way God teaches us about time.

—Thomas C. Oden

God gives every human being—every precious image-bearer who has ever lived—a gift of years. During this gift of years, we're called to keep in step with Jesus. We learn to walk in Jesus's shoes.

The rationale God employs in allocating these years remains a mystery to me. Some image-bearers receive six months, some three years, some twenty, some fifty, some seventy, some even more.

Sometimes extravagantly wicked people receive a long gift of years. I don't know why. They wreak havoc as their years pass by and seemingly die peacefully in their sleep, smiles on their faces. I'm reminded of Job's words. He was puzzled about the same thing. "Why do the wicked live on, growing old and increasing in power? . . . They spend their years in prosperity and go down to the grave in peace" (Job 21:7, 13).

God gives other image-bearers such a short time to live. "You should have given them more time, Lord," I say to myself. Those most gifted seem to receive too few years, while the shallow, the wicked, the self-indulgent, the selfish, and the cruel are doled out a trove of years, which they squander vapidly and unreflectively.

Finally, after criticizing God's wisdom, I come to my senses. For I, too, have been shallow, wicked, self-indulgent, and selfish. If years were awarded based on who qualifies for a long life, we'd all be living a very short time. Our gift of years is just that, a gift, from the air we breathe to the food that sustains us each day, to the work God gives us over the course of our lifetime; all is gift.

A better question to ponder, it seems, is this: What are we doing with the years we've been given? We aren't responsible for what we have not been given. We are responsible for what we have received. A Latin phrase comes to mind: *cum gratia officium*, with gifting comes responsibility.

Perhaps from God's perspective—the long view of eternity—five years well spent equals, or indeed surpasses, seventy or eighty years lived in a spiritual, emotional, and physical wasteland. Only God knows what equals what. God's mathematics are best left to God.

We may be tempted to heed our culture's siren call to seek happiness, meaning, and purpose in a comfortable, soft, undemanding life, one that slowly numbs us to the beauty, wonder, and demands of the kingdom of God.

God asks us to receive our gift of years thankfully and thoughtfully, and to live them well, however long or short our gift may be. Our gift of years races by in a flash. They are a glowing speck on the radar screen of eternity. How often older folks comment, "Where have the years gone?" Now in my seventies, I find myself asking the same question.

The psalmist reminds us "to number our days, that we may gain a heart of wisdom" (Ps. 90:12). "Show me, LORD, my life's end and the number of my days; let me know how fleeting my life is. You have made my days a mere handbreadth; the span of my years is as nothing before you" (Ps. 39:4–5).

How sad, how foolish, to allow our gift of years to flow thoughtlessly through our fingers like sand through an hourglass.

As you contemplate your life with God, does it look like a gift? Our life experiences, some of them excruciatingly difficult and painful, may cause us to doubt. "This is a gift?" we ask in our pain and confusion, our hearts wrenched out of shape. It's fair, even natural and healthy, to ask this question. For things happen that dreadfully hurt us. We may end up disappointed and disillusioned. With life. With others. With ourselves. With God.

Thankfully, God possesses the wondrous ability to redeem time— our time—on our behalf. God never runs out of time. Though we may act foolishly, seemingly squandering the gift of years given to us, God can take the last year, month, hour, or minute of our lives and redeem an entire lifetime.

So, if you're tempted to think that meaning or hope for your life has gone up in smoke, that the years gone past are irrecoverable or irredeemable, think again. God delights in making old things new. I think Paul was smiling when he wrote, "So from now on we regard no one from a worldly point of view. Though we once regarded Christ in this way, we do so no longer. Therefore, if anyone is in Christ, the new creation has come: the old has gone, the new is here!" (2 Cor. 5:16–17).

## Pause and Reflect

Pause for a moment and examine your gift of years. What's already happened, what's occurring now, and what might God still have in store for you? Pray this:

> **Lord, I turn to you in faith. Redeem my life. Redeem my years. Bring something new and good out of them.**
>
> **Reflect on what struck you during this prayer.**

## A Life-Changing Conversation

When I arrived at UCLA for my first year of college, I thought I should follow the premed track. Why? Well, I had lots of family members who were doctors. My maternal grandfather was a doctor: John Steinbeck's urologist. I had two uncles who were doctors, one a pathologist and the other a psychiatrist. I have three cousins who are doctors. So, without consulting anyone, I decided to become an MD. I took it for granted that if I were to maintain my dad's approval—or perhaps gain it—medicine was the path to follow.

My first quarter at school, I enrolled in courses to prepare me for the premed track. I hated them. I hadn't liked biology or chemistry in high school, and my dislike continued in college. I'd never been good at math. Yet I imagined my dad nodding in approval as I slogged my way through these courses—some as general education requirements I couldn't avoid and others to lay the groundwork for getting into medical school. What happened? I bombed.

What was I to do? I decided to transfer. I could start over somewhere else. A clean slate would be just the thing. To do so, I would need to call Dad. Here's how the conversation went:

"Hi, Dad. How's it going?"

"Fine here. How are you?" I hemmed and hawed a bit and then spoke of transferring.

"Why you going to do that?" he asked.

"Well, I guess I don't want to be a doctor."

"Why do you have to be a doctor?"

"You don't want me to be a doctor?"

"When did I ever say that?"

"I don't know. I just thought you wanted me to be one. So many others in the family are doctors."

"Listen to me, son. Do whatever you want to do. If you want to be a garbage collector and would be happy doing so, that's fine with me."

"Really?"

"Really. I just want you to be happy."

This short conversation changed my life. It was the one story I told at my dad's funeral.

I took Dad at his word. I started taking more courses in English and history. Indeed, I became a history major on a prelaw track, was accepted into law school my senior year, and thought I had found my vocation.

How about you? How are you expending your gift of years? What vocation has God offered you? Did you welcome it or resist it? Did you find yourself comparing what God offered you with what he offered others and find yourself at the short end of the stick? Even at the very end of our lives we can receive a new vocation from God. Dying well, for instance, is an exalted vocation.

## A Life Map

Here's a specific exercise that may prove helpful as you ponder what's occurred so far in your gift of years. I call it a life map. Creating one is profitable for young and old.

First, divide your life into decades. I've just turned seventy; I was born in 1950. So I have seven decades to map: 1950–60, 1960–70, 1970–80, 1980–90, 1990–2000, 2000–2010, and 2010–20. You may have more decades to map, or perhaps less. Plot each decade using the following categories:

## Significant People

Who were the significant people in your life during each decade? Were they positive or negative influences on your life? Why? What did they say to you? What experiences did you have together? Were these significant people sources of joy or sorrow, flourishing or floundering?

As specifically as possible, identify these people decade by decade. Do they bring a smile to your face or a frown? Do you feel reactions in your body when you think of them? Why do you still remember them after all these years?

Let me give you an example of something at the very beginning of my life that's very significant. For the first week of my life in March 1950, I was separated from my mother. An error was made by her obstetrician during childbirth, and my mom was given way too much anesthetic. It flowed from her into me. So, for the first week of my life, my mom and I were separated.

I've since learned that separation after birth is a recipe for an angry baby. And this is just what I was. I cried and cried. I threw tantrums. My mom later told me that as I moved into my second year, I'd lie down and bang my head on the floor. This anger continued for many years. Learning the circumstances of my birth, however, shed light on the later struggles I experienced with anger in my first and second decades.

In terms of people, when I think of my maternal grandfather, Boppa, I feel happy. He saw how troubled I was as a little boy. My mom later told me that on my bad days, Boppa would pick me up from the floor, sit me in his lap, softly rock me, and murmur into my ear, "My dear, dear boy, my dear, dear boy."

Boppa understood, in a manner I didn't, why I was so angry. For he, too, had struggled with anger and depression.

## Pause and Reflect

Again I ask, who have been the significant people for you, decade by decade? They might be parents, friends, enemies, abusers, teachers, coaches, pastors, colleagues, or bosses. Put their names down on paper. Get them in front of you.

Then offer a prayer:

Lord, show me the meaning of my life with these people. What must I forgive? What must I forget? What must I remember? Where were your grace and mercy working in these relationships? Where did I think your mercy and grace were lacking? Help me, Lord. I need clarity in my gift of years as I learn to keep in step with Jesus.

## Significant Life Experiences and Events

Now, decade by decade, list your significant life experiences. These times will likely be both positive and negative. Perhaps there was a sickness, an accident, a death, or a tragedy, and its effect has rippled across the years. My parents' divorce was a major life experience for me.

One of my happiest experiences was a Philadelphia Phillies–Milwaukee Braves game I attended with my dad at Connie Mack Stadium in 1962. We had seats right next to the dugout of the Braves, my favorite team.

Those tickets must have cost my dad a pretty penny. I still remember walking through a stadium corridor and seeing a major league field for the first time. How green the grass was! Organ music rippled through the air. Vendors were already selling popcorn, cotton candy, and beer.

Dad and I walked down the steps to our seats. And there they were, only a couple of feet from me—my baseball heroes, Eddie Mathews and Hank Aaron. They stepped onto the field for batting practice and stretched. I watched intently as they playfully sparred with their bats. I drank in batting practice and the game itself. I never wanted it to end.

Have there been days or experiences like that for you? Note them. Ponder them. What was God offering you? What does God want to draw to your memory? How have these life experiences shaped your personality and the ingrained habit patterns—emotional and otherwise—that mark your life today?

Another experience comes to mind. I see myself as a little boy, maybe four or five, holding an ice cream cone and walking with my dad near our home in North Hollywood. Suddenly my hand tips, and my ice cream falls to the hot pavement. I recall my tears. And I recollect my dad calming me down and buying me another cone.

"Why," I ask myself, "do I still remember that experience in my seventieth year?" However insignificant you might initially rate an event or experience, if you still remember it today, it's meaningful for you and fodder for reflection.

## Significant Books and Films

Are you a reader? Are there significant books that have cultivated the landscape of your mind? Just this morning I was thinking about the ten books C. S. Lewis listed as most significant for his life. Among them were George MacDonald's *Phantastes*, G. K. Chesterton's *Everlasting*

*Man*, Virgil's *Aeneid*, Rudolf Otto's *Idea of the Holy*, and James Boswell's *Life of Samuel Johnson*. It's an interesting list. What have been important books for you?

Dallas Willard commented to an interviewer that the book that most deeply touched him was relatively unknown. It's *Deeper Experiences of Famous Christians* by James Gilchrist Lawson. Willard remarked that the book was of interest to him because it described the process of transformation in various Christians' lives.

When I read the book, I was impressed by the life of John Fletcher, a contemporary of John Wesley. Fletcher "made it a constant rule to sit up two whole nights in the week for reading, prayer, and meditation." He ate very little, and Thursday was his fast day. I asked myself why he practiced these specific disciplines. Fletcher's life, through the medium of Lawson's pen, got me thinking.

Willard was deeply impressed by the Roman Catholic martyr Savonarola. Savonarola's "drive toward holiness, toward a different and a supernatural kind of life—a life 'from above'—and his readiness to sacrifice all to achieve such a life" touched Willard.[1]

The breadth and quality of our reading shapes our ideas and our lives. Poor books form and foster poor lives; good books nourish and grow us, often in unexpected ways.

Not all of us are big readers. Fair enough. If you're a more visual learner, are there films or TV shows that have played a significant role in your perceiving, thinking, learning, and living? I remember going to see my first movie with Boppa. It was *The Flight of the Phoenix* and starred Jimmy Stewart. Even as a very young boy, I found that the film stimulated my thinking about courage and perseverance during great adversity. Other films in the fifties and sixties positively affected me: *Ben-Hur*, *Spartacus*, *Lawrence of Arabia*, and *The Bridge on the River Kwai*. Notice any common themes in these movies? What might they tell you about my developing personality?

*In Cold Blood* and low-budget horror films like *The House on Haunted Hill* watered a troubling thirst within me for darker things and the supernatural.

## Significant Ideas

As a thought experiment, try to pinpoint, decade by decade, the various ideas that continue to influence you today. Did they emerge recently? Or are they older? In what decade did they appear? Are there ideas that you once found important but now you've discarded, like a lizard shedding its skin? Why did you do so? Should they remain in the dustbin of your mind or be retrieved for reexamination?

Your significant ideas are closely related to what you consider valuable, praiseworthy, or repugnant. Other ideas may lurk in the shadows of your mind, a kind of mental pollution. Can you identify some? Don't hurry through this exercise. Take your time. Idea mapping may take a few months, even a year.

Once you've identified the important ideas influencing your intellectual, emotional, physical, and spiritual formation, try to map carefully when they first developed. For instance, I've asked myself what ideas developed in me in my first two decades.

I remember how strongly my father felt about discrimination. Dad befriended the only Jewish man who lived in our neighborhood, Lou Obermiller. My mother's ideas about God affected me both positively and negatively in these early years. What ideas began to develop in your mind during your first decade? Were they flowers or weeds?

Continue this exercise decade by decade. As I mapped my second decade—the years when my family moved from the West to the East—I realized this was the time when my love for reading appeared. I joined a history book club for kids. I read biographies of Davy Crockett, Daniel

Boone, Jim Bowie, Clara Barton, George Washington, Abraham Lincoln, Betsy Ross, and Thomas Jefferson. I still recall my excitement as I waited for the next book to arrive in my monthly installment. The ideas these books contained, accurate or not, shaped my young mind and how I viewed the world. I now am shocked to notice there's not a single African American in the group.

From 1960 to 1970 I also began to think more about God. I listened to my mom's George Beverly Shea albums and liked to watch Billy Graham on TV. I sometimes cried when people came forward as the crusade choir sang "Just as I Am," though I'm not sure I understood clearly what was going on.

In New Jersey—quite a change from California and Arizona—we attended a church in the Christian liberal tradition; what I was taught on Sunday morning was not very helpful. Simultaneously, I began to expose myself to darker ideas that weren't helpful at all. In the late sixties I immersed myself in the music of the Doors. Jim Morrison's lyrics lured me toward darkness rather than light.

How about you? What ideas and intellectual explorations occurred in your second decade? Continue this mapping exercise up to your present age.

Once you have completed your life map, slowly ponder its mountains and valleys, its oases and deserts. The terrain of each image-bearer's life possesses its own unique contours. Once you've completed charting your gift of years, which may require a year or two, take another six months to ponder and pray over what you have discovered.

## Pause and Reflect

What ideas now populate your mental universe? How did they develop?

## An Important Case Study

The landscape of the apostle Peter's life—his life's terrain—included Jesus as the most significant person Peter would ever meet. Jesus, the incarnate Son of God, understood Peter's physical, emotional, and spiritual gifts well. After all, Jesus had created Peter. Peter's gifts, Jesus realized, were endangered by his volatile, impulsive, prideful personality. Peter needed to learn more about his own strengths and weaknesses. Peter didn't realize this growth in self-awareness was necessary. Jesus did.

Jesus selected Peter, a very interesting and gifted man, to lead the apostles, and Peter would be the rock on which Christ would build his church (Matt. 16:17–19). Yet Jesus realized that Peter would wreak havoc as a leader unless the deep cracks and fissures in his personality were made whole. Jesus created Peter to be an agent of healing, not harm; for this transformation to occur, Jesus grows Peter's self-awareness and weeds the garden of Peter's self-deception. The weeding will be painful for Peter and difficult for Jesus.

Jesus grows Peter's self-awareness by deliberately placing him in situations designed to reveal the cracks in his personality. In our first example, Peter finds himself literally out of his depth.

In Matthew 14:22–29, we find the story of Jesus walking on the surface of the Sea of Galilee, one of Christ's nature miracles. Here's the setting: Jesus has just finished feeding the five thousand. Matthew relates that "immediately Jesus made the disciples get into the boat and go on ahead of him to the other side, while he dismissed the crowd. After he had dismissed them, he went up on a mountainside by himself to pray" (Matt. 14:22–23). Was Jesus thinking about Peter as he prayed?

The disciples begin their travel across the sea in very windy weather. Matthew comments that the "boat was already a considerable distance from land, buffeted by the waves because the wind was against it," when near dawn, Jesus approaches the disciples, walking on the water.

The disciples are terrified as Jesus approaches. "'It's a ghost,' they said, and cried out in fear" (Matt. 14:26). "It is I," Jesus shouts out. Peter immediately asks if he might approach him on the water.

Now, what does Peter's request teach us about Peter? He's impulsive. He's courageous. And he trusts Jesus—at least to a certain extent.

Jesus knows exactly what's going to happen as the scene unfolds. He knows all the disciples in the boat are watching the scene. No one else has dared follow Peter. He knows Peter's going to sink. Jesus realizes Peter will return to the boat like a drowned rat—embarrassed, disgraced, and discouraged.

Still, knowing Peter will experience all these painful things, Jesus invites Peter to come to him on the water. Jesus literally asks Peter to step into his shoes, shoes Peter is not yet prepared to wear. In the process he lovingly hurts Peter. Why does he do this? What's the point? "Peter, you are impulsive. You believe you are strong and courageous. But you are weaker than you think. You believe you're trusting in me when you're really trusting in yourself. Peter, I must move you to a deeper understanding of who you are. And the stormy Sea of Galilee is a good place to start."

Do you see Peter, now sitting soaked to the skin in the boat, enduring the stares of his friends, none of whom had dared follow him on the water to Jesus? The whole group is just as weak as Peter.

The other disciples look to Peter as their leader; they'll be quick to follow his example. In the months to come they'll continue to watch him closely and are apt to follow Peter's example; Jesus knows this. He'll teach the other apostles as he teaches Peter. These lessons will be difficult for everyone. Transformation always is. Keeping in step with Jesus always includes these tough lessons.

The school of hard knocks remains in session in Matthew 16. The apostolic band is now gathered at Caesarea Philippi, and Jesus asks them all an important messianic question. "Who do people say the Son of Man is?" (Matt. 16:13). The disciples offer a Whitman's Sampler of possibilities. Some folks say Jesus is John the Baptist. Others think he is Elijah. Still others, Jeremiah or one of the prophets. Jesus pushes the point. "But what about you?" he asks. "Who do you say that I am?" And as we know, it's Peter who identifies Jesus correctly.

"You are the Messiah, the Son of the living God" (Matt. 16:16). Peter's answer pleases Jesus, and he declares Peter "blessed," for Jesus's Father has revealed Jesus's messianic identity to Peter. The Father, Son, and Holy Spirit all have plans for him.

How exhilarated Peter must have felt, not only to have received Christ's blessing but to be promised that "you are Peter, and on this rock I will build my church, and the gates of Hades will not overcome it. I will give you the keys of the kingdom of heaven; whatever you bind on earth will be bound in heaven, and whatever you loose on earth will be loosed in heaven" (Matt. 16:17–19).

Peter's blessing is rich. His future seems bright. God has given him insight into Jesus that the other disciples have not received. Yet when Jesus speaks of suffering, dying, and crosses, horrible realities that lie ahead for him as the Anointed One of God, Peter takes Jesus aside and begins to "rebuke" him (Matt. 16:22).

Peter is spectacularly blind to the Father's purpose for Jesus, his incarnate Son. And Jesus is not pleased. "Get behind me, Satan! You are a stumbling block to me; you do not have in mind the concerns of God, but merely human concerns" (Matt. 16:23).

Notice the bent, sinful dynamic operating in Peter's personality. When Peter doesn't understand something, when someone or something doesn't make sense to him theologically, spiritually, or providentially—even teachings from the mind and mouth of Jesus—Peter resists. He rebukes. He doesn't listen.

Peter's default position in difficult situations or when taught difficult things is to believe he knows more than he really does. And it is this self-deception, this swollen pride in his own capabilities and knowledge, this unwillingness to be taught, that Satan spots and exploits.

There are grave flaws in Peter's personality—intellectual, emotional, and spiritual weaknesses that must be addressed and healed if Peter is to minister to others safely, sanely, and powerfully. Can you imagine how painful Jesus's words must have been for Peter? He stands rebuked for allowing the devil to speak through him. Sometimes Peter is spot on. And sometimes he's terribly wrong.

Peter is not yet a rock. He is a mere pebble. A difficult journey with Jesus lies ahead for Peter, a demanding, occasionally excruciating pilgrimage. Because Jesus loves Peter, he willingly travels with him into the valley of tribulation. He is walking with Peter. Peter has yet to learn to walk with Jesus. He must learn the steps of obedience and love.

The next stop for Peter occurs in Matthew 26:31–35. The evening when Jesus's passion will begin has arrived. The disciples and Jesus have gathered in an upper room to prepare the Passover meal. Jesus has taught the apostles for the past three years to prepare them for the next three days. But they have proven to be slow learners.

Jesus realizes that his disciples are still weak, self-deceived, ignorant, fearful, and proud. He clearly understands they will soon fail him at his point of greatest need. "Then Jesus told them, 'This very night you will all fall away on account of me, for it is written: "I will strike the shepherd, and the sheep of the flock will be scattered." But after I have risen, I will go ahead of you into Galilee'" (Matt. 26:31–32). These are hard words, terrifying words, discouraging words, but they end with a word of hope: resurrection.

True to form, Peter tells Jesus he's dead wrong. Not only does Peter directly contradict Jesus in front of all the disciples; he compares himself favorably to the rest of the group. "Even if all fall away on account of you, I never will" (Matt. 26:33). They must have loved that.

As deep darkness descends—figuratively and with the deepening of night—the cracks in Peter's character widen. He is a hollow man full of hollow words: "You can count on me, Jesus. I promise. I'll never let you down."

All the while, the other disciples listen and watch. Perhaps some are angered by Peter's proud and boastful comparison. Still, they are quick to mimic Peter and promise they won't desert Jesus. Eardrums are hard. Brittle. No one is listening. Few are attentive to the devilish horror soon to be unleashed.

When all hell breaks loose in the Garden of Gethsemane, how does Peter respond? He is quickly—almost immediately—overwhelmed by events. His character is frail and soon will snap as the horrific circumstances of Jesus's passion unfold. What did Peter sorely need to weather the storm? Obedience, openness, receptivity, attentiveness, and faith.

Peter has lived with pride's cancer for too long. A tumor has metastasized to Peter's personality, infesting his mind, heart, and body. Divine radiation treatment—God's white-hot light and love—must be extensive and deep.

How Jesus must have suffered in seeing how little his disciples had learned over the past three years! And there was their leader—the "rock"—grossly self-deceived, both about himself and about God's purposes for Jesus, the Anointed One of Israel.

In my mind's eye I see an IV bag, filled with the vapid promises of Peter, dripping into the bloodstream of the whole group. "You can count on me," Peter promises. Yet within hours Peter disintegrates, terrified by the words of a *paidiske*, a young girl of perhaps thirteen or fourteen (Mark 14:66–70). Peter crumbles and denies three times that he knows Jesus, the very thing he promised he would not do.

We know the story of these tragic events well: the agony of Gethsemane, the mockery of a show trial, the brutality of a Roman scourging, a long, lonely trek bearing the weight of the cross through Jerusalem, the horror of crucifixion, and burial in a borrowed tomb. By all appearances everything has gone wrong.

Luke describes the chilling scene as Peter repudiates Jesus for the third time: "About an hour later another asserted, 'Certainly this fellow was with him, for he is a Galilean.' Peter replied, 'Man, I don't know what you're talking about!' Just as he was speaking, the rooster crowed. The Lord turned and looked straight at Peter. Then Peter remembered the word the Lord had spoken to him: 'Before the rooster crows today, you will disown me three times.' And he went outside and wept bitterly" (Luke 22:59–62).

Can you imagine Peter's distress, his agony, his despair? The cracks—indeed, crevasses—in Peter's personality are now fully exposed. Peter's self-deception is revealed for all the world to see. And his Lord, his friend, stares.

The extent of Peter's desertion is shocking. Even after Jesus and Peter exchange glances—at the very moment of Peter's third denial—Peter's fear overwhelms him. His world is disintegrating. Over the next hours Peter's worst fears are fulfilled; Jesus dies on a Roman cross while Peter hides to save his skin.

With Jesus's death, the horror must have peaked for Peter; the point of no return had arrived. Jesus was dead. The story was over, the friendship ended. And Peter had utterly failed. Surely, Peter must have thought, all that remained for the rest of his days—his gift of years—was a life of quiet desolation; things could never be made right.

Ever feel like that? The mistake is too great, the sin too enormous, the failure too shattering. "If I could only reverse the clock, turn back time, and start over again. If only I could have a second chance."

Thankfully, in the light of Jesus's resurrection from the dead, we see that second chances are possible, and third chances, and fourth and fifth chances. We can start over as many times as we need, for repentance is always possible. How do we know this? Peter's gift of years stands as a pristine example of the promise and possibility of human transformation. It is indeed possible to keep in step with Jesus. His shoes will finally fit.

An encounter between the resurrected Jesus and Peter on the shoreline of the Sea of Galilee illustrates the pathway to change for Peter, and for us.

## John 21 and Luke 5

Let's set the scene. Peter knows that Jesus has been raised from the dead. In fact, he's seen him, if ever so briefly. The most important conversation between Jesus and Peter has yet to take place; perhaps there hasn't been time or the privacy needed.

Peter has returned north to Galilee with other disciples; he's now home, where he grew up. As John explains, the disciples have returned to fishing—their earlier vocation before Jesus called them to a different way. "So they went out and got into the boat, but that night they caught nothing" (John 21:3). Peter still seems to be the leader, even after his failure, for it's he who suggests they go fishing; the other disciples readily agree.

The night's fishing proves unsuccessful, though. Just as dawn breaks—"Early in the morning"—Jesus appears on the shoreline. He's about one hundred yards from the boat, and the disciples don't initially recognize him. All they discern—perhaps in the morning mist—is a figure standing on the beach.

"Friends, haven't you any fish?" Jesus calls out. "No," the disciples respond. "Throw your net on the right side of the boat and you will find some." They follow Jesus's instructions, and their net is quickly filled with fish. Indeed, the catch is so huge that they're "unable to haul the net in because of the large number of fish" (John 21:6).

Have you noticed that what's happening is a replay of an earlier experience Peter, James, and John had with Jesus? We find it in Luke 5. It's one of the earliest encounters these three had with Jesus.

The story begins with Jesus teaching on the shoreline of the Sea of Galilee. Luke tells us that people "were crowding around him and listening to the word of God" (Luke 5:1). Peter, along with his fishing partners James and John, are cleaning their nets and listening to Jesus. The crowd is large and pressing into Jesus as he speaks. Without asking permission, Jesus climbs into Peter's boat and continues teaching.

When Jesus finishes speaking, he commands Peter to head out for more fishing. "Put out into deep water, and let down the nets for a catch" (Luke 5:4). Did Peter skeptically roll his eyes at Jesus's request? Peter knew the right time to fish. Jesus was a teacher, not a professional fisherman. Yet Peter knew enough about Jesus to follow his advice. "But because you say so, I will let down the nets" (Luke 5:5). James and John are now in a boat nearby, watching.

Can you picture the muscles in Peter's arms rippling as he lets the nets down into the water? As they disappear into the deep, did Peter really expect to catch anything? Probably not. Once the nets reach their depth, Peter pulls them up quickly, expecting them to be as empty as when he first lowered them into the water.

Suddenly Peter feels weight and movement in the nets. His muscles strain as he tugs the nets to the surface. Finally, as the nets draw near the surface, Peter perceives the silver of fish enfolded in the netting. This is no small haul. The nets start snapping as Peter signals James and John "to come and help them, and they came and filled both boats so full that they began to sink" (Luke 5:6–7).

What a scene! Nets snapping, fish jumping, boats swamping. Recall that these are the same three apostles who will exercise special leadership among the twelve. Peter will someday be the rock on which Christ builds his church. He plays the leading role in the first eight chapters of

Acts and writes two letters that remain in print today—1 and 2 Peter. At this point, though, Peter is more liquid hot lava than rock.

As for John, he receives a long gift of years, and his brother James a short one. John writes a Gospel and three apostolic letters: 1, 2, and 3 John. The final book of the New Testament, Revelation, is likely penned by John. He lives the longest of all the apostles and according to the church's tradition is the only one who dies nonviolently. Apart from Judas Iscariot, John's brother James has the shortest ministry and briefest life. He dies a martyr, executed by Herod (Acts 12:2).

The future ministries of these three men are different and the time allotted for their gift of years dissimilar; for each to fulfill Christ's call on his life, however, their distinct personalities must be healed, honed, and empowered by Christ; a crucial aspect of this shaping process is the wild catch of fish on the Sea of Galilee.

Peter falls to his knees in his swamped boat, shocked by what has happened. In a moment of graced honesty, he admits who he is: "'Go away from me, Lord; I am a sinful man!' For he and all his companions were astonished at the catch of fish they had taken, and so were James and John, the sons of Zebedee, Simon's partners" (Luke 5:8–10).

Is Peter saying, "Lord, you are more than I ever imagined you to be. And you don't know who you're dealing with. I'm trouble. I'm molten lava. Best to keep your distance"?

Thankfully, Jesus always knows whom he's dealing with, whether it be Peter, James, John, you, or me.

## Pause and Reflect

Jesus offers possibilities to us—his precious image-bearers—to which we're often blind. Yes, we all have deep character flaws. Yes, we're dangerous people if we remain as we are. But our past and present don't limit what Jesus can do. He sees differently than we do. And he offers a different way to us.

Why are we holding back? Why are we afraid? Jesus beckons us into the future, our individually wrapped gift of years. He did the same for Peter—at the very time Peter warned Jesus to leave him alone. Though Jesus knows Peter will fail him at the time of his greatest, most profound need, he still calls Peter to follow.

Have you been tempted to think your sins and mistakes have eliminated the possibility that your gift of years will have lasting goodness? Why in the world would you think such a thing? Peter's life demonstrates that God is in the business of transformation.

## Follow Me

Jesus beckons Peter—and us—to keep in step with him on a different way. "Don't be afraid; from now on you will fish for people," Jesus says to the kneeling, confused Peter (Luke 5:10).

Jesus also speaks to us: "Don't be afraid, my precious image-bearer. I have something for you that we can do together. Your gift of years is not yet over. Trust me."

When Peter again finds himself fishing in the Sea of Galilee (John 21), it's likely that three years have passed since that first great catch of fish in Luke 5. Again, Jesus stands on the seashore and asks Peter to let down his nets for a catch. Jesus is replaying the tape of Luke 5. He desires to restore his relationship with Peter, who is now transforming into rock, not dangerous, fast-flowing lava.

First, though, before full restoration can occur, there's a difficult conversation ahead for Peter and Jesus. Peter's past failures can't simply be swept under the rug. Healing, forgiveness, and restoration will come not by ignoring what has happened but by Jesus and Peter walking through their past together.

Jesus calls the disciples to cast their net into the sea; he is quite specific in his instructions. "'Throw your net on the right side of the boat and you will find some.' When they did, they were unable to haul the net in because of the large number of fish" (John 21:6).

Suddenly it dawns on the disciples that it is Jesus standing on the shoreline. Peter can't help himself. He jumps into the sea and starts swimming toward Jesus.

Let me ask you a very direct question: If you had failed Jesus as miserably as Peter did, would you swim toward him? I've often thought I'd start swimming in the opposite direction!

Yet Peter's love for Jesus, a love deeper than his failure, impels him toward shore. Peter understands that Jesus will know what to do with all his stuff: his fear, his pride, his failure, his sin.

When the boat arrives at the shore, Jesus is there waiting. "When they landed, they saw a fire of burning coals there with fish on it, and some bread. Jesus said to them, 'Bring some of the fish you have just caught.' So Simon Peter climbed back into the boat and dragged the net ashore. It was full of large fish, 153, but even with so many the net was not torn" (John 21:9–11).

Can you see Jesus watching Peter? How much had passed between them! The time has now arrived for a good talk. A difficult talk. A restoring talk. A cleansing talk. A transforming talk. For Jesus is going to offer Peter a different way through the gateway of forgiveness.

First, though, they must all eat together. "'Come and have breakfast.' None of the disciples dared ask him, 'Who are you?' They knew it was the Lord. Jesus came, took the bread and gave it to them, and did the same with the fish" (John 21:12–13).

Jesus is restoring table fellowship with his friends. In his own unique way, he's saying, "The past will not determine the present and future for us. You are my friends, my apostles. And friends eat together."

The breakfast must have been a fairly quiet affair. Glances pass among the disciples. Some stay busy, stoking the fire or cooking more fish. Occasionally, they peep at Jesus. Mild pleasantries are exchanged.

In John's Gospel, we're told of a much longer conversation that ensues between Peter and Jesus. The goal of the conversation? A fresh start for Peter in his relationship with Jesus. The past will be left in the past; Peter is now safe for ministry. In John Chrysostom's words, Jesus "does this to show him that he must now be joyful since the denial was behind him . . . the life you said you would lay down for me, now give for my sheep."[2]

Did you notice that Jesus asks Peter to reaffirm his love for him three times (John 21:15–17)? Why? Peter denied Jesus three times. Jesus walks Peter through each denial and asks Peter to affirm his love at each point of failure. The church father Ambrose comments, "He is asked three times whether he loves the Lord in order that he may confess him three times whom he had denied three times before his crucifixion."[3]

Cyril of Alexandria reinforces Ambrose's insights: "We must understand a renewal as it were of the apostleship already given to Peter, washing away the disgrace of his fall that came in the intervening period and obliterating his faintheartedness that arose from human infirmity."[4]

Revisiting the past was no doubt difficult for Peter. Jesus's first question must have been quite painful. "When they had finished eating, Jesus said to Simon Peter, 'Simon son of John, do you love me more than these?'" (John 21:15).

Do you recall Peter's insistence at his last meal with Jesus that "even if all fall away on account of you, I never will" (Matt. 26:33)? Peter brashly compared himself to all the other disciples, yet crumbled when the time for faithful courage arrived. Jesus is gently reminding him.

Thankfully, Peter is maturing. His self-awareness is growing. Peter is much more aware of his weaknesses, as well as strengths. This growth in self-understanding has transformed Peter's personality—hot, streaming lava—into solid rock. Rock is needed, for Jesus is committing the care of his sheep to Peter. Theodore of Mopsuestia comments, "It is necessary that you [Peter] carry their burden, and protect them, and comfort them in their weakness and nourish them with the grace that was given to you."[5]

How hard it is to acknowledge transparently our failures and sins! Still, when we embed our struggles in God's grace and recognize how we have grown through them, our heart enlarges empathetically for our fellow pilgrims. Romanus Melodus, for instance, notes that if Peter ever was tempted to judge another proudly or unfairly, he had only to remember his own testing and failure. "If conceit attacks you, hear the sound of the cock's crow, and remember the tears with whose streams I washed you, I who alone know what is in your heart . . . love those whom I love, sympathizing with sinners."[6]

We should heed an important wordplay in the conversation between Jesus and Peter. The first two times the Lord asks Peter if he "loves" him, John uses the Greek verb *agapeo*, the word most often used in the New Testament for God's immense, unconditional love. Jesus is urging Peter to love him with a deeper, wider love, a love that reflects God's love for Peter (John 21:15, 17).

The third time Jesus asks Peter if he loves him, John uses the Greek verb *phileo*, which is commonly used to express the love friends have for each other. Jesus is asking Peter if he would again be his friend. Clearly, Jesus wants to be friends with Peter, but he also wants his love to widen and deepen to reflect the depth of God's love.

## A Solemn Prediction

Let's move beyond the question and response section of Peter's conversation with Jesus. After exhorting Peter to "feed my sheep," Jesus solemnly predicts the manner of Peter's death. "Very truly I tell you, when you were younger you dressed yourself and went where you wanted; but when you are old you will stretch out your hands, and someone else will dress you and lead you where you do not want to go" (John 21:18). John then remarks, "Jesus said this to indicate the kind of death by which Peter would glorify God. Then he said to him, 'Follow me!'" (John 21:19).

Paul and Peter were executed by the Roman government at roughly the same time, probably during the Neronian persecution in 64 AD. Paul received a mercifully quick death, beheaded as a Roman citizen. Peter didn't share Paul's Roman citizenship and instead suffered crucifixion outside Rome's city walls. Recall how Peter feared crucifixion at the time of Jesus's death.

Peter has dramatically changed over the past thirty years. The church father Jerome notes that when the Roman execution squad arrived at the site of Peter's crucifixion, Peter said, "I don't deserve to be crucified in the manner of my Lord. Crucify me upside down."[7] The Roman soldiers—professional killers like those at Jesus's crucifixion—readily obliged. As Peter dies, I see him looking up and imagine Jesus looking down, along with the angels. They are applauding. "Well done, Peter. Well done. You used your gift of years so well. Welcome home."

Augustine aptly comments, "Peter accomplished later on by the grace of God what he had previously been unable to do by self-reliance."[8]

## What Is God Offering You in Your Gift of Years?

Peter's gift of years was spent largely in Christian ministry. So have mine. Vocations in full-time ministry, though, are more the exception than the rule. And that's fine with God.

Imagine a young girl gifted by God with a love for bugs. Those suffering from arachnophobia may find it hard to believe, but God creates some image-bearers with just such a love. This young bug-loving girl has been graced with a lively curiosity, intelligence, mental discipline, and adventuresome spirit. As she grows up, she spends hours outdoors, prowling for her small critter friends. She looks for bugs, reads books about bugs, and draws pictures of bugs. In high school her interest in entomology grows.

When she heads off to the university, she chooses biology as her major with a minor in entomology. Graduate school is her next step. Finally, she earns a PhD in entomology, awarded for her research on African wolf spiders.

Is our entomologist PhD a second-class citizen in the kingdom of God? Absolutely not. For the very God that full-time ministers serve is the one who created and delights in the insect world. I easily imagine Jesus holding a flashlight on a nighttime search for spiders as he and our PhD friend search under rocks and peer into holes looking for spiders. When they find one, Jesus exclaims, "Cool, isn't it?"

"You bet," our gifted entomologist responds. "You really knew what you were doing when you made that one."

## Pause and Reflect

For a moment, think, pray, and dream—broadly, not narrowly. What might God desire for your gift of years, however many may remain? He has a different story in mind for each of us. Perhaps start your reflection by asking a very simple question: What do I like to do? Like our entomologist friend, you're thinking or doing something—maybe something you can't imagine anyone else being interested in—yet you say to yourself, "I was made for this. This is my niche." Consider your circle of interests. What rises to the surface?

Manual work will interest some folks; working with ideas will interest others. There is no right or wrong here, no better or worse.

Do you have a love for cooking, animals, philosophy, mechanics, airplanes, gardening, cars, drawing, books, math, or poetry? What do your interests tell you about you, God's unique image-bearer?

Don't worry about what others might think about your niche, your propensities, your interests, your loves. They are not the judge of your life. God is.

## A Change in Direction

Here's what happened to me. In high school I realized I liked to write. I also started to occasionally speak in a public setting, and people seemed to listen. In my pre-Christian days, I planned to use my verbal skills to practice law after my undergraduate work at UCLA.

Then something unexpected happened. I entered the kingdom of God, either shortly before or shortly after I arrived to attend university in California. After becoming a Christian, I still planned on going to law school.

Sometime in my junior year I started teaching a Sunday school class for young people at a local church in Pacific Palisades. As I taught, a spiritual gift bubbled to the surface of my life. It seemed to piggyback on my ability to speak and write.

I distinctly remember the day a well-known writer happened to visit my Sunday school class. When class ended, she walked quickly up to me. I knew who she was and was surprised when she unexpectedly thumped me on the chest with her finger and said, "You're meant to teach."

She caught me off guard. I'd never considered this possibility. I was already accepted into law school. When my senior year ended, I planned to move to San Diego to study law at the University of San Diego Law School. And suddenly, unexpectedly, under God's grace and providential care, a new possibility opened up before me. Over the next few months I prayed, pondered what others were saying about my teaching gift, and continued to teach my Sunday school class.

Let's consider my situation more abstractly: What was happening? First, I tried doing something I hadn't planned on doing. Someone asked me to teach a Sunday school class, and I said yes. As I started teaching, I really enjoyed what I was doing. Not only that, but my community—the students in the class and close friends outside of it—confirmed that I was good at what I was doing. The Holy Spirit was blessing my teaching. Considering these factors, I continued to take Bible classes at a little Bible school just off the university campus, while I finished up my studies at UCLA. Finally, I changed my plans for the future. I ended up attending seminary rather than law school, and I'm glad I did.

In my situation, I moved from law to a more religious or spiritual vocation. Some of you might move in the opposite direction. If God's directing, that's absolutely fine.

My advice is to think and pray through what the Lord is asking you to do with your gift of years. First, ask yourself what you like to do. Not what you don't like to do. Too often, especially when we ask what the Lord wants us to do with our lives, we think negatively: *If I do what God wants me to do, I really won't like it.* Sacrifice is inevitable when we follow Jesus, but the sacrifice is coupled with the abilities, gifts, and desires that God has implanted in each of us.

Where do you feel at home? What's your niche? Let's return to our entomologist friend. Since she was a little girl, she's loved insects. She followed that love as a Christian into a PhD program. Quite evidently, she won't be preaching every Sunday morning. She might well be doing something equally important: introducing God's image-bearers to one of the most interesting and beautiful aspects of God's creation. In studying entomology, she's fulfilling God's call on her life, just as another image-bearer might go to seminary or earn a PhD in theology.

To sum up, as we live our gift of years, as we keep in step with Jesus, we ask ourselves what we like to do, remain open to a wide range of possibilities, surround the process in prayer, and consult our community of friends and associates. We value their opinions, for we are not the only ones in relationship with the Holy Spirit. And we accept responsibility for what we've been given, not for what we haven't received.

## What Are We Responsible For?

Let's consider Jesus's parable of the bags of gold in Matthew 25. In older translations it's known as the parable of the talents; a talent was worth about twenty years of a day laborer's wages.

In Jesus's story a man leaving on a journey entrusts one servant with five bags of gold (Matt. 25:15). Another servant is given two bags. Still another is given one bag.

After a long time, the man returns from his journey and asks each servant to give an account of what he's done with the gold he's been given.

The servant who received five bags has gained five more. The same is true of the servant who received two bags; he has gained two more bags. The third servant, however, is rebuked severely, for he feared his master and simply buried his one bag in the ground.

The stern master does not hold the servants responsible for what they have not been given. The servant given two bags is not responsible for gaining five more. He's simply held responsible for what he's been given. The first servant was given more, and hence is responsible for more.

The fault of the "wicked, lazy" servant—the one who had been given only one bag of gold—was not that he had been given less. It was that he was not responsible with what he had been given.

The overarching point of the story? We are not held responsible for what we have not been given. We are responsible for what we have received. This principle shows how silly comparison is in the kingdom of God. Yes, our gifts entail responsibility—for what we've been given. Nothing more and nothing less.

Older folks like me may feel regret as the end of our gift of years looms before us. We may have made bad decisions. Perhaps we have squandered our years and the gifts given to us. What to do? We take a day, rehearse the past with God, confess our sins, and move into the future. God is not done with us yet. New beginnings are always possible.

Thankfully, God is in the business of redeeming people, including their past. God redeems the time we have lost as we offer it to him, for God loves to do so. Old things become new in the hands of God (cf. 2 Cor. 5:16–18; 6:16–21).

God redeems the years of his precious image-bearers as we lean into him with faith, hope, and love. As Paul puts it in his letter to the Romans: "And we know that in all things God works for the good of those who love him, who have been called according to his purpose" (Rom. 8:28).

Old things can become new up to the moment of our last breath. Think of Paul's words in Romans 11:33–36; ponder them in the context of your own gift of years, with all its complexities, disappointments, fulfillments, and beauty: "Oh, the depth of the riches of the wisdom and knowledge of God! How unsearchable his judgments, and his paths beyond tracing out! Who has known the mind of the Lord? Or who has been his counselor? Who has ever given to God, that God should repay them? For from him and through him and for him are all things. To him be the glory forever! Amen."

So if you're on the back stretch of your gift of years and imagine your vocation is complete—or your life is a disappointment or a failure—think again. What if the years now complete were given to you as preparation for the last five minutes of your life? Or the last week? Or the last month? Or the last six months? Or the last year?

What are the glories and beauties God plans to extrude from your life as its end draws near? Keep your eyes and heart open. God knows and sees things in their totality. We rarely receive more than a glimpse. And that's fine. God knows what to do and when to do it.

## Stewards and Sinners

God's precious image-bearers—you and me—are not only stewards of the gift of years and the personal gift mix that God has graced us with. We are also sinners. We exercise our gifts through our personality, with all its strengths and weaknesses.

Yes, we are all curved in on ourselves. We are *incurvatus in se.* Hence, for us to be safe, sane, healthy gift bearers, we must simultaneously engage in a process of spiritual formation. Gifting and character formation are to be married together, or our gift of years may well blow up in our faces.

Ponder how celebrities are idolized in American culture and around the world. What is a celebrity? Someone who has become famous. Celebrities may be complete rascals: murderers and thieves still qualify for *People* magazine. A celebrity may surely be a praiseworthy person and have a solid, loving character. But character development is not a requirement for most folks seeking celebrity or for those who admire it.

How frequently we read of Christian celebrities who've "fallen" in one way or another. Genevieve Carlton lists "legendary pastors who fell from grace": Ted Haggard (premarital sex, adultery, gay sex scandal); Jim Bakker (financial fraud, sexual abuse); Bill Gothard (sexual harassment); Bob Coy (multiple affairs, pornography addiction); Dave

Reynolds (child pornography); Jimmy Swaggart (adultery, prostitution, pornography); Robert Tilton (financial misuse of funds); Mark Driscoll (plagiarism, allegations of emotional abuse and misogyny); Josh Duggar (sexual molestation).[9] Allegations of sexual harassment against Jean Vanier, Bill Hybels, and Ravi Zacharias have recently been confirmed.

What dynamic underlies these tragic moral failures among Christian leaders? Most often we have a Christian who is extremely gifted. In most cases, Christians such as these are well known for a reason, and the reason is sometimes laudable.

Fame and its accoutrements—wealth, prestige, power, and sexual opportunity—weigh heavily on gifted but malformed personalities. Cracks in Christian leaders' characters surface, and finally break, apart from a spiritually disciplined life. Three specific sins frequently appear: financial shenanigans, misuse of power, or sexual sin. Sometimes they are blended in a toxic mix.

## Pause and Reflect

It's easy to point the finger at someone else. How are you doing in terms of the big three: money, sex, and power? What grade would you give yourself?

Richard J. Foster wisely observes, "The crying need is for people of faith to live faithfully. This is true in all spheres of human existence, but is particularly true with reference to money, sex, and power. No issues touch us more profoundly or more universally. No themes are more inseparably intertwined. No topics cause more controversy. No human realities have greater power to bless or to curse. No three things have been more sought after or in need of a Christian response."[10]

Foster wrote those words in 1985. Has the situation changed for the better in the Christian community? In our own lives? For some, yes. For too many, no.

"If there is no inner-life," Foster warns, "however great may be the zeal, the high intention, the hard work, no fruit will come forth; it is like a spring that would give out sanctity to others but cannot, having none to give; one can only give what one has."

Saint Paul was aware of the relationship between character development and the exercise of spiritual gifts. He cautions that whomever we consider for a position of leadership in Christian ministry "must not be a recent convert, or he may become conceited and fall under the same judgment as the devil" (1 Tim. 3:6).

Ponder the years Paul spent nurturing Timothy's character and gifts. Very early in their relationship, Paul recognized Timothy's gifts and budding character. Timothy's community spoke well of him (Acts 16:2). Paul discerned Timothy's spiritual gifts, recognized his promising character, and then spent years with Timothy, developing both. We see a master of the spiritual life training his beloved apprentice.

Consider Paul's words to Timothy as Paul's own gift of years draws to a close. Soon Timothy will step into Paul's shoes and assume much of Paul's ministry. Paul continues to speak to Timothy about the importance of sound doctrine, but he also stresses the importance of character formation in Timothy and other possible leaders.

Love is the goal, Paul writes, "which comes from a pure heart and a good conscience and a sincere faith" (1 Tim. 1:5). Earlier prophecies about Timothy are now being fulfilled. Paul asks Timothy to remember these prophecies, "so that by recalling them you may fight the battle well." Paul urges Timothy to hold "on to faith and a good conscience" (1 Tim. 1:18–19). Twice Paul stresses the importance of a pure conscience, the moral awareness planted within us by God. He knows our conscience can grow and mature or stiffen and die.

Is it a foregone conclusion that God's image-bearers inevitably fall from grace? Thankfully, no. Christian history is replete with folks who lived their gift of years well with God and ended their pilgrimage as holy, loving, faithful people. Billy Graham, Mother Teresa, Edith Stein, and Charles de Foucauld come to mind.

### Pause and Reflect

**Who are on your list of Christians who've borne the burden of fame well? Of course, we can also identify friends and family who have run their race well and crossed the finish line to the applause of saints and angels. Try compiling a list.**

I'm thankful that we don't have to be well known for God to see us. "I see you," the Lord says softly to millions of image-bearers each day. "I applaud your faithfulness. One day I will call you home, and your beauty will be seen by all, the beauty of faithfulness, hope, love, courage, chastity, and perseverance. Few noticed you as you lived your gift of years with me in this present evil age. But I did. Your faithful life will never be forgotten. I saw you. I applaud you. Welcome into the kingdom prepared for you."

God's overarching goal for his precious image-bearers is a graced life of faithfulness to Jesus and love for God and neighbor, whether we live lives of obscurity or recognition. To live lives that ring true, lives in step with Jesus, lives where our words and actions fit together. To live in a way that encourages and stimulates others to seek a different way—the way of Jesus—for their gift of years.

CHAPTER SIX

# Read Christ into Your Heart

In meditation we should not look for a "method" or a "system,"
but cultivate an "attitude," an "outlook": faith, openness,
attention, reverence, expectation, supplication, trust, joy.

—Thomas Merton

Take a look now at the subtitle for *A Different Way*: *Recentering the Christian Life Around Following Jesus*. In the chapters to come, including the present one, we focus on specific practices—often termed spiritual disciplines—that build on the ground we have covered so far and enable us to recenter our steps as we follow Jesus throughout our gift of years. The first of these practices is learning to read in a different way.¹

Each morning, I spend time with the Scripture. Many of you do, too. I read it, ponder it, and often, thanks to encouraging listening apps such as Hallow and Dwell, I listen to it. I try to be creative in my listening and reading. Once, over ninety days, I listened to all the Old Testament prophets, Isaiah through Malachi, a chapter or two a day depending on the length of the passage. When the ninety-day cycle ended, I tapped an icon on the app and began the cycle again.

Some days I listen to the Gospels. Or I might listen to Paul, Peter,

John, or Jude. I listen to the Psalms. Once a year I listen to the Pentateuch—the first five books of the Bible. Other times over the year, I may listen to historical books like Judges or 1 Kings. At the present moment, I'm immersed in listening to 2 Samuel. Occasionally, my listening focuses on specific biblical characters like Deborah, Mary, or David. From the previous chapter, you'll know that I've spent quite a while with Peter. My appreciation and love for him has grown from pondering his life. Listening has enhanced our relationship.

Sometimes, I simply listen to a single chapter or set of verses over and over. This morning, sitting in my favorite chair, I repeatedly listened to Isaiah 1; I did nothing else except listen. I simply tapped "repeat mode" on my Dwell app, and the chapter kept playing.

Often as I listen, I read the biblical text with my eyes; I engage in an ocular and auditory reading, employing two senses rather than one. YouVersion allows me to listen and read texts in different languages. I lived in France for five years, and now each morning I can listen and read in French. Verbum, a wonderful Catholic app, presents texts in Greek and Latin, for those readers with background in these languages. Hallow enables Catholics to pray the rosary in English and Latin. I'm thankful for the way all these creative apps are making the Bible readily available.

I love listening to biblical texts. Listening focuses my attention. It slows me down. For one stretch a year or two ago, I listened repeatedly to Jesus's Sermon on the Mount. I periodically changed my routine as I listened. One morning I listened to the entire sermon, Matthew 5–7. On another, I listened to only one part of the sermon. This works well with the beatitudes, Matthew 5:3–11.

As I listened, I sensed Jesus's sermon slowly seeping into me. Jesus's mind was dripping into my mind and, with these holy drops, into my heart. My mind and heart, by God's grace, were slowly immersed in the mind and heart of Christ.

As I read and listen to the Scripture—during the early morning hours or perhaps at other times of the day—the analytical side of my brain is surely involved. I'm processing information, analyzing the grammar of sentences, following arguments, and tracing key themes. After years of reading texts, Christian and others, these are ingrained reading habits for me. What are your reading habits?

## Study and *Lectio Divina*

When Jesus addressed issues in his famous sermon concerning the fulfillment of the law of Moses, murder, adultery, divorce, oaths, loving one's enemies, and so on, I explored how these topics were understood and adjudicated in Jesus's ancient Jewish context. I practiced the spiritual discipline of study—a discipline more analytic than synthetic—as I mined the text for its nuggets.

When I analyze a text, I purposely distance myself from what I'm reading. I step back, pull the text apart, and examine its various parts. "How does all this fit together?" I ask.

The discipline of study provides brakes and buffers for our imagination as we seek spiritual insight and transformation. Solid biblical interpretation helps us crack open the text like a nut. It serves as a spiritual searchlight, used by the Holy Spirit to assist us as we explore a text's depth.

In study, we may consult ancient biblical interpreters such as the church fathers to help us make sense of the Bible. Modern biblical commentaries can also help. Yet we don't stop with the discipline of study. If we only analyze the Scripture in terms of its syntax, historical and cultural background, authorial intent, and so on, without *feeding* on the riches our interpretation has revealed to us, we ironically may starve spiritually as we study. Study sets the table and prepares the meal. In *lectio divina* we enjoy the feast.

So, if I am not to starve, I must link a different kind of reading to my study, a spiritual discipline known in Latin as *lectio divina* ("divine," "spiritual," or "devotional" reading). Jean Leclercq describes *lectio divina* as a way of reading "entirely oriented toward life, and not toward abstract knowledge."[2]

Let's return for a moment to my morning listening to the Sermon on the Mount on Dwell. As I listened to the text, I used my ears to "read" the text. As I did so, Jesus's sermon settled ever more deeply in me, filtering through my mind into my heart. Christ's words percolated in me, like the bubbling of hot water through coffee grains.

The metaphor of percolation describes the rich, slow soaking that occurs in *lectio divina*. To change metaphors, in *lectio divina* I'm fertilizing and watering my mind and heart, much like a gardener tending her garden or flowerbed.

*Lectio divina* is, in Eugene Peterson's words, "a way of reading that refuses to be reduced to *just* reading but intends the living of the text, listening and responding to the voices of that 'so great a cloud of witnesses' telling their stories, singing their songs, preaching their sermons, praying their prayers, asking their questions, having their children, burying their dead, following Jesus."[3]

Consider for a moment a cluster of participles that illustrates well the heart of *lectio divina: pondering, ruminating, chewing, embracing, addressing, imitating, responding, following, repenting, eating, digesting, revering, meditating, praying, hearing, reflecting, considering, listening, remembering.*

All these verbal nouns suggest a movement toward Scripture that is more than study, a reading that is slow, hungry, attentive, and prayerful. We read with the eager expectation that God wishes to address us—address you, address me—in this particular book, chapter, or verse. God is lovingly offering specific words, phrases, stories, exhortations, prayers, encouragements, and sometimes rebukes for each precious image-bearer to embrace, devour, digest, imitate, or obey, as if all one's life depended on it.

*Lectio divina*, then, is a slow-paced, meditative reading of Scripture, a way of reading the Bible with the goal of personal transformation and faithful following of *a different way*. It helps us keep in step with Jesus.

We are created in the image of God, but the image we presently reflect is too often distorted, bent, skewed, twisted. *Lectio divina* helps straighten us out so that we mirror the beauty of Christ more clearly. Spiritual reading repairs and restores our character; it is an avenue of healing for the spiritual genes that mutated with the fall of Adam and Eve into sin. You might picture *lectio divina* as a form of spiritual gene therapy.

Medieval Christians sometimes described *lectio divina* as *otium sanctum*, "holy leisure." When I first ran across this phrase in Foster's *Celebration of Discipline*, it was new to me. I was surprised to find leisure described as holy. Are you?

Ponder for a moment the word *holy*. The Hebrew word for *holy* is *qadosh*. Something or someone is *qadosh* if "set apart from the common or profane." For example, if I curse using God's name, or treat God's name as a common thing, I'm profaning it. "Oh, my God!" would qualify. When I speak God's name this way, I'm treating it like any other common thing. I violate the fourth commandment: "You shall not misuse the name of the LORD your God, for the LORD will not hold anyone guiltless who misuses his name" (Exod. 20:7).

Think of the burning bush that captured Moses's attention as he walked through the desert. Before the angel of the Lord manifested his flaming presence in that particular bush, it was a common bush, much like the other desert shrubs.

Everything changes as the angel of the Lord flames in the bush, setting it on fire but not consuming it; the bush is no longer a common desert shrub. God's holiness radiates from its shoots, limbs, and roots across and into the surrounding desert terrain. Moses approaches the bush, and God warns him to remove his shoes. "'Do not come any closer,' God said. 'Take off your sandals, for the place where you are standing is holy ground'" (Exod. 3:5). The ground is now *qadosh*.

*Lectio divina* is not common reading, the reading I engage in as I speed-read the *New York Times* on my phone. Rather, it is a fiery, holy reading that can set us afire with God's holiness. It does so in a surprising way, sometimes by simply slowing us down. It is an invitation to practice holy leisure.

## Holy Munching

How surprising to find leisure (*otium*) described as holy (*sanctum*). The holy leisure of *lectio divina* is quite specific: we are slowly chewing on Scripture. Can you picture yourself munching on a text, grinding it between your teeth, much like a cow chews its cud?

The vivid metaphor of Bible munching came to life for me when we lived near the French Alps in Gex, France. Behind our apartment building in Gex was a large pasture, home for our local bovine friends from the spring to the fall. Occasionally, the kids and I walked over to the pasture fence, gazing at the cows from a distance. We looked at them, and they stared at us, slowly chewing their cud.

If I had a few sugar cubes, their interest would rise, and one or two cows would slowly amble over, hoping for a treat. I'd place a sugar cube on the palm of my hand, hold it out, and a wet, leathery tongue would sweep it off. It disappeared down the cow's throat; satisfied, dreamy eyes stared at me, begging for another cube. Finally, when all my sugar cubes were on bovid deposit, the cows resumed chewing their cud. Can you see them? They munched slowly, meditatively, in no rush to swallow. *Lectio divina* is much like this: a leisurely munching on a biblical text.

Other metaphors for *lectio divina* come to mind. Baron von Hügel compared *lectio divina* to melting a lozenge in his mouth. That's a good descriptor of *lectio divina*. Just last night I enjoyed a See's lollipop; I could have hurriedly cracked the candy and swallowed it, but that would have needlessly shortened my enjoyment. Instead, I let the lollipop melt in my mouth; my pleasure lengthened. Are there scriptural lollipops the Lord is offering to you?

Consider Psalm 1. The psalmist doesn't simply read the law. He delights in it. *Lectio divina* resembles the psalmist's delight in the beauty of God's law. We read a text slowly, allowing time for delight to develop. We're in no rush. We simply gaze, much like the reader Rainer Maria Rilke describes. He "does not always remain bent over his pages; he often leans back and closes his eyes over a line he has been reading again, and its meaning spreads through his blood."[4]

Rilke's words perfectly describe a good friend of mine. Every Friday afternoon we spend an hour or so reading Thomas Aquinas together. Now, reading Aquinas is never a speedy affair. We read the *Summa* line by line out loud. To complete our reading will take us quite a few years, but as we often say to each other, "Why rush?" Every now and then as we read, my pal morphs into the very person Rilke describes. He starts swaying, leans back, and smiles over a word or phrase. Who would have imagined reading Aquinas could be a form of *lectio divina*? I think Thomas would smile.

My favorite description of *lectio divina* comes from Eugene Peterson. It's worth quoting at length:

Years ago I owned a dog who had a fondness for large bones. For-
tunately for him we lived in the forested foothills of Montana. In
his forest rambles he often came across a carcass of a white-tailed
deer that had been brought down by the coyotes. Later he would
show up on our stone, lakeside patio carrying or dragging his
trophy, usually a shank or a rib; he was a small dog and the bone
was often nearly as large as he was. Anyone who has owned a dog
knows the routine: he would prance and gambol playfully before
us with his prize, wagging his tail, proud of his find, courting our
approval. And of course, we approved. We lavished praise, telling
him what a good dog he was. But after a while, sated with our applause, he would drag the bone off twenty yards or so to a more
private place, usually the shade of a large moss-covered boulder,
and go to work on the bone. The social aspects of the bone were
behind him; now the pleasure became solitary. He gnawed the
bone, turned it over and around, licked it, worried it. Sometimes
we could hear a low rumble or growl, what in a cat would be a
purr. He was obviously enjoying himself and in no hurry. After
a leisurely couple of hours he would bury it and return the next
day to take it up again. An average bone lasted about a week. . . .
[M]y dog [was] meditating his bone.[5]

Peterson insightfully comments, "There is a certain kind of writing
that invites this kind of reading, soft purrs and low growls as we taste
and savor, anticipate and take in the sweet and spicy, mouthwatering
and energizing morsel words—'O taste and see that the LORD is good!'
(Ps. 34:8)."[6]

Christians have meditated the bones of Scripture for a long time.
Ancient Christians like Origen, Basil the Great, John Cassian, Gregory the Great, and Benedict of Nursia practiced *lectio divina*. Folks
who joined Benedict's monastic community were expected to learn

to read if they couldn't already, for Benedict wanted all community members reading texts. He not only wanted his monks to read texts; he wanted them to read slowly, to imprint what they read on their minds and hearts.

Reading in the ancient world was slow, demanding work, for few texts were readily available. Scarcity of reading material accentuated the importance of memory work as a monk read. Jean Leclercq refers to "the phenomenon of reminiscence." Reading out loud assisted this memory work and could be physically demanding, much like a good workout. "They read usually," Leclercq writes, "not as today, principally with the eyes, but with the lips, pronouncing what they saw, and with the ears. Listening to the words pronounced, hearing what is called 'the voices of the pages.'"[7]

Michael Casey explains, "The monks tended to read slowly, probably vocalizing the words as they read. Often significant passages would be committed to memory; only a few scholars had the possibility of taking notes for permanent reference. With so few titles available, favorite works would be re-read many times. Because there were few reference books or commentaries, the monks had to learn to sit with difficulties and obscurities and try to puzzle out for themselves the meaning of the page before them. Reading became a dialogue with the text."[8] Listening well to a text required the monks to be attentive, receptive, and trusting, a ready vessel to receive the feast offered by a text.

Like other areas of the spiritual life, *lectio divina* is an act of trust. We trust that the Holy Spirit desires to speak to us, even in those parts of the Bible we find boring or offensive. We trust that other writers are smarter, more gifted, and wiser than we; we trust that they are worth our time and effort. We trust that God has scattered jewels for us in the writings of an early Christian bishop like Ignatius of Antioch, a desert dweller like Antony the Great, or medieval saints such as Julian of Norwich or Teresa of Ávila.

## Wise Reading or Absurd Living?

Henri Nouwen recognizes the connection between listening and transformation. Nouwen's thoughts can easily be applied to *lectio divina*. Modern people, Nouwen notes, inhabit an extremely noisy environment. Intrusive racket impedes our ability to listen well. Nouwen points to "our worried, overfilled lives." We "are usually surrounded by so much outer noise that it is hard to truly hear our God when he is speaking to us. We have often become deaf. . . . Thus our lives have become absurd."

The connection between deafness and absurdity is worth noticing. Poor listening and absurd living are bedmates. Indeed, as Nouwen observes, our English word *absurd* is etymologically related to the Latin word *surdus*, meaning "deaf." Nouwen comments, "A spiritual life requires discipline because we need to listen to God, who constantly speaks but whom we seldom hear."[9]

As we learn to listen to texts, we dive deeper and deeper into the depths the Bible offers and contains. Some of us, though, will want to swim in the shallows for a while. We're just beginning to know the Bible, and spiritual cramping can catch us off guard if we don't start slow and develop our swimming muscles.

Let's return to our munching metaphor. We may need to become familiar with the menu before we sit down to eat. We take the time, then, to peruse the Bible's table of contents and ask, What parts of the Bible are unfamiliar to me?

I mentioned earlier in this chapter that I listened for three months to the Old Testament prophets on the Dwell Bible reading app. Why? I had asked myself an important question: "Chris, what parts of the Bible do you need to know better?" The prophets immediately came to mind. There were sections of the prophets that I knew fairly well, but I hadn't thoroughly explored lots of prophetic teaching. Over the next year or so I plan on continuing to listen from Isaiah to Malachi. I sense a deepening occurring in me as I soak my mind and heart in these prophetic texts.

In my listening immersion I'm noting texts I definitely want to slow down and ponder; these are good candidates for future *lectio divina*. Some are relatively new to me; I wouldn't have discovered these tasty morsels apart from soaking in the prophets as a whole.

You might try this reading method yourself: first, broad reading; some might want to read the Bible over a year or two's time. Dwell, Hallow, and other Bible apps provide reading plans that will help you do so.

Others may want to camp with specific texts for a long stretch. You set up your tent, the Holy Spirit lights a campfire, and you roast the meat the Spirit offers. Relax, stretch out your legs, and enjoy the meal the Spirit has prepared. Nourish your mind and heart. And with the filling, growth will occur. You will have taken one more step in learning to live a different way. You're keeping in step with Jesus, for he loved the Scriptures.

What kind of food has been your spiritual diet so far in your life with God? Junk food sickens us. It clogs our arteries and adds weight. Jesus offers us healthy, life-giving food. In *lectio divina* we settle down with him for a long, wonderful meal.

Much like Peterson's dog, in *lectio divina* we gnaw on Scripture's bones and feed on Christ's marrow. As we feed on Christ in Scripture, we savor him, digest him, assimilate him. The food Jesus offers grows us—and over the years we mature. A mere sapling grows into an oak.

## Information Is Not Enough

We've all met people who possess significant knowledge of the Bible and yet seem unchanged by what they've read. They're not much fun to be around. John Ortberg comments, "Take any person you know whose knowledge of the Bible is, say, ten times greater than that of the average unchurched person. Then ask yourself if this person is ten times more loving, ten times more patient, and ten times more joyful than the average unchurched person." Ortberg's point is a good one. Information alone is not enough to live a different way. "Knowledge about the Bible is an indispensable good," Ortberg acknowledges. "But knowledge does not *by itself* lead to spiritual transformation."[10]

Nouwen again is helpful. He notes the connection between listening—think of listening to a text on Dwell or Hallow—and obedience, that is, a changed life: "The word *obedient* comes from the Latin word *audire*, which means 'listening.' A spiritual discipline is necessary in order to move slowly from an absurd to an obedient life, from a life filled with noisy worries to a life in which there is some free inner space where we can listen to our God and follow his guidance."[11]

This is where consistent *lectio divina* can make a big difference in our lives. This discipline helps us *process* or *digest* the information God offers us in the Scripture or other devotional texts, in a manner and at a pace that enables us to assimilate our reading into our spiritual digestive system. Too much food at too rapid a rate causes indigestion. Not enough food and we begin to starve.

The example of a cow chewing its cud again is relevant. I've learned that cows actually have more than one stomach. This enables them to repeat their chewing and digestion. I know it sounds gross, but cows bring up what they've already chewed to munch once again. This repetitive chewing enables a cow to derive the last ounce of nourishment from the grass she has eaten. How similar to *lectio divina*!

A commonplace in the ancient Latin-speaking world was *repetitio mater studiorum est* ("repetition is the mother of all learning"). No ancient readers would ever question the importance of repetition and memory work if they were to grow intellectually and spiritually from their reading.

> ## Pause and Reflect
>
> **As you practice *lectio divina*, enjoy the freedom of repeating your reading as many times as you want. Memorize this phrase: "No rush. Repeat, remember, and relish."**

I'm reminded of a story I heard about a pastor who was approaching spiritual burnout. He had worked too hard for too long, 24/7, and his well was dry. He was living on fumes and very near to leaving the ministry. Our exhausted pastor approached a close friend and shared his struggle. "I think my faith has died. I read the Bible and it's like drinking sawdust. My mind and heart are dry as a bone."

His wise friend listened, pondered, and prayed silently. He didn't scold or offer easy solutions. He simply suggested that his burned-out friend read Paul's letter to the Ephesians once a day for thirty days. "Don't try to do anything more than this. It shouldn't take more than twenty minutes."

"It's not going to do any good," his despondent friend grumbled.

"Maybe it won't. Just give it a try."

"All right," replied the discouraged pastor. "I suppose it's worth a try."

"While you're reading, I'll be praying," his friend encouraged.

Well, for the first five readings or so, things went just as our tired pastor expected they would. Paul's words seemed dry and dusty. But the pastor kept his promise to his friend. He continued to read Ephesians once a day. By day ten, Ephesians slowly began speaking to him. The Spirit was gently at work. By the twentieth reading, the text was once again alive, singing music to him he hadn't heard for a long time. Forgotten themes were resurrected in our tired pastor's mind and heart. He felt his fatigue slowly lifting. No longer was our despondent pastor in the dumps; his spiritual eardrums were once again supple and vibrating. Something good was happening in him. His well was slowly filling with living water, the wonder and beauty of Christ. By the thirtieth reading his spiritual life was significantly restored and renewed. He felt back on track.

Ephesians once a day for thirty days was just the right prescription. The Spirit blessed the repetitive reading of the text. As a side benefit the pastor deposited Paul's entire text in his memory bank. In the future, Ephesians was available for withdrawal, a verse or chapter now available on call. So many good things happened as Ephesians percolated through the pastor's mind and heart. Renewed life and reinvigorated ministry were the happy, graced result.

## Chewing on the Gospels

For a moment, let's focus specifically on *lectio divina* and the Gospels. Matthew, Mark, Luke, and John narrate Jesus's words, life, and ministry, with each Gospel possessing its own characteristics and emphases.

When I meditate on a passage from Jesus's life, in Eugene Peterson's words, I'm fusing together my story and Christ's story. I'm welcoming "the opportunity to revolutionize the whole tenor of the segment of history that is my little life."[12] Imagine that. With this spiritual discipline, through the Spirit's empowerment, I can meld my life's story with that of Jesus, the most important life in human history.

Have you battled fear in your life? I have, especially in my earlier years. If fear has been an issue for you, try fusing your fear to Christ's power and love by meditating on Jesus's stilling of the storm, recorded in Mark 4. As the stormy sea rages out of control, the terrified disciples fear for their lives. The boat, their only refuge from the waves, could capsize at any time. Yet there lies Jesus, asleep with his head on a cushion in the stern of the boat.

Jesus knows who he is, and he knows his Father. He sleeps, perfectly at peace in circumstances that his disciples consider completely out of control. When Jesus wakes to the fearful cries of his friends, he quickly quiets the storm with a stern word of command. "Quiet! Be still!"

Note, too, the pointed question Jesus then asks the disciples: "Why are you so afraid? Do you still have no faith?" As stillness covers the sea, the terror of the disciples switches to perplexity, even confusion. "Who is this?" they ask. "Even the wind and the waves obey him!" (Mark 4:39–41). We hear their question and ask it for ourselves: "Who are you, Jesus?"

Use a *sanctified imagination*, as Foster puts it, to imagine yourself with Jesus in the boat. Perhaps imagine yourself as Jesus. You are the one sleeping on the cushion. What did Jesus experience as he woke from his sleep? What was his expression as he looked at the disciples and the sea around him? What is your expression as you take his place? What are you feeling? What are you learning with Jesus in the boat?

Or situate yourself in the boat as an unseen observer. Can you feel the boat rocking in the wind? Ocean spray splashing against your face? Do you see the dark clouds hovering over you? Lightning flashing? Thunder booming? What are you *thinking and feeling* as you watch Jesus sleeping so soundly? Use your imaginative skills to open yourself to all that is happening in the storm. What does the Holy Spirit wish to say to *you* in this story about Jesus?

This spiritual, imaginative reading of a text is an inventive, receptive reading. As we read the Gospels, our life story gradually welds itself to Jesus's story. Our consciousness, as Michael Casey puts it, will increasingly conform to the mind of Christ, as will our actions. "When our minds and hearts are formed according to Christ," Casey writes, "then our actions can be vehicles of grace to others. The precondition is, however, that our consciousness is shaped to agree with that of Christ. And this is precisely the role of *lectio divina*. It is a school in which we learn Christ. . . . *Lectio divina* helps us to encounter Christ, it initiates us into the way of Christ."[13] The Gospel narratives percolate within us, like hot water through coffee grounds.

If we're tempted to flee from the truth, *lectio divina* helps us turn and embrace it. If sin has distorted our thinking, *lectio divina* serves as a channel of grace, forgiveness, and healing. It engages our mind redemptively, forming new thought patterns to replace old ones. *Lectio divina* gently and slowly guides us to the only one worthy of our trust, the God who has created us for himself.

*Lectio divina* uses Jesus's words and actions to *form* Jesus in us. It is formative reading designed to redeem and sanctify our thoughts. We sit at Jesus's feet, listening, reading, meditating, praying, contemplating, and then acting in line with what we've learned. Our reading aligns us with the steps of Jesus.

We need to be patient, with ourselves and with the text. The soul likes to move slowly.[14] As for the Bible, some texts are clear, delightful, accessible, and taste good. There is little bone to crack, for instance, in Psalm 23. The sweet-tasting marrow is readily available. Other texts are less accessible, bony, hard to crack, and well-nigh indigestible. "Why would the Holy Spirit want me to know this?" we ask, as we read through a difficult book like Leviticus, Judges, or Joshua. How, in any discernible way, is Christ present here? That's a good question. Use your questions as prayers as you read and listen.

Always remember that the Father, Son, and Holy Spirit have inspired these particular sentences and stories; God has set them apart as sustenance for our spiritual transformation. As we transition from study to *lectio divina*, meditation on Scripture transfuses the marrow of the Bible into our spiritual bloodstream.

We study, we memorize, we ponder, we meditate, we pray, we act. Image-bearers called to significant involvement in social justice and mission will especially need to allocate time for *lectio divina*. Social activism without *lectio divina* burns people up like kindling.

Bryan Stevenson, Gary Haugen, Ron Sider, Justin Welby, Jonathan Wilson-Hartgrove, Lisa Harper, and Shane Claiborne are great examples of folks whose commitment to social justice and mission is fused to a rich inner life with Jesus.[15] John Perkins, Martin Luther King Jr., Christena Cleveland, Barbara L. Peacock, Willie Jennings, Dorothy Day, Natasha Sistrunk Robinson, Elizabeth Conde-Frazier, Samuel Escobar, and Orlando Costas also come to mind.[16]

We meditatively read Scripture not to avoid the world but to move into our world powerfully and wisely, to avoid any disconnect between what our eyes read, ears hear, mouths speak, and arms and legs practice.[17] To meditate a text is "to read a text and to learn it 'by heart' in the fullest sense of this expression, that is, with one's whole being: with the body, since the mouth pronounced it, with the memory which fixes it, with the intelligence which understands its meaning, and with the will which desires to put it into practice."[18]

While *lectio divina* or *meditatio Scripturarum* (meditation on Scripture) is most easily done with passages from the Gospels, we can also meditate on New Testament letters like those of Paul. John Chrysostom, archbishop of Constantinople, would form "a mental image" as he read Paul's words. Even the salutation of a letter came to life in Chrysostom's sanctified imagination. "For truly, when I hear, 'Paul the apostle,' *I have in my mind* the one in afflictions, the one in tight struggles, the one in blows, the one in prisons, the one who was night and day in the depth of the sea, the one snatched up into the third heaven . . . the one who prayed to be anathema from Christ for the sake of his brothers and sisters. Just like some golden cord, *the chain of his good deeds comes into the head of those who attend with precision along with the remembrance of his name."*[19]

Jesus's Jewish audience would have understood the importance of *meditatio*. Indeed, Margaret Mitchell explains that *meditatio* "is used generally to translate the Hebrew *haga*, and like the latter it means, fundamentally, to learn the Torah and the words of the Sages, while pronouncing them usually in a low tone, in reciting them to oneself, in murmuring them with the mouth. This is what we call 'learning by heart,' what ought rather to be called, according to the ancients, 'learning by mouth,' since the mouth 'meditates wisdom.'"[20]

Eugene Peterson reiterates Mitchell's point: "*Meditatio* is the discipline we give to keeping the memory active in the act of reading. *Meditatio* moves from looking at the words of the text to entering the world of the text. As we take this text into ourselves, we find that the text is taking us into itself. For the world of the text is far larger and more real than our minds and experience."[21]

Carefully ponder Peterson's words, especially "We find that the text is taking us into itself." This is what the Lord desires for us, for the Lord inspired the Bible for us not only to study *but to inhabit*. If we allow the text to take us into itself, we are allowing God, in a very profound way, to take us into himself. What could be better than that? *Lectio divina* is God's magnet to pull us home, God's tracking device to find lost image-bearers, God's GPS to guide them home and keep them on course.

Jean Leclercq sums things up well: "To speak, to think, to remember, are the three phases of the same activity. To express what one is thinking and to repeat it enables one to imprint it on one's mind. In Christian as well as rabbinical tradition, one cannot meditate anything else but a text, and since this text is the word of God, meditation is the necessary complement, almost the equivalent, of the *lectio divina*."[22]

## Practical Steps into *Lectio Divina*

Here are a few concrete steps you can take into the wonderful spiritual discipline of *lectio divina*, so-called spiritual, devotional, divine, or meditative reading.

- Set aside time. Twenty minutes a day should do the trick. To find these valuable minutes, you'll probably need to step back and analyze your whole day. If your calendar is filled to the brim, you may have to get up twenty minutes earlier than normal. Or if you're a night owl, you might want to rearrange how you're using the evening hours. *Every movement toward God requires a sacrifice of some kind, however small it may be.*
- Consider these twenty minutes a gift of love from you to God.

    Lord, I desire to be with you. I give these minutes to you.
    Use them as you will. I want to draw near to you through
    the book you have written. As I read, I offer myself to
    you. Help me, Lord. I can't accomplish this on my own.

- Don't burden yourself with undue expectations for what you must accomplish during your spiritual reading. *Lectio divina* is a highly relational reading, a reading couched in love. Simply receive whatever the Lord offers you in a text, even if the Lord's gift stings. He knows what is best. Devotional reading is a gift, not a task.
- Keep your eyes open for the "little pools of silence" offered to you each day by your loving Lord.[23] They are there. Have ears to hear and to receive. The silence that strengthens our reading is available. Consider some concrete steps into silence. Learn to use technology more wisely. Turn off the TV. Stop

reading emails every ten minutes. Limit your texting and time on Facebook and Twitter. "Don't send" can be quite as helpful as "Send." Your friends and associates will survive. And when you finally do communicate with them, what you say will more likely be safe, wise, gentle, and kind.

- Have a journal at hand for noting questions or insights that come as you read. Note the day and the text you're munching on. As time passes, occasionally review what the Lord is "texting" you during *lectio divina*! Feel free to "text" back in your prayers. Occasionally write out these prayers in your journal. You're learning the language of love, the language of *lectio divina*.

- If you find yourself distracted as you read meditatively, rather than engaging in hand-to-hand combat against the distractions, simply write them down as they occur. A point will come when the distractions lessen in intensity. Every now and then, use the distractions you've recorded as your *lectio divina* for the day. Are there patterns you discern in what's been distracting you? Recurring distractions might contain a message. Sailors used to leave messages in bottles. God might have a message for you in a distraction.

- Seriously consider Foster's words about a "sanctified imagination." Work at developing one. Yes, the human imagination makes some folks uneasy and is not always reliable. Won't we imagine things that aren't true? The possibility surely exists. We can also reason or think in faulty ways and reach false conclusions. Do we stop thinking because we might make a mistake? No.

- Our imagination is a significant means God has given us for developing our relationship with him. We use our imagination when we enter the world of Homer, Shakespeare, Dante, John Donne, Dorothy Sayers, or Flannery O'Connor. Our perspective widens and understanding deepens as we use our imagination in a holy way.

- A safety net for our imagination is careful thinking and mature biblical interpretation. We may imagine God has said we can sleep with a friend, but that's not God's voice speaking, as much as we imagine it to be. God has already told us sleeping around is off-limits. God doesn't speak out of both sides of his mouth.

- Consider getting acquainted with a biblical character through *lectio divina* coupled with the discipline of study. Take six months or a year to get to know Jesus's mother, Mary; David; Isaiah; Hannah; Deborah; or other biblical characters who have caught your attention.

- When you read other devotional texts, you might spend a year of concentrated reading and prayer with Julian of Norwich, Teresa of Ávila, John of the Cross, Charles de Foucauld, or other image-bearers whose writings have stood the test of time. There's a reason these writers are still in print. Many are now available in modern, accessible translations.

- Remember that *lectio divina* invites us to *enter* the story we're reading. In study we take a step back from the text to analyze. In devotional reading we embrace the text. We give it a hug. You might assume the role of a biblical character in the text you're reading. Become Mary at the foot of the cross, Peter in the boat with Jesus on the stormy sea, or David fighting Goliath. What might you learn if you assumed the role of Goliath, Saul, Manasseh, Athaliah, or Jezebel? The possibilities for learning and growing seem endless.

- Surround your meditative reading with prayers for growth and protection from spiritual attack. The devils won't be happy with your desire to draw close to God, but that's their problem, not yours. Try this prayer:

Lord, as I meditate on this text, surround me with a wall of light four feet thick.[24]

• Finally, pray for truckloads of grace as you read. Pray for the courage to receive whatever God desires to say to you in your reading. Share your learnings with your spiritual director or your close friends if this seems appropriate or wise. We can be self-deceived, and our closest friends are likely to spot this.

It is now time to examine our prayer life more thoroughly. We will do so in chapter 7.

CHAPTER SEVEN

# Commune and Communicate with God

> Simply put, prayer is all the ways in which we communicate
> and commune with God. The fundamental purpose of prayer
> is to deepen our intimacy with God. Early in the spiritual
> life we experience this intimacy primarily through the
> words we say to God, and there is deep satisfaction in it.
>
> —Ruth Haley Barton

Have you noticed that the connecting thread—the common theme—woven through *A Different Way* is learning to keep in step with Jesus? As we come to the mystery of prayer in this chapter, imagine Jesus with you. He is interested and excited about your desire to learn more about prayer; Jesus is eager to share with you what he learned about prayer during his short sojourn on earth. Link arms with him, then, as you journey into the mystery of prayer together. There are specific ideas and questions about prayer we will explore and specific practices of prayer I hope you find helpful.

Over twenty-four years of teaching at Eastern University, I often talked with students about prayer. As we talked, we learned together. In my Foundations of Christian Spirituality course, for two weeks, we particularly focused on prayer; this was one of my favorite sections of the course, and I think it was also for the students.

In the first session on prayer, I invited students to share the questions they'd always had about prayer. Since most students came from a Christian background, they were fairly familiar with prayer as an abstract concept, though few had entered deeply into prayer. Perhaps this was related to their age. Most were just getting started with God.

As the years passed, what increasingly caught my attention was that the same questions kept coming up. I've reduced the students' recurring questions down to the top five. Perhaps you, too, have wondered about questions like these:

1. If God already knows what I'm thinking, what I need, and what I desire, why do I have to pray?
2. Why should I bother God with the petty details of my life?
3. What's going on when God says no to my prayers?
4. Why don't we get all we ask for?
5. Why am I so distracted when I pray?

These five questions were consistently raised each semester. Take a close look at the list. Four out of five questions are related to two specific kinds of prayer: petition (praying regarding our own needs, concerns, and desires) and intercession (praying for others). The Holy Spirit, for instance, intercedes for us, and we can intercede for others in a similar way. Paul writes, "We do not know what we ought to pray for, but the Spirit himself intercedes for us through wordless groans" (Rom. 8:26). Epaphras, a faithful minister to the Colossians, constantly wrestled in prayer for them (Col. 4:12).

Distraction disrupts petition and intercession. I can be so distracted! Often the moment I begin to pray, I sense the humming of mosquito wings in my mind. Things I haven't thought about for months suddenly bubble to the surface of my consciousness. The to-do list for today—one that I've ignored for hours, if not weeks—suddenly becomes a high priority. I bet you've experienced some of the same things as me. What is one to do?

Of course, there are many more ways to pray than petition and intercession. Richard J. Foster, in his insightful book *Prayer: Finding the Heart's True Home*, discusses twenty-one types of prayer. He devotes two chapters to petitionary prayer and intercessory prayer; occasionally I'll be drawing on his insights. Other chapters in Foster's book, though, expand our prayer horizons beyond intercession and petition. For instance, Richard devotes a chapter each to meditative prayer and contemplative prayer, ways of praying that don't have asking and receiving as their core emphasis.

Because many readers of this book likely have questions related to intercession and petition, we'll focus on these two types of prayer in this chapter, while sometimes addressing other issues involved in prayer. I do encourage you, though, to read Foster's book on prayer. It's the best book I've read on prayer by a modern writer.

## Questions and Concerns about Prayer

What a strange, wondrous means God has ordained and created for communion and communication between him and his precious image-bearers. As I continue to learn and experiment with prayer in my personal life and in my work with Renovaré, I realize that my learning in prayer and about prayer will never end. I've simply dipped my toe in the ocean; there are untold depths yet to explore.

My students shared the difficulty of praying while living in their complex, rapidly changing, noisy, info-saturated, cluttered world. They often struggled to set apart five minutes a day for God. Indeed, these few minutes would have been the exception for them rather than the rule.

Such is the case with many of us. Then, when we do manage to find a moment of silence and attempt to pray, we fumble, mumble, gaze out the window, struggle to maintain our attention, and often walk away from our attempts to pray discouraged, dumbfounded, and disillusioned.

We ask, and heaven seems deaf to our requests. Our petitions or intercessions seem to mean little to God. I've already shared in this book the disappointment I experienced when my prayer for the healing of my parents' marriage was not granted. God's seeming lack of attention and concern created distance between us.

Writing about prayer is difficult, because prayer is enveloped in mystery; prayer's breadth, depth, and intimacy resists capture in human language. Yet isn't this also true of intimate human relationships? When I try to describe my love for my wife, Debbie, words fail. Poetry rather than prose draws closer but still falls short of what my heart desires to express. How much more we sense our limitations when we speak and write of the principal love language between God and human beings!

So, initially at least, prayer appears peculiar, odd, even bizarre. I speak to God, yet I don't see God. I've never heard an audible voice from God, though I have sensed God communicating to me in other quite specific ways, sometimes in English, and once in German.

I, like my students, once wondered if God is really interested in the petty details of my life. Is God really concerned that I find a parking space? Doesn't God have more important things to be concerned about?

"Am I talking too much in my prayers?" I sometimes asked. Does the Lord wish I would just quiet down a bit?

Isn't prayer supposed to be a conversation rather than a monologue? If it's a dialogue, how do I know when God is speaking? How can I learn to discern God's voice and distinguish it from the lingering effects of last night's spicy pepperoni pizza?

Let's simply acknowledge that when it comes to prayer, we're beginners and will always be beginners. Thomas Merton's wise counsel
comes to mind: "One cannot begin to face the real difficulties of the
life of prayer and meditation unless one is first perfectly content to be a
beginner and really experience himself as one who knows little or nothing and has a desperate need to learn the bare rudiments. Those who
think they 'know' from the beginning will never, in fact, come to know
anything. . . . We do not want to be beginners. But let us be convinced
of the fact that we will never be anything else but beginners."[1]

## Learning to Walk

Think of a youngster learning to walk. She toddles as she takes her first
steps. She is a toddler, after all. Brian Doyle describes watching a young
girl "waddle and yaw across the sea of the quadrangle grass; each step
is a new adventure and each, you can tell, still a newish idea for the legs
and feet, which are still getting the hang of the thing; and the girl herself is entertainingly *not* in control of the engineering but seems to be
riding along happily on top of her legs and feet, delighted to be moving
upright. She sits down suddenly, with an almost audible plop; she leans
a little too far to starboard, and capsizes briefly; her feet lose their way
and she stumbles and goes down face-first in the grass; but she scrab-
bles up again diligently, weaving and waltzing a little, and meanders for
another ten feet or so before gravity again hauls her down to examine
the dense green mattress of the lawn."[2] Similarly, I imagine the Holy
Trinity chuckling as we take our first steps in prayer.

We all suffered a few bumps and bruises as we learned to walk. Wise,
loving parents, hovering over their baby to prevent serious harm, know
they must give her enough freedom to step, then walk, then run. In like
manner, God delights to see his precious image-bearers taking their

first steps in prayer, while fully aware there will be challenges ahead and much to learn for his beloved children. By God's grace it won't be long, though, before they're keeping in step with the Spirit.

## Begin with the Grace of God

God's grace surrounds, supports, and empowers us as we pray; even when we stumble in our prayers, God still gladly accepts our frail offerings, mumble though we may.

Thankfully, we don't have to pass a theology exam before we dare to pray, though a knowledge of the Bible and some theology and history surely helps. God knows our hearts better than we do and accepts the offering of the heart, even when the thoughts expressed in our prayers are garbled and foggy. Jesus accepts us where we are, delighting in our baby talk. He is eager to teach us the grammar, content, and rhythms of prayer.

A story from Jewish folklore reminds us that God understands the intent of our prayer, even when our thinking may be confused.

There once was a shepherd who nightly offered God a bowl of milk to drink at the end of the day, an offering of love and devotion. Moses, though, was upset by the foolishness of the shepherd's gift and was quick to set the shepherd straight. Didn't the shepherd realize that God was "pure spirit" and "does not drink milk"?

The shepherd was surprised by Moses's teaching and remained awake one night to see if God indeed did not drink milk.

The shepherd hides, the night comes, and in the moonlight the shepherd sees a little fox that comes trotting from the desert, looks right, looks left, and heads straight toward the milk, which he laps up, and disappears into the desert again.

The next morning Moses finds the shepherd quite depressed and downcast. "What's the matter?" he asks.

The shepherd says, "You were right. God is pure spirit and he doesn't want my milk."

Moses is surprised. He says, "You should be happy. You know more about God than you did before."

"Yes, I do," says the shepherd, "but the only thing I could do to express my love for him has been taken away from me."

Moses sees the point. He retires into the desert and prays hard. In the night a vision appears to Moses in which God speaks to him. "Moses, you were wrong. It is true that I am pure spirit. Nevertheless, I always accepted with gratitude the milk which the shepherd offered me, as the expression of his love, but since, being pure spirit, I do not need the milk, I shared it with that little fox, who is very fond of milk."[3]

Be encouraged that all prayer starts with God's initiative, undergirded at every moment by God's grace. The shepherd plainly loved God, and his love motivated him to leave milk for God in the desert. God gladly accepted his gift. If we demand perfection in prayer, of ourselves or others, paralysis will soon set in.

## Family Language

Conversation with God is similar in many ways to human conversation. If I'm speaking to God, I'm probably speaking in English. I'm using nouns, verbs, adjectives, adverbs, conjunctions, and particles to communicate my thoughts to God. I communicate through my voice or other uses of my body such as nodding, gesturing, writing with a pen, or tapping on a computer keyboard.

Let's get more specific. What kind of language does God invite us to use in talking with him? How did Jesus talk with his Father? He used family language. For instance, at the time of Jesus's testing and betrayal in the Garden of Gethsemane, Jesus calls his Father Abba. "Going a little farther, he fell to the ground and prayed that if possible the hour might pass from him. '*Abba*, Father,' he said, 'everything is possible for you. Take this cup from me. Yet not what I will, but what you will'" (Mark 14:35–36).

Did you notice that Mark leaves Abba in Aramaic and then translates it into Greek? He does so to emphasize the intimacy that characterized the relationship between Jesus and his Father, and how unusual it was for a Jew to address God this way. God the Father was Jesus's Abba, the Aramaic word for Papa or Daddy. The point? Jesus used family language in prayer as he asked God to deliver him from the hour of his suffering.

"Well," we might respond, "that's fine for Jesus. After all, he was God incarnate. But that's a bit too close for me. I'm not sure I should talk to God like that. And to be honest, I had a hellish home life with an abuser for a father. When I hear the word *Father*, I see an enemy, not a friend."

Fair enough. Thankfully, Jesus's Abba is our friend, not our enemy, though for some of us it will take time for this truth to sink in.

## Pause and Reflect

For those who've had wicked, abusive fathers, pause and imagine the father—or mother—you always wanted. That desire for a loving mom or dad is implanted in you by God. It's valid and praiseworthy, not something to be denied, repressed, or regretted. Thankfully,

God is an unimaginably good Father and not one whit like an abusive parent.

Paul encourages Roman Christians to address God as Abba. He writes, "The Spirit you received does not make you slaves, so that you live in fear again; rather, the Spirit you received brought about your adoption to sonship. And by him we cry, 'Abba, Father.' The Spirit himself testifies with our spirit that we are God's children. Now if we are children, then we are heirs—heirs of God and co-heirs with Christ, if indeed we share in his sufferings in order that we may also share in his glory" (Rom. 8:15–17). Paul couldn't be clearer. We have been adopted into God's family, the communion of the Holy Trinity. The Abba Jesus speaks to in the Garden of Gethsemane is our Abba, and in prayer we are invited to address him as such.

Paul makes the same point when he writes to the Galatians. "Because you are his sons, God sent the Spirit of his Son into our hearts, the Spirit who calls out, 'Abba, Father.' So you are no longer a slave, but God's child; and since you are his child, God has made you also an heir" (Gal. 4:6–7). We have been adopted into God's family. When we pray, then, family language fits our status as God's children. It nurtures intimacy with God. Indeed, sometimes in prayer we will not speak at all; we will simply be together—we with God and God with us—enjoying each other's presence, like a daughter and father or husband and wife, sitting by a fire, entirely at ease.

I admit that the first time I addressed God as Abba, it felt strange and awkward. The more I did so, though, the more it seemed natural and right. I had learned a new linguistic habit in prayer—encouraged to do so by Jesus and Paul—and my relationship with God was further healed and strengthened. I hope yours will be, too, as family language works its way into your prayer vocabulary.

## The Invitation into Communion with the Trinity

Let's focus more closely now on petitionary and intercessory prayer. Richard J. Foster describes petitionary prayer as "our staple diet. In a childlike expression of faith we bring our daily needs and desires to our heavenly Father."[4] In prayer, we present our "needs and desires" openly, fully expecting God to respond as our loving Father. Still, questions arise. Let's begin to examine them.

How might the family language of prayer help us answer the number one question Eastern students always posed? "If God already knows what I'm thinking about, what I need, and what I desire, why do I have to pray?"

Family language in prayer indicates and illustrates the intensely personal nature of God. Before the creation of the universe, before the first atom explodes into existence, before there are angels, stars, comets, planets, meteors, oceans, trees, human cells, butterflies, hippos, or puppies, God is alive.

God already is but in an utterly incomprehensible mode of being. How can we describe the being of God, both before and after creation? God is, as Father, Son, and Holy Spirit. Hence, God always is in relationship and communion. God has never been lonely, for God by definition is personal communion. God exists, has always existed, and will always exist as Father, Son, and Holy Spirit. God's essence is the Father, Son, and Holy Spirit. Ponder that for a minute or two.

There is no essence of God behind the Father, Son, and Spirit. Rather, to be God is to be Father, Son, and Spirit. In the language of the creeds, "one God, three persons." Consequently, God is immensely, intensely personal. We, God's image-bearers, are personal creatures, because our creator is personal, to a degree and with an intensity that surpasses our ability to comprehend.

Thus, as God's precious image-bearers, we're hardwired for relationship with God. The primary means God has designed for nurturing that relationship is prayer. In a word, prayer is intensely relational because God is intensely relational. Whatever questions we wisely ask about prayer, then, will find their resolution within the context of God's immensely, intensely personal relationship with each of us.[5]

The apostle John writes that "God is love" (1 John 4:16). To be God, then, is to be love in communion. God invites us into this communion of love through faith in Jesus. In Jesus and through Jesus, God graciously chose to expand the borders of the divine communion. We've been adopted into the family; we've been invited into the communion. There could not be any more personal, more intimate relationship than this.

Now let's return to the first question about prayer on my students' list: If God knows what I'm thinking, what I need, and what I desire, why pray? Why ask?

The answer is as simple and profound as this: God likes to be asked, for the asking nurtures the relationship. If healthy, loving parents like to talk to their children, they do so because they bear God's image. They love hearing their child's questions and comments. They love to be involved in their kids' lives, for their love for their kids is embedded in them by God. Asking, whether between kids and parents or between humans and the Triune God, "enhances and deepens the relationship. . . . Love likes to be told what it knows already. . . . It wants to be asked for what it longs to give."[6] Asking, receiving, and sharing—the fabric of petitionary and intercessory prayer—enrich our relationship with God.

Josh, my youngest son, turns thirty-three tomorrow. As I think of him and my mind drifts across the years, I'm reminded that the experiences and conversations Josh and I have shared have deeply enriched our lives together. One of these times occurred when Josh was around six.

## A Little Boy and a Long Flashlight

In the early nineties my wife, Debbie, and I attended a weekend retreat at our local church, the Church of the Good Samaritan in Paoli, Pennsylvania. We brought Josh along with us. I think he was around six. We knew the church had activities planned for the youngsters and hoped Josh wouldn't be too bored.

When Friday night's adult session ended, we said good-bye to our friends. It was time to collect Josh. We headed to his Sunday school room and found him buzzing with excitement.

"Dad, Dad!" Josh exclaimed.

"Yeah, Josh. What's going on?"

"Dad, guess what we're going to do tomorrow night."

"I don't know. What?"

"Dad!" he nearly shouted. "We're going to circle our chairs, and the teacher's going to cover them with a blanket. It will be like a cave underneath. Then we're going to crawl into the cave, and she's going to turn out the light."

"Wow," I said. "That sounds exciting."

"That's not all, Dad! We're all going to bring flashlights. And when she turns out the lights, we're going to turn our flashlights on inside the cave! We have to remember to bring a flashlight from home. Don't forget."

"Wow!" I said. I was getting a little fired up myself. "We'll be sure to do that."

There stood my little boy, quivering with excitement, and I couldn't help but join in. He was my boy, after all. I still remember the moment, over a quarter of a century later.

The next night we returned to church. The only flashlight we'd found at home was a big yellow one, long and heavy.

Josh cradled the flashlight in his arms during the drive to church.

When we arrived, we walked into church together, his left hand in my right. We headed down the hallway. The adventure was soon to begin.

Josh excitedly pulled me down the hall, his right hand swinging back and forth with the heavy flashlight. If he'd hit anyone with it, he might have broken that person's leg. Josh walked with determination and excitement. We were experiencing one of the highlights of his six-year-old life. I wished I could crawl under the blankets with him.

A few steps from the classroom door, Josh stopped. He caught his breath, looked up at me, gripped my hand even more tightly, and said, "Dad, this is going to be great!"

And it was. As Josh's joy expanded, so did mine.

Ponder once more with me the intensely, immensely personal nature of God. There is nothing in our lives that disinterests God, nothing petty, nothing unimportant. Absolutely nothing. Why should this surprise us? My experience with Josh reflects in some small but significant way God's ceaseless experience with his precious image-bearers, his kids. Perhaps that's why Jesus was so entranced with children, always attentive to them while others regarded them as unimportant.

God will never say to us or our prayer, "You know, I'm just not interested." For God, the Holy Trinity, is eternal, immensely personal communion. God loves it when we talk to him and discuss what concerns us—interests and requests he already knows fully—because the very asking, the very conversation, the very sharing, enhances our relationship. Our willingness, then, to bring the smallest question, concern, and desire to God makes good theological and biblical sense. This is not maudlin sentimentality but spiritual reality.

## Pause and Reflect

Are there areas of your life or personal concerns or desires that you'd like to share with God but have felt they were too small, too insignificant, too minor, too trivial? List them on a piece of paper. God might well be more interested in them than you are! If we think God is only interested in the big stuff in our lives, we've effectively eliminated most of our lives from God's concern or interest, for the vast majority of our gift of years consists of small stuff. Actually, from God's perspective, the small stuff is the big stuff.

C. S. Lewis reminds us that if we don't consider the small stuff, the seemingly trivial things, as important subject matter for our prayers and petitions, we'll be ill prepared to face the big stuff when it finally arrives. "Perhaps," Lewis writes, "as those who do not turn to God in petty trials will have no habit or such resort to help them when the great trials come, so those who have not learned to ask Him for childish things will have less readiness to ask him for great ones. We must not be too high-minded. I fancy we may sometimes be deterred from small prayers by a sense of our own dignity rather than God's."[7]

## The Perplexity of Unanswered Prayer

We all have experienced unanswered prayers. Some readers might respond, "I'm not sure you're right. God answers all prayers. Sometimes God says yes, and sometimes God says no." Is this response helpful? For many, it's actually hurtful. A flippant, insensitive, shallow response to the question of unanswered prayer helps no one.

Do abstract answers satisfy as we pray for food, for our sick child, for clothing or housing, for meaningful work, for a marriage that is splintering or shattering on the rocks, for the restoration of a relationship we long to see healed? Lewis again is wise: "The distance between the abstract 'Does God hear petitionary prayers?' and the concrete 'Will He—can He—grant our prayers for George?' is apparently infinite."[8]

Ponder Lewis's words on unanswered prayer: "Every war, every famine or plague, almost every deathbed is the monument to a petition that was not granted. At this very moment thousands of people on this island are facing as a fait accompli the very thing against which they have prayed night and day, pouring out their whole soul in prayer, and, as they thought, with faith. They have sought and not found. They have knocked and it has not been opened. 'That which they have greatly feared has come upon them.'"[9]

At times, it does seem God has given us a stone when we asked for a loaf of bread (cf. Luke 11:11–12). We have all received a no to a petition in prayer, and these noes can break our hearts and stretch our faith, almost to the breaking point.

Are plausible answers available concerning unanswered prayer? With the help of Richard J. Foster, let's lean into the questions, answering those we can and accepting that some will remain unanswered.

P. T. Forsythe writes, "We shall come one day to a heaven where we shall gratefully know that God's great refusals were sometimes the answers to our truest prayers." Foster comments that "many times our prayers are indeed answered, but we lack the eyes to see it. God understands the deeper intent of our prayers and so responds to the greater need, which, in its time and in its way, solves our specific prayer concern."[10] I learned this in my friendship with Reba Yoder.

## You're Not Listening!

Think of a Christian you know whose deepest desire is to live a life of faithfulness to Christ, to embody in her body and mind as fully as possible Jesus's desire for her gift of years. I knew someone like this. Her name was Reba Yoder.[11]

I met Reba in the mid-1990s. She was a student in my class. During a lecture, I touched on the issue of suffering and the role suffering plays in our spiritual formation into the image of Christ. As I spoke, I noticed an older student, perhaps mid-forties, listening intently. At the end of class, she came up and introduced herself: "Hi. My name's Reba Yoder. I liked what you had to say. I've got cancer." This greeting was what I came to know as classic Reba: direct, honest, and open to God and others. "Nice to meet you, Reba. I'm so sorry about the cancer."

Over the next few years, Reba and I became very close friends. We prayed fervently, consistently, imploringly to God that her cancer would be healed. For a while, during a wonderful period filled with joy and expectation, Reba's cancer went into remission. We thought she might have been healed, and hope expanded in our hearts like a balloon. Our spirits soared as the future appeared to open to Reba like a flower stretching its petals to the sun.

Then, at first almost imperceptibly, Reba began to feel tired. Old, worrying symptoms reappeared. Perhaps, we thought, Reba was just working too hard. She decided to take a short vacation to Oregon, hoping the rest and change of scenery would do her good. Then the phone call came, one I will never forget: "Hi, Chris. It's Reba. It's back."

My heart sank like a stone. "Oh, Reba. I'm so sorry. We won't give up, though. We just need to pray even harder for your healing. God hasn't forgotten you."

"I know that," Reba replied, somewhat curtly. "But we're going to pray differently."

I didn't like the direction the conversation was headed. I longed for Reba to be healed. I wanted her around for years to come. I didn't want to hear anything about praying differently.

"What do you mean, praying differently?" I asked, my voice tinged with impatience, anxiety, and sadness.

"We are going to pray that I die like a Christian," Reba replied.

"No, we aren't," I said to myself. There's no way I'm going to pray that prayer. Reba was just discouraged and tired; she wasn't seeing clearly. She only needed some encouragement.

"Reba, I know this is discouraging. But we don't want to give up. Christ has heard our prayers in the past. This cancer's not the last word."

I attempted to convince Reba that we should continue to pray for her physical healing. She listened for a while, I'm sure biting her tongue, but finally she'd reached the end of her patience.

"Stop it," she said angrily. "You're not listening."

Reba was right. I wasn't listening. I wasn't listening because I didn't want to accept that Reba's pilgrimage on earth was nearing its end. I wanted her around for a long time. I wanted her there for her children, for her husband. I wanted her to see the birth of her grandchildren.

I wanted to dance a jig with Reba. Instead, Jesus had decided—for reasons of his own he has not shared with me—that our last dance together, one he would join in with us, would be a slow, solemn, sad waltz. Occasionally it would be beautiful beyond words, sometimes unspeakably sorrowful. What strange music Christ sometimes sings to us!

So, over the next few months, Reba listened to Christ and discerned more clearly the words he was speaking to her. Indeed, we both came to believe that Jesus was answering the deeper intent of our earlier prayers for Reba's healing: a deeper transformation was occurring, one that would continue into the age to come. I still struggled to accept this deeper healing, because I knew, as did Reba, it would involve partings—if only for a time. And I didn't want to say good-bye.

As Jesus and I waltzed with Reba, our dance gradually slowed to its last delicate steps. Joe Modica, the chaplain at Eastern, and I promised

Reba we would visit her each Friday until her earthly dance with Christ ceased its grace-filled rhythms. And so we did.

On our hourlong drive to Reba's home, Joe and I pondered together the puzzling ways of God with his precious creatures. We never figured out why God chose to waltz Reba out of this world when she could have done and received so much good; to this day I don't know why.

There are so many things, I've come to believe, we must leave in God's hands, basing our trust on the strange and wondrous truths revealed to us in the incarnation, ministry, cross, and resurrection of Jesus. Two thousand years earlier Christ himself had danced with his Father the waltz he now stepped gently with Reba. Jesus has never distanced himself from our sufferings. He will never ask his disciples to endure something he has not first undergone. He invites us to enter his sufferings with him, just as he does with us (Luke 14:25–33; Col. 1:24; Mark 8:31–38).

If I chose to judge simply by appearances, Reba's sickness and death looked to be an act of divine foolishness, indifference, or cruelty, as God extravagantly spent Reba's short gift of years. By all appearances there was a much better path God could have walked with Reba: one of restoration, happiness, joy, and healing.

Yet Reba discerned, in a manner I didn't at that time, that God was at work deep down, under the surface of things, fertilizing her roots through the Spirit. Fruit and flowers were blossoming in the garden of her suffering—if only I had eyes to see. But how difficult it is to look and discern beyond appearances and longings, especially in the midst of pain and parting.

Christ's willingness to suffer for her strengthened Reba's determination "to live and die like a Christian." He had provided the pattern on the cross and asked Reba to walk in his cruciform footsteps. Her faithful disposition, openness to Christ, and increasing ability to discern how Christ was choosing to work were forged in the fire of pain, loss, trust, and faith. She was never alone. Christ was present with her in her sorrowful, holy dance, continually taking the lead.

Reba listened, and Jesus spoke. She refused to limit how God must speak and respond to her prayers regarding her cancer. She had prayed clearly and at times loudly for healing. And at the end of her life, she firmly believed she was soon to experience a deeper, lasting healing. She invited Christ to hear the deeper intent of her prayers—to live a life of courage and faithfulness with Jesus—and he did.

## Shortsightedness, Self-Deception, and Prayer

Richard J. Foster teaches that sometimes we can be shortsighted in our prayers. We see only what's right in front of us; the larger picture escapes us. We are, after all, finite creatures with limited perspective. "Oh, Lord," we pray, "I know this would be the best thing for me. Be merciful to me. Hear my prayer. Please. Hear my prayer."

The Lord, much wiser than we are, knows that our prayer can't be answered as we wish, for we may not be ready to receive what we are asking. It's difficult to see clearly when we're directly involved in the outcome of our prayers.

Often, Foster comments, our asking is not in our best interest. Or in the best interest of someone else. Sometimes our character does not yet match what our request requires. So the Lord with great mercy responds, "Not now, child, and perhaps never. Lean into me. Trust me. You may ask again in the future. Or perhaps by that time you will have no need—or desire—to ask the same thing."

Our old nemesis, self-deception, sometimes influences the requests we make and the answers we hope to receive. Unavoidably, I bring my character into prayer with me. This doesn't mean I should stop praying, for praying is a principal means God uses to heal and reshape our character more fully into the image of Christ. It does mean, though, that shortsightedness and self-deception occasionally mark my prayers—and yours. I'm thankful God graciously and lovingly protects me from the skewed, foolish prayers I sometimes pray. As Lewis puts it, "If God had granted all the silly prayers I've made in my life, where should I be now?"[12]

## Pause and Reflect

**Have there been instances when you were shortsighted in your prayers? How might God have protected you from shortsightedness by not answering your prayer or by delaying the answer?**

## Prayers in Conflict?

Imagine all the prayers ascending to God every moment of the day and night. People around the world are praying all the time. If so, it surely seems possible that the prayer of one person might collide or conflict with the prayer of another. What do you think?

Here's what I mean. When my daughter Nathalie was around ten years old, she sometimes went with her church youth group to North Philadelphia to distribute lunches to poor folks who were hungry.[13] As she did so, she made new friends, her perspective on life broadened, and her love for the poor deepened. She learned that winter was an especially hard time for her new friends, many of whom had no shelter from the elements.

One winter's evening at home, it started snowing heavily. I was with Nathalie in her bedroom, a time when we liked to talk a bit, pray, and bid each other good-night. Before we prayed, we gazed out the window at the large white flakes floating down. We could spot their outline through nearby streetlamps. The room felt cozy and warm. We sat in silence, caught up in the beauty of a nighttime snowstorm. Finally, it was time to pray. I still remember Natty's sweet prayer: "Oh, Lord, let it snow, snow, snow. It would be so nice if we didn't have school tomorrow. In Jesus's name. Amen."

I inwardly smiled as I listened to the sweet prayer of my ten-year-old daughter. And then I asked a hard question. Mean-spirited theologians do this kind of thing. "Natty, do you think your friends downtown are praying for lots of snow?" Rather than punching me—I deserved it— Natty sat still and pondered. Finally, she said, "No. They'll be cold. And the snow will make them colder."

For a moment we were silent together. Then for the next few minutes we talked about how our prayers might sometimes conflict with other people's prayers. We decided we shouldn't stop praying for fear of making a mistake, but that we should keep in mind there's lots of folks praying around the world, and sometimes our prayers might conflict with someone else's prayers, or even be detrimental to them.

Only God can make sense of all that's being prayed all the time; only God can discern what's best. I'm sure that sometimes when I've received a no in prayer, someone else received a yes, and that's fine with me. Of course, the opposite is also true. I wonder when a yes to my prayer meant a no to someone else's. Only God knows. I think we need to give God a little leeway in how he responds to our prayers.

There's a lot more going on than meets the eye when we pray. Don't judge how God is acting on the basis of appearances. Rachel, a dying schizophrenic, helped me learn this lesson.[14]

## "I'm So Blessed. Thanks Be to God."

Let me introduce you to someone we'll call Rachel, a patient at the New Jersey geropsychiatric hospital where I served as director of pastoral care in the late 1980s.

Make no mistake about it: working at a geropsychiatric hospital is difficult. Not only are patients suffering from a vast host of psychiatric illnesses, but they are also tormented by a wide variety of end-of-life issues: frequent illness, loneliness, fear of death, deep remorse over past mistakes that seem beyond repair, and so forth.

One month at the hospital was particularly difficult. The sheer weight of suffering I encountered daily weighed heavily on me.

I recall, for example, walking into a unit at the hospital. A patient down the hallway spotted me as I walked toward her. She was strapped in her chair to keep her steady as she ate her breakfast. Suddenly, she started screaming and banging her head into her breakfast tray. "Rev. Hall, Rev. Hall, I don't want to die. I don't want to die." Susie was all alone. She had been an abuser of other people and been abused by them. Her family had written her off. And now she was dying. I rushed up to her, cradled her head in my hands to prevent further injury, and said softly, "I know, Susie, I know."

I'd been praying for Susie and other patients for months, and it seemed that God was refusing to listen. I asked and asked and asked for healing and the restoration of hope, and still patients appeared to grow worse, mentally and physically. Indeed, Susie died a few days after this incident. I buried her. A few family members came, the very people who had refused to visit her while she was still living.

Shortly after Susie's death I decided I'd seen enough. Another long day at the hospital had passed and things looked the same. Discouraged, sad, and angry, I simply wanted to go home. How quickly I fell into the sin of presumption.

What is presumption? I presumed—based on appearances—that God was not working at the hospital, that patients were not being helped, that my prayers were not being heard, that God didn't care.

At the end of one workday, I was sitting in my office fuming at God and the circumstances at the hospital. Suddenly, my office phone rang. It was my boss, the clinical care director. "Chris, Rachel has just been admitted into the ICU unit at Easton Hospital. She's in bad shape. Could you visit her on your way home?"

"I'd be glad to," I lied.

The last thing I wanted to do was to visit a dying schizophrenic. I was sick of suffering, sick of pain, sick of sadness, sick of death.

I drove to Easton, parked in the hospital parking lot, and steeled myself for more agony. The nurses at the ICU unit smiled and nodded as I walked past. I had no expectations that God was at work here or anywhere else. I was tired, discouraged, angry, and frightened. I just wanted out. I can distinctly remember thinking, first in my office and later as I entered Rachel's ICU room, that God was not working. "You're not working. You don't care," I grumbled internally. God had not listened to my prayers. God didn't care about these suffering people. I wanted out, plain and simple.

When I entered Rachel's ICU room, things looked just as I expected. My last vestige of faith slipped away. The scene was horrifying. Rachel was strapped to her bed with pieces of linen cloth gently tied around her wrists. Both her arms had been tied loosely to her bed frame because in her confusion she kept pulling out her IVs. A respirator had been inserted in Rachel's throat because she couldn't breathe on her own. Her eyes were swollen and distended, seemingly in terror. I glanced at the monitor listing her vital signs and realized that Rachel's life was ending. Her body was shutting down. What help could I possibly offer to a dying schizophrenic?

I walked over to Rachel's bed. She looked up at me with enlarged, frightened eyes that begged me to help her. I reached out for her left hand. "Rachel, can I say a prayer for you?" She frantically nodded yes. As I prayed the expression on her face never changed; her distended eyes—frantic, frightened, seemingly despairing—communicated horror, not hope.

And what did I have to offer her? The short, sad prayer of a faithless chaplain. "Lord, please help Rachel in her time of need. Touch her body. Touch her spirit. Relieve her suffering. Be with her throughout the night. Amen." I squeezed her hand and turned to leave. I didn't want to see any more suffering, any more dying.

Rachel's left hand caught my sleeve. I turned, and she stared at me with the same frightened eyes. She began to raise and lower her left hand, signaling to me that she had something she wanted to say to me. Her hand, though restrained, had about a foot of wiggle room. I placed a piece of paper on a hospital clipboard, slipped a pencil into Rachel's hand, and held the clipboard in front of her.

She wrote slowly for about five minutes, struggling to form every letter. Her expression never changed. By all appearances she was still a terrified, lonely, dying schizophrenic. I thought to myself, *You should have known better.* She could tell you were lying and didn't care about her. She knew you were just going through the motions. You deserve to get chewed out. And that's just what I thought Rachel was doing as she wrote minute after minute.

Finally, she stopped writing. I took the pencil from her hand and lifted the clipboard to read her message. Rachel had managed to write five sentences in what looked like stilted letters. I still have the message she wrote me some thirty-three years ago.

First line: I love my Jesus.
Second line: Thanks for visit.

*You shouldn't be thanking me*, I thought to myself. *If you only knew what I was thinking as I was praying. I just wanted out.*

Third line: Your Jesus loves you too.

This was the line that both broke my heart and filled me with wonder. Had Rachel sensed my struggle, my discouragement, my anger over so many prayers that by all appearances had been unanswered?

Suddenly, Rachel's ICU room was densely filled with the presence of God—not visibly present, but tangibly present. I actually turned to see if someone was standing behind me. An angel, perhaps? No. The only people present in the room were Rachel, a faithless chaplain, and God. The thump of the respirator was the only sound.

Jesus had lovingly borrowed the mind and body of a dying schizophrenic to remind me, "I'm working at the hospital. I'm working in and through you. I love Rachel. She's going to be fine. Stop judging by appearances. Trust me."

Fourth line: I'm blessed.

Blessed? You look so frightened, so alone, so discouraged. Don't you realize you're dying?

Fifth line: Thanks be to God.

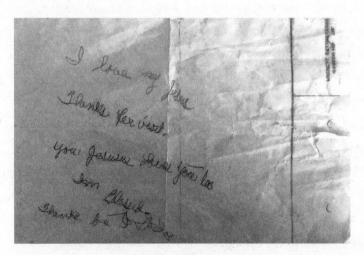

Rachel's note in the ICU.

Jesus's message to me through Rachel seemed to be this: "Thank me, Chris, for those things you do understand. Thank me for the forgiveness of your sins. Thank me for the beauty of my creation. Thank me for all the gifts I have sprinkled into your life: your family, your friends, your vocation, your health, and the times I speak clearly to you. I have spoken to you in the past and I will do so in the future. But please, stop trying to figure out matters I have not chosen to explain to you. Trust me, my son. Trust me."

## Healing Does Happen

I've shared two stories concerning physical healing where prayers didn't seem to be answered, that of Reba and that of Rachel. If these were the only stories I told you about healing and prayer, you might conclude that healing in prayer rarely occurs, or that I'm expanding the meaning of healing so broadly that any no to a prayer for healing might actually qualify as a yes. So let me tell you a story about a dramatic physical healing in my own life.

It was the late 1980s. We had returned from France, and I was attending graduate school at Regent College in Vancouver, British Columbia. A pastor friend of mine in Southern California had been invited to speak to a group of Kenyan Christians but couldn't make the trip. He contacted me and asked if I could go in his place.

I had never been to Africa. It sounded like fun. I asked, "Who will I be going with?"

"There's another pastor from the Vineyard Fellowship down here who'll also be going. But you'll be doing most of the speaking. His name is Barney Hamady."

*Barney Hamady*, I thought, *that's an interesting name.*

Our conversation ended, and I began to make plans for the upcoming trip, some four months away.

While preparing for the trip, I prayed for God's blessing. My prayer was fairly generic. "Lord, bless this trip. Even now help me with what

I should say." As the trip drew nearer, I prayed for safety and health. Suddenly, out of the blue, I sensed the Lord speaking to me: "Have Barney Hamady pray for you." These words were more than a vague impression. They were very specific.

It's a stretch to say I gave deep attention to the words, but I thankfully tucked them in the back of my mind. I continued planning, praying, and packing. Finally, the day to leave arrived, and I boarded my flight for Nairobi.

I'd been told I would teach a seminar with around 250 people attending, so I was surprised to discover my first assignment was to speak to ten thousand men in the Kenyan bush during their spiritual renewal week. The following week five thousand women would gather, and again I was the main speaker.

I would be connecting soon with the Vineyard pastor, and I thought I knew what to expect. Over the years I had developed terrible stereotypes of charismatic believers as loud, naive, deceived, and ignorant.

Then I met Barney.

He had an earthy sense of humor, was well read, and was a good listener. His mind was deeply grounded in Christ, biblically informed, and flexible in terms of how and when he expected God to work. The platitudes and plastic Christianity I expected to see and hear never appeared. In my surprise and shock, I forgot the words I had heard so clearly in Vancouver: have Barney Hamady pray for you.

The day arrived for me to speak to the men's group in the bush. Some had walked fifty miles to attend. Two days before the event, I visited a kind Kenyan pastor and his family who lived in an isolated area. Water for their home was supplied through a borehole.

When we shared dinner and water was served in glasses, I asked if I should not rather drink water from a sealed bottle.

"No, no," the pastor responded. "The water in your glass comes from a borehole. It's very clean. The rock cleans it."

I took a long drink.

After a night's rest in a straw hut outside the pastor's home, I headed back to the missionary compound where Barney and I were staying. The men's event was two days away.

How can I put things delicately? On the day I was scheduled to speak, I awoke around 6:30 and realized I had a problem that could only be resolved by a sprint to the bathroom—a journey that occurred every five minutes or so for the next two hours. The big "D," dysentery, had arrived.

In four hours, I was supposed to speak to ten thousand people, but my sickness was worsening by the minute. "What am I going to do, Barney? I'm supposed to speak in front of all these people, and I can't move more than five feet from the bathroom or real disaster will strike, for me and everyone else."

The minutes passed. The time for our departure drew near. We mumbled a handful of prayers, and Barney finally said, "We need to go." I grabbed a roll of toilet paper, and we climbed onto the bed of an old pickup truck, settled down into two rocking chairs, covered ourselves with blankets to protect ourselves from the dust, and off we went. With each bump of the truck my lower half jiggled, but things held firm.

After an hour's drive, we arrived in a large valley. Seated on the ground waiting for me were ten thousand men. I walked gingerly from the pickup truck to my speaking spot in the center of the valley. A loudspeaker was hanging from a tree. My interpreter handed me a mic, and I greeted the crowd. "I'm afraid I'm not feeling well today. Will you pray for me as I speak?"

"Ayee!" the crowd responded in Swahili. "Yes!"

I started speaking. I can't recall what I said. I do remember that while I spoke, I felt calm, peaceful, and free from the nausea that had been plaguing me. After forty-five minutes I ended, the crowd dispersed, and I went home with Barney. By the time we got back to the compound, my health problems had returned, and they continued as the week proceeded.

As the day drew near to speak to the five thousand women, I increasingly weakened. The only thing I could manage to keep in me was soda containing glucose. I spent the day before the event in the small living room of a missionary's home. Walking back that evening to my room required Barney supporting me on one side and Jackson, my Kenyan host, on the other. How was I supposed to speak the next day? I could hardly walk.

Then the words I had heard so clearly in Vancouver drifted back into my memory: "Have Barney Hamady pray for you." *Yes,* I thought to myself. *That's right. How could I have forgotten?*

That Friday night, sitting on my bed beside Barney and Jackson, I asked softly, "Barney, will you pray for me?"

"Sure."

I stretched out my hands in front of me, to show my willingness to accept whatever the Lord would offer or do. Jackson was sitting on my left. Jackson had been taught that healing had stopped at the close of the first century. I'm not sure what he was expecting, but he seemed to join willingly in Barney's prayer.

I expected that when Barney prayed, it would be loud, dramatic, and insistent. Yet Barney's prayer was simple, quiet, direct, and expectant: "Lord, Chris has to speak tomorrow. A lot of folks are walking a long way to hear him. And he's sick. Please heal him." That was it. And he prayed just once.

To be honest, I had expected more from Barney. Something a little louder perhaps? I do believe Barney expected something to happen. He just didn't feel he had to raise his voice for God to respond. There I sat between Jackson and Barney, my arms slightly extended, palms open and raised—and felt a bit disappointed in Barney.

Then it started. Something like an electric current began to stream into my left arm. My arm muscles began to flex in response. It began to swing methodically, slowly, back and forth. There was no pain, but I did feel distinct heat. In one of my wiser moments, I decided to accept what was happening rather than resist it, and the current continued to stream into my arm for ten to twelve minutes.

Barney offered only one brief prayer while the current continued: "More power, Lord."

In my mind's eye, while the power flowed into my arm, I remember seeing the beauty of God, the beauty of the Trinity manifesting itself to me as a blending of stunning colors. Finally, this, too—a vision of some kind?—slowly dissipated. Lastly, I fell back on the bed.

"Wow," I said to my two friends, one who fully expected something like this to happen and one who thought this kind of thing had ceased hundreds of years ago, "that was wonderful."

"Yeah," Barney responded, "the Holy Spirit was jumping all over you." I glanced at Jackson, and he was staring at me with an expression of utter surprise. Eventually Jackson went home, and Barney and I went to bed.

After his initial comment, Barney said nothing about what had happened. Indeed, he did not seem all that interested. *What could be more normal?* he seemed to be thinking. As we drifted off to sleep, I asked, "Barney, do you think I'm healed?"

"I don't know," he mumbled, his mind clicked off, and he was out like a light.

Eight hours later I awoke healthy, healed, and energized. My dysentery had disappeared. I was able to speak later that day without hindrance, weakness, or difficulty.

Two or three days after the healing occurred I asked myself whether anything really happened. Was there some other explanation? Had I really been healed? Suddenly a very distinct word came: "Don't you do that." With this direct word came the awareness that the muscles in my left arm were still sore from the healing current. "Don't doubt what I have done for you."

It's fair to ask, as many readers might well be doing, "Well, why hasn't God spoken to me like that? What makes you so special?"

I have no idea. Actually, I'm reluctant to share these stories, because I don't want people to walk away disappointed and disillusioned with God or with themselves. Yet I would be lying if I said these things didn't happen. They did. To me. And I've been pondering them for years, am thankful for their occurrence, and sometimes ask why they don't happen more often. These were gifts from God, words and acts that greatly facilitated what God desired to do through me for the sake of other precious image-bearers.

## Self-Contradictory Prayers

Foster mentions self-contradictory prayers. What do self-contradictory prayers sound like? Try this one on for size: "Lord, give me patience quickly." Or: "Lord, teach me compassion, without my having to suffer." Or: "Lord, please give me a healing ministry, but I don't want to ever get sick."

Do you get the point? Does patience ever come quickly? It's a contradiction in terms. Can I ever become a deeply compassionate person if I've never suffered? Can I gain insight into sickness if I've never been ill?

Around 1983, while I was pastoring a church with two friends in France, I felt a nudge from the Holy Spirit to begin a healing ministry of some kind. At least that's what I thought the nudge meant. I started to study passages in the Bible about healing. I studied Jesus's healing ministry. I read lots of books about healing. And I developed a low-grade fever that lasted for months.[15]

*That's great*, I thought to myself. *I want to learn how to help people get well, and I get sick. I never get sick. What's the deal?*

Well, maybe that was the point. I have a "strong constitution," as my wife puts it. I've been blessed with a sturdy immune system. I'm now seventy-two, and I've never been admitted into a hospital. It was as though the Lord said to me, "I'm glad, son, that you want to have a healing ministry. But there is knowledge you need that only sickness can provide. I want you to know what it's like to have a chronic illness, one that goes on for a long time. I want you to grow your compassion. So, you're going to be sick for a while. In the long run, it will be good for you."

I was surprised by how long the low-grade fever lasted. It was just high enough for me to feel lousy but not so high as to necessitate extreme measures. I just felt bad, for month after month. People in the church were sympathetic but not terribly enthusiastic about having me pray for them. When I approached people whom I knew to be ill, they'd shuffle off or say, "You know, I'm feeling much better. Thanks for the offer."

Finally, the fever passed. What had I learned? For one thing, I learned what it's like to be sick. I learned how discouraging illness is, especially when it drags on for day after day. My heart softened for people who have serious, long-term illnesses. And I learned that the Lord had a different ministry in store for me than that of healing. In my specific case, God was training me to be a companion with those who are sick and dying rather than a healer. Or to put it better, the healing I would learn to offer was different than the healing I thought would occur.

## The Problem of Distractions

Let's take a closer look at a problem I mentioned earlier, that of distraction in prayer. We get distracted. Have you ever felt when you began to pray, as Henri Nouwen puts it, that your mind suddenly starts jabbering and howling like "a banana tree filled with monkeys"? Thank goodness, this problem is nothing new. Try not to be discouraged.

A desert father by the name of Agathon taught that distractions often are an aspect of a larger spiritual battle in which we're constantly engaged. Agathon links distractions to supernatural interference and resistance to our prayers. "For every time a man wants to pray, his enemies, the demons, want to prevent him, for they know that it is only by turning him from prayer that they can hinder him from his journey."[16]

Our minds, even apart from spiritual interference, tend to flit about like a hummingbird. How can we learn to lengthen our concentration and attentiveness in prayer while preparing meals, driving to work, taking care of kids with their many demands, finishing business deals, solving calculus problems, sinking a free throw, or engaging in the other challenges, demands, and joys of life in the twenty-first century?

How can we maintain mental steadiness and attentiveness? Our ancient brothers and sisters suggest that we keep "something special before our eyes as a kind of formula to which the errant mind can be recalled after numerous detours and wanderings and into which it can enter, as into a safe harbor, after repeated shipwrecks."[17]

So, for instance, if you find yourself distracted, try repeating a short line from a psalm. Something as simple as "Lord, make haste to help me" (Ps. 70:1, ESV) will do the trick. Or when your attentiveness wanders, pray a short prayer like "Lord Jesus Christ, Son of God, have mercy on me, a sinner." Short, direct prayers like this help tether the mind. The hummingbird comes to rest. With practice, your distractions will begin to dissipate.

### Pause and Reflect

Ponder these two questions: When do I get distracted? What distracts me? Try writing down your distractions.

For the first few times you do this in prayer, it may seem that all you're doing is writing down distractions. But after a week or two, there will be nothing more to write down, for our distractions tend to be repetitive. In time, you'll have a nice distraction list. If a distraction appears while you're praying, you can simply glance down, take a peek at your list, and say to yourself, "I can deal with this when my prayer is finished. I've written it down."

Keep your distraction list. God may well be speaking to you in your distractions. Patterns may appear. And the patterns may be important. Some distractions may be related to specific issues or thought patterns worthy of our attention. Add new distractions when they occur.

How have your habitual thought patterns affected, positively or negatively, your specific prayers and prayer life in general?

John Cassian, after a conversation with Abba Isaac, offers Isaac's practical cautions and advice for keeping our thought life outside of prayer. "Before we pray, we should make an effort to cast out from the innermost parts of our heart whatever we do not wish to steal upon us as we pray. For instance, if I want my heart to be pure when I enter prayer, I need to be attentive to temptations to impurity outside of prayer."[18]

Isaac compares the soul to a "light feather." Feathers float in the air easily if not "weighed down by a sprinkling." When they are damp, though, their ability to float disappears. So, Isaac teaches, our sins can weigh us down and "assail" the soul, hindering its natural buoyancy. The remedy? Isaac suggests we learn to live wisely. Make a disciplined effort to draw the mind away from patterns of thinking that easily weigh it down. In a word, a healthy prayer life entails certain yeses and noes outside of prayer that we stick to with the help of others.

Wisdom outside of prayer assists wisdom, attentiveness, and discernment in prayer. I remember one of my first Bible teachers defining wisdom for me: "Chris, wisdom is knowing how to live," a knowledge available to us in our relationship with Christ through an immersion in Jesus's teaching and form of life.

After all, Christ created the world. Jesus knows what works and what doesn't. He understands our hardwiring, our spiritual, emotional, and physical DNA. If we attempt to live against the grain of the universe Jesus has created, we'll end up scraped, bruised, frustrated, and disillusioned. Life will make little sense, nor will our prayers. And among other things, we'll be extremely distracted. Yes, "true life involves living in a particular way."[19]

Gradually, with God's grace and the help of friends, we learn to say no to those influences and appetites that—in our most honest moments—we know are choking our desire to know God and to pray. I can remember James Houston, for instance, saying in a class at Regent College in the late eighties: "You can't read *Playboy* and expect to have a fruitful prayer life." You could have heard a pin drop. How much more so in our pornified culture today.

By God's grace and the power of God's Spirit, we learn to embrace the concrete means God has ordained for living a different way, the classical spiritual disciplines. At the top of the list is prayer, our lifeline to the immensely and intensely personal God we worship as Father, Son, and Holy Spirit.

# CHAPTER EIGHT

# Slow Down, Quiet Down

Spiritual formation is the slowest of all human movements.

—James Houston

To receive the grace of God, you must go to a desert place and stay a while. There you can be emptied and unburdened of everything that does not pertain to God. There the house of our soul is swept clean to make room for God alone to dwell. . . . We need this silence, this absence of every creature, so that God can build his hermitage in us.

—Charles de Foucauld

If you love the truth, love silence.

—Saint Isaac the Syrian

We've got to slow down to catch up.

—Carolyn Arends

Jesus led his life in Israel at a slow pace. He remains a slow mover and rarely seems rushed. The pattern of modern people's lives is quite different, especially in the West. Why are we moving so fast? Why is the pace of our lives so frenetic? Why are our lives so noisy and crowded? Have speed, busyness, and constant clatter increased our happiness and joy?

Deb and I walked up to the train platform, and there she rested, the TGV, long and lean. The TGV is France's bullet train, *le train de grande vitesse* ("the train of great speed"). It looked like a long projectile, sleek and streamlined.

We stepped on board, settled in our seats, and waited excitedly. Soon we'd be traveling at 120 miles per hour through the French countryside. I'd never traveled that fast while still on the ground and wondered what it would be like.

The train started to move, slowly crawling out of the station. As it gained speed, we felt little movement inside the cabin, although the countryside outside our window began to speed by faster and faster. When we reached top speed, my eyes hurt if I tried to focus on houses or trees; we were simply moving too fast for our eyes to track with our speed.

We gave up trying to enjoy the scenery. In effect our speed blinded us to what was directly outside our window. The sound of the train traveling at high speed didn't prevent conversation, but it did make it difficult. Things were too loud and too fast for us to do much else than sit and look at one another. Yes, we reached our destination very quickly. We just didn't see much along the way.

Our experience on the TGV is a parable of sorts for the pace at which many of God's precious image-bearers are leading their lives in the twenty-first century. Our lives move at TGV speed, but God moves at a much slower pace. How ironic to live at a pace where, in a manner of speaking, we leave God trailing behind. If we move too fast in too loud an environment, we miss much along the way, inattentive to the gifts that God generously offers each day.

There are beauties and wonders very near us that we only see and appreciate if we slow down and quiet down, gifts such as "a perfect rose or the scent of honeysuckle, the embrace of a friend, the taste of bacon."[1]

## The Rhythm of Jesus's Ministry

Jesus's life and ministry demonstrate a distinct rhythm, one that illustrates the importance of slowness, solitude, and silence in a spiritually healthy and mature image-bearer's life. If we are to keep in step with Jesus, we'll likely need to slow down and quiet down.

As Jesus is the model for his image-bearers, surely following his example, the manner in which he lived, and the habits and practices that characterized his life, is the heart of wise spiritual formation. In a nutshell, if Jesus lived a paced life, with significant periods of solitude and silence marking his life's rhythms, can we ignore his practice and hope to live a different way with God?

Jesus was an extremely busy man, sent by his Father to accomplish the most important work in human history. For Jesus, there was always something to do, someone to heal, something to teach, someone to exorcize and free from the power of evil. Luke describes Jesus's work in Luke 5:15: "Yet the news about him spread all the more, so that crowds of people came to hear him and to be healed of their sicknesses."

Still, Jesus never seems rushed as he carries out his Father's will. He doesn't work at a hectic pace. He moves through time focused on whatever his Father offers him along the way; his path and field of vision are straight and clear. On Jesus's way into Jerusalem, for instance, he sees the tax collector Zacchaeus in a sycamore tree: "Zacchaeus, come down immediately. I must stay at your house today" (Luke 19:5).

### Pause and Reflect

What or whom might you see if you lived a more paced life and transitioned from rushing to walking, from frenetic activity to a slower, less hectic rhythm through your day?

Why have you chosen to live at such a fevered pace, rushing from one person, thing, or event on to the next? What are you hoping to accomplish?

Take time to ponder the pace of your life and how things came to be this way.

If you lived at a slower pace, might you actually accomplish more rather than less?

Let's look again at Jesus's life. Luke points us to two specific practices that made all the difference for Jesus. After describing how busy Jesus is in Luke 5:15, Luke surprises us in the very next verse: "But Jesus often withdrew to lonely places and prayed" (Luke 5:16). These different practices—pace, solitude, silence, and prayer—provided the scaffolding and support for Jesus's active ministry.

The rhythm of Jesus's ministry is clear: intense, focused, paced ministry; silence, solitude, and prayer; intense, focused ministry; silence, solitude, and prayer. The question facing all of us is plain. We dare not avoid it. If Jesus found it necessary to withdraw regularly into silence, solitude, and prayer, why would we imagine we can live or love well apart from the very practices that nourished the incarnate Son of God? If Jesus rarely if ever rushed, what can I learn from him about the dangers of hurry and the blessings of slowness?

Consider Jesus's relationship with three of his best friends: Mary, Martha, and Lazarus. Jesus receives word from Mary and Martha that Lazarus is ill: "Lord, the one you love is sick" (John 11:3). Mary and Martha want Jesus to come quickly to address this dire circumstance, but Jesus remains where he is for "two more days," for he discerns God's deeper intent for this perilous situation. "Lazarus is dead, and for your sake I am glad I was not there, so that you may believe. But let us go to him" (John 11:14–15).

Jesus knew what to do and when to do it. His heart, mind, will, and body were aligned with his surroundings, the people he loved, and his Father's will, because of the fundamental rhythms of his life.

### Pause and Reflect

**Take time to ponder these questions: What noises and voices are echoing through the corridors of my mind and heart that must be stilled? What truths must I settle on, like a hen softly resting on her eggs? What might birth within me if I would simply slow down, quiet down, and settle down? Are there any possibilities and prayers incubating in me that can only be birthed in silence and solitude?**

Slowness, silence, and solitude offer a framework for prayerfully discerning the influences affecting how we think and live; the pressures and pace of our environment can easily deflect us from the values of Jesus's kingdom.

Each day, through the various media and technology available to us, we hear voices, read words, and see images that shape us consciously and subconsciously. Some are quite positive, others much less so. Neil Postman points to Aldous Huxley's warning in *Brave New World*:

What Huxley teaches is that in the age of advanced technology, spiritual devastation is more likely to come from an enemy with a smiling face than from one whose countenance exudes suspicion and hate. In the Huxleyan prophecy, Big Brother does not watch us, by his choice. We watch him, by ours. There is no need for wardens or gates or Ministries of Truth. When a population becomes distracted by trivia, when cultural life is redefined as a perpetual round of entertainments, when serious public conversation becomes a form of baby-talk, when, in short, a people become an audience and their public business a vaudeville act, then a nation finds itself at risk; culture-death is a real possibility.[2]

In C. S. Lewis's *Screwtape Letters*, Uncle Screwtape, an experienced devil, coaches his nephew Wormwood to tempt his patients with mental laziness—laziness fostered by attachment to mere diversions. If the temptation succeeds, spiritual destruction is not far off: "You will no longer need a good book, which he really likes, to keep him from his prayers. . . . [A] column of advertisements in yesterday's paper will do."[3] Once the victim is trapped by mental laziness,

> You can make him do nothing at all for long periods. You can keep him up late at night, not roistering, but staring at a dead fire in a cold room. All the healthy and outgoing activities which we want him to avoid can be inhibited and nothing given in return. . . . The Christians describe the enemy as one "without whom Nothing is strong." And Nothing is very strong: strong enough to steal away a man's best years, not in sweet sins but in dreary flickering of the mind over it knows not what. . . . It does not matter how small the sins are provided that their cumulative effect is to edge the man away from the Light and out into the Nothing.[4]

With every hour watching TV or surfing our favorite website, media debris slowly drifts to the floor of our conscious and unconscious mind. Periodically, the floor needs sweeping. Slowness, solitude, and silence provide the broom and dustpan.

Slowing down deepens our attentiveness to, as Joyce Huggett puts it, the "pools of silence" God offers us every day. "Whilst washing up, ironing, hoovering [vacuuming], dusting, gardening, walking to the post, driving to the shops, or traveling by public transport . . . I would try to listen to God as intently as in my place of prayer. It worked."[5]

Slowness and silence foster our ability to see what is right in front of us: sprinklings of God's blessing, care, and love. Hollow attractions and diversions, many promoted by our preoccupation with technology and social media, numb our awareness of the beauty of the common.

Huggett suggests we develop the discipline of the "godly pause": "When taking paper out of my typewriter or making myself a cup of coffee or waiting at traffic lights, I would turn my mind God-wards quite deliberately. Often God would communicate his presence to me in some felt way."[6]

Mary Pipher reminds us that most

real life is rather quiet and routine. Most pleasures are small pleasures—a hot shower, a sunset, a bowl of good soup or a good book. Television suggests that life is high drama, love and sex. TV families are radically different from real families. Things happen much faster to them. On television things that are not visually interesting, such as thinking, reading, and talking, are ignored. . . . Instead of ennobling our ordinary experiences, television suggests that they are not of sufficient interest to document.[7]

Yes, there's a good phrase to remember: "our ordinary experiences." Slowing down and quieting down ennoble them.

## Learning to Live a Different Way in Contemporary Society

In the introduction to Richard J. Foster's chapter on meditation in *Celebration of Discipline*, he writes this: "In contemporary society our Adversary majors in three things: noise, hurry, and crowds. If he can keep us engaged in 'muchness' and 'manyness,' he will rest satisfied."[8]

Ponder with me, for a moment, the influence of crowds. Our families, peer groups, local communities, work environments, and national context influence us daily. An occasional long step away from the crowd helps us regain our balance and focus. A key question to ask is this: Is my normal environment helping me love other people or not? To be more specific, are there so-called normal aspects of my environment—my familial, cultural, political, or ecclesial context—that from the perspective of Jesus's kingdom are abnormal at best and sinful at worst?

I think of the history of slavery in the United States and the racism that still infects our culture. For hundreds of years racist perspectives and actions toward African Americans, Native Americans, Asians, and Hispanics characterized American society. They still do.

The deaths of precious image-bearers like Trayvon Martin, George Floyd, and Breonna Taylor have focused Americans' attention on the evil of racism. Thankfully, Americans are increasingly willing to admit that what seemed normal—whites are superior—is genuine looniness.

## Pause and Reflect

**What aspects of American culture considered as normal might you identify as abnormal from the perspective of Jesus and his kingdom?**

**What comes to mind for you? Of course, this question can be applied to other cultures as well.**

Foster also mentions noise and hurry as devilish tools and tactics. How so? Noise distracts. Noise drowns out. Noise diverts. Distraction averts our attention from the most important things. It strangles attentiveness. Loving God and neighbor is the heart of the matter for Jesus:

this is the most important thing. Should we be surprised that the devil uses noise and hurry to divert and distract us from our highest calling?

Once again, we turn to Uncle Screwtape for a demonic perspective. He warns his nephew Wormwood that he must never allow those he tempts to experience two things: music and silence. Noise "alone defends us from silly qualms, despairing scruples, and impossible desires. We will make the whole universe a noise in the end. We have already made great strides in this direction as regards the Earth. The melodies and silences of Heaven will be shouted down in the end. But I admit we are not yet loud enough, or anything like it. Research is in progress."[9]

It's fair to say that the devil's research is bearing abundant fruit in the twenty-first century. We now live in the noisiest period in human history. Screwtape and Wormwood couldn't be more pleased.

## Hurry Sickness

What about hurry? Of all that Foster might have chosen to highlight as devilish, why would he choose hurry ("noise, hurry, and crowds") as one of the big three? John Ortberg provides a succinct and wise answer: "Love and hurry are fundamentally incompatible. Love always takes time, and time is one thing hurried people don't have."[10]

*Psychology Today* defines hurry sickness as "a behavior pattern characterized by a continual rushing and anxiousness; an overwhelming and continual sense of urgency." It's a sickness "in which a person feels chronically short of time, and so tends to perform every task faster and to get flustered when encountering any kind of delay."[11]

A national survey in *USA Today* "revealed that the vast majority of Americans feel they are busier this year than last year and they were busier last year than the year before, and for better or worse, the pace of life is speeding up to make us feel trapped in a 'time crunch.'"[12]

I recently listened to a short talk by Tony Campolo on the Red Letter Christians website. Tony commented on the coronavirus pandemic's isolating effect, yet he believed the new pandemic environment might offer unexpected benefits. He encouraged listeners to consider how slowness and silence might be very good things to experience, though initially somewhat uncomfortable.

Campolo spoke of attending a conference in Florida at which Bill Gates was speaking. To no one's surprise Gates was extremely excited about new computer advances that enabled ever-faster access and processing of information. A man in the audience from India raised his hand and asked Gates a simple but direct question: "Mr. Gates, how can you help the people in my village to slow down?"

It's no doubt true that rapid access to information has helped many. Thousands of lives have been saved through the speedy dissemination of knowledge on a global scale. Yet there are aspects of human life that simply can't be rushed. When we try to rush them, life blows up in our faces.

The simplest things in life teach us this lesson. A cake must be baked for a sufficient time at a precise temperature. If we remove it too quickly from the oven in our desire to taste its sweetness, all that reaches our eager taste buds is uncooked dough. Insufficiently baked cake may deceive us with its golden-brown surface, but thorough baking demands time and patience.

I remember the excitement I experienced as a little boy living in Phoenix. I had just bought a pack of carrot seeds for fifteen cents. I carefully tilled a small patch of soil in my backyard, watered it, dropped my carrot seeds into the ground, and covered them gently.

How hard it was to wait for the carrots to grow! Each day I cultivated my little garden, eagerly waiting for the shoots of my carrots to break the soil's surface. "What's going on down there?" I asked myself. "This is taking too long. Is something wrong? Maybe I should take a look just to make sure everything is all right."

I succumbed to temptation and hurriedly dug beneath the surface. There were my carrots. They had just begun to develop. And my impatience had snuffed out their burgeoning life.

So I'd like to pose some hard questions. How fast are you moving? Do you need to slow down to reach your destination safely and enjoy the view along the way? I think of my experience on the TGV.

How can we regain our center, our grounding, our balance? Our internal gyroscopes are wildly spinning. We've lost our way. How can we reset them by the power of the Spirit?

John Ortberg asked a trusted friend—my guess is that it was Dallas Willard—what he needed to do to maintain his spiritual health. The answer? "You must ruthlessly eliminate hurry from your life."

"That's a good one," John replied. "What else?"

"There is nothing else. You must ruthlessly eliminate hurry from your life."[13]

*Ruthlessly* is quite an adverb. I looked it up. Here's the definition: "Without pity or compassion; mercilessly; unsympathetic." So if I'm understanding Ortberg's mentor correctly, I must be ruthless with hurry in my life. I must not make excuses for why I hurry through day after day. I must show hurry no compassion. I must kill it. How about you?

How do we know if we have hurry sickness? Ortberg lists a number of symptoms of hurry sickness that are worthy of our attention. I found I had a number of them. I must have hurry sickness.

1. Do you find yourself constantly speeding up your daily activities?
2. How about multitasking? I recall pulling up at a red light and noticing a good friend in the lane next to me. He had the day's paper spread over his steering wheel. I honked my horn, gave him a concerned look, and self-righteously wiggled my finger: "Naughty, naughty."

3. Do you ever count the number of cars in front of you on the freeway? "Sure," I say to myself. "Who doesn't?" If you move beyond counting cars to changing lanes, having carefully computed the fastest lane, you might well have hurry sickness. Ouch. I feel my temperature rising. Is that a fever I sense?

4. How about looking for the fastest checkout lane at the grocery store? I do this all the time. Not only do I look for the fastest lane—Ortberg may have the same problem—but I find myself competing with folks in the line I thought was going to be slower than mine. I just did this the other day at Wawa, a local convenience store. I felt a sense of disappointment as the person who was where I would have been checked out first. I had lost. I probably have hurry sickness.

5. How about putting your clothes on inside out or backward? You could be in trouble. I'm an expert at this with underwear. I thought I did this because I'm old. Maybe my diagnosis is wrong.

6. Have you ever slept in your daytime clothes to save time in the morning? Oh my. Call the doctor.

7. Do you have a hard time saying no? Absolutely. I'm a people pleaser. I don't want to let people down. What are the hidden costs in my life every time I say yes when no would have been a wiser response?

8. Are you so tired at the end of the day that you have no time, energy, or love for those who matter most to you? Ortberg calls this "sunset fatigue."

What happens to us when hurry sickness remains undiagnosed and continues for a lengthy period? We burn out. We crumble. We disintegrate. We get depressed. Our nervous system implodes. Consider the case of Juanita Rasmus.

Juanita is the copastor of Saint John's United Methodist Church in downtown Houston. In her book *Learning to Be: Finding Your Center After the Bottom Falls Out*, Juanita discusses "the stress of living in a do-do-do world." For a number of reasons, Juanita found herself enmeshed in a pace of life and a list of demands that ultimately proved too much for her and her nervous system. Finally, she crashed. Juanita experienced a severe nervous breakdown.

"Friends and family reflected on how wound up I was," Juanita shares. "Relationships suffered—I didn't have time to 'waste' talking to friends about getting together. I had things to do and places to go. Though I valued my friendships, my to-do list took priority over my to-be list. I was running on empty. And since I was meeting my deadlines, for the most part, I never noticed the growing problem."[14] Suffice it to say, Juanita's body did. She succumbed to a significant, life-changing depression.

Thankfully, Juanita recovered and is ministering again today. Part of Juanita's healing process involved extended periods of silence and solitude. "Silence is amazing," Juanita writes. "It's like a marinade to put on chicken, fish, or beef. There are times when I'm like the fish in marinade, easily overcome by the silence."[15]

As Juanita slowed down and quieted down, her self-awareness grew and matured. "In the silence the nuances of my personality have been revealed for what they are. . . . Marinating in the silence is allowing me to see me. This is heavy shit, but I don't feel punishment, which is what I've always expected in these moments. I feel regret, remorse, and a bit disoriented by my new awareness, but believe it or not I also feel a great deal of gratitude."

Juanita was helped by Richard J. Foster's words concerning busyness: "Busyness is not of the devil. It is the devil." In silence and solitude, Juanita learned to slow down and quiet down. Her spirit has been renewed; her body has been healed. She has recovered and is in a much better place than when she ministered to others in such a frenetic, driven manner.

Juanita's prayer: "Okay, Lord, marinate me in your silence so that I'm transformed into something fulfilling, life-giving, and memorable."[16] You might try praying Juanita's prayer with her. Is the Lord inviting you into silence, to extended periods of quiet and solitude when you can simply marinate in the wonder, beauty, and love of God? No TV. No radio. No internet. No social media. Simply silence.

I'm trying to live, think, and work more slowly. As I walk from my office to another room of the house, I purposely walk slowly. As I sit at my desk writing, I'm gradually learning to slow down. Occasionally I simply sit and ponder. During Zoom calls I'm trying to grow my attentiveness, focusing on the person across from me and not on the next call to be accomplished. I'd like to say I've moved from speed to slowness, but I'm not there yet. I am taking steps in that direction, though, and in time they will add up.

I'm developing a new habit: intentional slowing. Am I accomplishing more than I did in my hurried moments? Maybe. Maybe not. I do sense I'm living, thinking, and acting in a healthier way. How patient Jesus has been as he waited for me to come to my senses. I can hear him saying, "You were always in such a rush. Why? I never lived that way myself, yet I accomplished what my Father asked me to do. Do the same with me. Don't get ahead of me. I'm a slow walker and a slow talker."

I remember teaching in the Cursillo Movement in Geneva, Switzerland, one weekend in the early eighties. At the beginning of the retreat, we collected wristwatches from retreatants as they entered through the monastery door. Most looked anxious as they dropped their watches into a box for safekeeping. "We'll keep track of time for you," we assured them. "You don't need to worry."

We also gently asked folks to observe silence from Friday evening through Saturday lunch. We considered our request as a gift, for most of these retreatants lived very busy, noisy lives. Some were leaders in worldwide corporations such as Caterpillar. Others worked at the United Nations, the World Health Organization, or the World Trade Organization. How busy these precious image-bearers were, even before the age of email, Twitter, Facebook, and Instagram.

During that Cursillo weekend, we gave our new friends three gifts: the gift of slowing, the gift of silence, and to a certain degree, the gift of solitude. By the time of their last communion service together on Sunday afternoon, God's Spirit had touched them deeply. Some shed tears. What might you experience if you purposefully slow down and quiet down?

## Pause and Reflect

Are there difficult problems, relationships, and issues—maybe three or four—that slowing and silence might help you to understand with greater clarity and perhaps resolve?

How might your horizons expand, and your understandings deepen, if you stayed put in a quiet place long enough for the learning to occur?

What might you see or learn if you periodically visited a quiet place for slow prayer and reflection?

Slowing and silence grow our attentiveness. They broaden our field of vision and help us discern what really matters and what doesn't. To whom or what have I given my attention this past week, month, or year? Why have I done so?

To develop focus and disperse distraction, though, requires an environment that sifts out influences, deflecting our attention from what really counts. As our eyes clear, what will we see? Who will we see? What needs? What beauties? The blurriness of eyes too long clouded by high-intensity foolishness demands a healing, quiet environment conducive to clarifying our vision and expanding our field of awareness and attentiveness.

## The Desert Dwellers

Christian history is replete with precious image-bearers who have pondered these same issues. Many in the communion of the saints can help us as we seek to live a different way. The desert dwellers have helped me; perhaps they can help you. Wise examples and prudent imitation can move us to a better, wiser, saner place.

From the late second century AD into the fourth century, a stream of Christians journeyed to the Egyptian and Judaean deserts to set up camp there. Why would they do such a thing? What did they hope to find? What were they seeking in the bleak, seemingly godforsaken hotbox of the desert? Women as well as men made their way to the desert. Why would they think this bare, boring, dangerous furnace might serve well as a learning space for mind, heart, soul, and body?[17]

At first glance, the desert dwellers seem to be rejecting Christ's teaching to be salt and light in the world (Matt. 5:13–16). Is this actually the case? Or might spiritual life and light flash brightly in this most unlikely and uninviting environment? Might life in the desert offer unexpected possibilities and opportunities for service and spiritual growth, prospects difficult to discover or embrace in an urban setting?

Picture the desert as "a space in which obedience to truth is practiced." Parker Palmer notes the importance of space in the lives of the desert dwellers and directs our attention to a well-loved desert abba or father, Abba Felix. "Abba Felix and his fellow seekers left the crowded cities to meet truth in the desert, one of the most open and spare spaces on earth. They went there not only to enter an outer space free of the cities' clutter but also to open up an inner space of heart and mind, free of inward noise. In desert emptiness the soul is able to settle on truth, to concentrate on that which is essential to salvation."[18]

Consider for a moment the distinctive, beautiful, and harsh geographical space inhabited day in and day out by ancient Christian desert dwellers. The desert offered early Christians intense, unremitting solitude and silence.

In their desert environment, Christian desert dwellers learned to attune their ears to Scripture and to prayer as they continually prayed the Psalms. They grew their attentiveness to God's voice and slowly learned the value of detachment. Things that once had seemed so important slowly sloughed off, like a lizard shedding its skin. The desert dwellers' embrace of God and love for other precious image-bearers expanded in their desert environment. They learned to suspect anything or any person that distracted, disrupted, or diverted them from their fundamental call to love.

Basil the Great, a church father who spent significant time in the desert, comments that "One cannot approach the knowledge of the truth with a disturbed heart."[19] The desert dwellers' restless and disturbed hearts slowly quieted down in their desert environment. For many, growing love and peace were the happy result of living and praying in this surprising learning space.

### Pause and Reflect

What's disturbing your heart or mind today? Perhaps you're feeling a general sense of unrest, uneasiness, discomfort, sadness, or confusion.

Is the Holy Spirit nudging you to a different way of thinking and living, perhaps an unexpected and invigorating way of reconfiguring your life as a conduit for the Spirit's love?

A desert environment, either literal or figurative, can help us in this new construction project, as unpromising as it may appear at first glance. "What can grow in the desert?" we ask. Tumbleweed? Cacti? Still, when the rains come, desert flowers suddenly appear.

Is the Holy Spirit gently tapping you on the shoulder? "Hey, friend. Might it not be time for you and me to get to know each other? And for you, dear one, to get acquainted with yourself? Allow me to guide you to a learning space that has helped other image-bearers to know me, and to know themselves."

For some ancient Christians, the desert's silence and solitude served as a magnet, raising the cracked filings of their personalities, habit patterns, and sins to the surface of their awareness. "Ah, so this is who I am. Who would have thought?" For others, values were clarified, and sins slowly dissipated.

## Pause and Reflect

Crazy voices inspire crazy lives. Can I pry just a bit? Whose voices have you listened to over the course of your lifetime? Why these particular voices? Think back on your life-mapping exercise. If you didn't engage in it, try listing now on a piece of paper the personalities, books, films, television programs, and music that have shaped your life and your response to life's opportunities and challenges; what titles, names, and ideas appear on your list?

Whose voices are you heeding in this present moment? Are they bringing perspective? Peace? Or fomenting confusion and craziness?

Are they nurturing love or provoking suspicion, resentment, and anger? The voices we habitually listen to may be positive or negative. What effect are they having on you—or me?

Folks journeyed to the desert to seek the silence and solitude necessary to surface key influences, people, and powers in their own cultural environment that had hindered their lives with God. There was time to focus on important things in the desert and no need to rush, for where was there to rush to? Opportunities for diversion or distraction were minimal, if not nonexistent. As the days and months passed, attentiveness to deeper, more important matters developed.

"Why did they do this?" Thomas Merton asked. Merton believed desert Christians increasingly discerned that the society in which they lived had, quite frankly, lost its mind. "Society—which meant pagan society, limited by the horizons and prospects of life 'in this world'— was regarded by them as a shipwreck from which each single individual man had to swim for his life. . . . These were men who believed that to let oneself drift along, passively accepting the tenets and values of what they knew as society, was purely and simply a disaster.

"They knew they were helpless to do any good for others as long as they floundered about in the wreckage. But once they got a foothold on solid ground, things were different. Then they had not only the power but even the obligation to pull the whole world to safety after them."[20]

Merton's words resonate with those of the apostle Paul: "Do not conform to the pattern of this world, but be transformed by the renewing of your mind" (Rom. 12:2). The great danger, one that often lurks below the surface of our consciousness, is to drift mindlessly along with the broader cultural consensus, passively floating downstream without heeding the white water ahead.

The desert dwellers heard the roar of the rapids and scrambled to shore. Or, to use Paul's metaphor, they sensed the tightening vise of a cultural consensus opposed to the teaching of Jesus; it was time to flee, many felt. To remain locked in their culture's corrosive environment was to surrender their minds and hearts to senselessness. For the desert dwellers, and it seems for Paul, a basic premise is this: a society can lose its mind. To help it regain its sanity, we may need to leave it, if only for a time.

When the movement to the desert reached its peak in the fourth century, the Roman world had become increasingly Christian. No longer was the church a minority community existing in a hostile cultural context. In 312 AD, Constantine converted to the Christian faith and subsequently emblazoned the cross on his legions' shields. Soon many conversions occurred, some genuine, some politically expedient. Many Roman senators, for instance, knew which way the wind was blowing and exchanged their pagan gods for the God of the Christians.

With the conversion of Constantine, the spiritual strength present in the Christian community during the sporadic though extremely intense persecutions of the mid-third and early fourth centuries began to dissipate almost imperceptibly as the Christian faith became culturally dominant. For some, the cross was viewed more as a signal of temporal power than redemption.

Literal martyrdom largely ceased for ancient Christians as Christianity was accepted in the Roman Empire of the fourth century, a culture that shortly before Constantine's time had not hesitated to persecute Christ followers. Some Christians perceived the need for a new type of martyrdom or witness, a bloodless one. The geography of the desert offered the opportunity for its development. Why a new martyrdom? Desert dwellers knew there was something in them that must die, something that needed to blossom, and a witness that should be borne.

Consider our own cultural environment today. How is the world squeezing us into its mold (cf. Rom. 12:1–2, PHILLIPS)? The desert dwellers purposely moved to a learning space that reduced the world's vice-like pressures.

Ponder what learnings can arise only in a desert environment. What might we learn that only a desert environment can teach us? About ourselves, the world, evil, sin, love, and God? How might the sands of the desert hone our lives and our character? How might the desert teach us to love God and neighbor more deeply, wisely, and effectively?

Many of us have never lived in a literal desert environment. Some, like me, may have spent time in a desert state such as Arizona and experienced the desert directly. Others have never had the opportunity or desire. No problem. We can validly expand the boundaries of a desert environment to include the various expanses and circumstances of our lives.

A cracked, abusive family environment is a desert. A long stretch in a lonely hospital room is a desert. A business that has failed is a desert. The reduced capacities of old age—physical, emotional, intellectual, and spiritual—are all a desert. The searing pain of loss is a vast desert. Life's inevitable disappointments are a desert, as are our disappointments and disillusionments with God. "Anything but this, Lord. Anything but this," we cry. And the Lord gently responds, "Ah, my child. For a time, this must be the only thing."

Yes, we will all experience the desert. It is inevitable. So rather than resisting, let us enter the desert together. What will we learn here that we can learn nowhere else? The desert strips, the desert cracks, the desert demands, the desert trains.

At first glance, it seems the desert offers so little. "Lord, why would you bring me to this place of all possible places? What do you desire to teach me here, in my desert experiences?"

Initially, it seems the desert is the least likely space to nurture our relationship with God. Yet there is a beauty, clarity, and focus the desert offers. "I offer you nothing," the desert says, "but a lonely space, a learning space. Come and dwell here. There is little here to distract you, little to divert your attention, little to entertain. Who will you meet here? You will encounter the real you, and by God's grace, the real Jesus. This will be a very good thing. You will meet the One who can teach you what you need, what you can safely set to the side, and most importantly, how to love."

Time in the desert significantly helps us gain the perspective and form the practices we need to simplify our lives—to live a different way as we keep in step with Jesus.

How might we faithfully keep in step with Jesus as we slow down and quiet down? Here's a very practical spiritual discipline you might find helpful. Consider a media fast. One day each week or each month take a step away from all social media: no email, no Facebook, no Twitter, no music, no TV, no radio. This suggestion may seem outrageous, but with a simple act of the will through the power of the Spirit, it's surely possible. My prayers are with you.

CHAPTER NINE

# Keep in Step with Jesus by Living More Simply

Many of my daily preoccupations suggest that I belong more to the world than to God. A little criticism makes me angry, and a little rejection makes me depressed. A little praise raises my spirits, and a little success excites me. . . . Often I am like a small boat on the ocean, completely at the mercy of its waves.

—Henri Nouwen, *The Return of the Prodigal Son*

I'm also learning the new freedom that comes—even while my stomach churns in rebellion—as I abandon my old script of asking, *What will people think?* They will think whatever they think, and I will go on and so will they. I have come to realize that I'm just not all that important, that my absence will not cause the great chaos that my ego had convinced me of.

—Juanita Rasmus, *Learning to Be*

We are made to feel ashamed to wear clothes or drive cars until they are worn out. The mass media have convinced us that to be out of step with fashion is to be out of step with reality. It is time we awaken to the fact that conformity to a sick society is to be sick.

—Richard J. Foster, *Celebration of Discipline*

s we begin to explore living more simply with Jesus, let me list a few questions that we can ponder together:

– What's the fundamental orientation of my life?
– To whom and to what do I give my ultimate allegiance?
– What does my concrete behavior over the past month indicate about what I value most deeply?

Now, after pondering these questions, let's take a look at four different translations of Jesus's command to seek first the kingdom of God from Matthew 6:33:

• "But *seek first* his kingdom and his righteousness, and all these things will be given to you as well" (NIV).
• "But *strive first* for the kingdom of God and his righteousness, and all these things will be given to you as well" (NRSV).
• "But *seek first* the kingdom of God and his righteousness, and all these things will be added to you" (ESV).
• "*Steep your life* in God-reality, God-initiative, God-provisions. Don't worry about missing out. You'll find all your everyday human concerns will be met" (THE MESSAGE).

Jesus's teaching is clear. He commands us to *seek first* the kingdom of God. Why does he say this? Jesus knows that our allegiances and values tend to drift as we live in the midst of this present evil age. The world around us continually attempts to squeeze us into its mold (Rom. 12:2, PHILLIPS). The Evil One exerts constant pressure on us, attempting to push us off course and away from the values of God's kingdom. And of course, we are *incurvatus in se*, curved in on ourselves. We are bent creatures and are apt to get our values confused.

Failure to seek first the kingdom of God leads to lives marked by underlying anxiety, confusion, disappointment, and despair. We lose our orientation. We likely respond to the siren call of values opposed to those of Jesus's kingdom. Our hearts are divided, tugged in two directions. Rather than experiencing the joy of a simple life, we are tempted to lead duplicitous lives and speak duplicitous words.

Trying to live in two kingdoms simply doesn't work. It is desperately difficult—the perfect recipe for stress, confusion, discouragement, and pain. I checked the Cambridge Dictionary and found the following list of words and phrases related to duplicity. None of them will make you smile:

- a crock of . . .
- artifice
- bad faith
- be a pack of lies
- canard
- feed somebody a line
- fib
- fiction
- flimflam
- forked tongue
- lie
- mythologize
- perjure
- polygraph
- stretch the truth
- white lie
- whopper

Ouch. Simply put, duplicitous people lie a lot, with their words and with their lives.

What characterizes duplicitous people? They speak out of both sides of their mouths. They're like chameleons whose skin color changes according to their environment. If they're with holy people, they act more holy than they really are. If they're with profane people, they act more profane than they really are.[1] Duplicitous people are fundamentally divided. They're double-minded. They haven't decided whose side they're on.

Imagine a line in the sand. On one side of the line stands Christ and his kingdom. On the other side stands the kingdom of this world, ruled by a different king, Satan himself. Duplicitous Christians straddle the line; they are divided in their allegiance. At certain times, in certain contexts, and with certain people, they gladly pledge their loyalty to the kingdom of God and verbally express their allegiance to Jesus. At other times, they cross over into the kingdom of this world. Back and forth. Back and forth. They're fundamentally divided in their loyalties. The result? Divided loyalties tire one out; it's exhausting to live in two worlds so different from one another. And when we live divided lives before a watching world, we surely give faith a bad name.

This is not the time to finger-point. All of us struggle with duplicity. In our most honest, transparent moments we sense the yawning gap between our words and our actions: we live as cracked people, divided people, bent people torn between two different kingdoms and kings.

Jesus insists on seeking first the kingdom because he longs for his followers to be straight talkers and straight livers. He wants our words and lives to fit together. He longs for our lives to ring true.

Learning to live simply with Jesus, then, concerns our heart's fundamental orientation before it concerns itself with anything else. Simplicity provides a conceptual framework and specific practices for learning to seek first the kingdom of God. It helps us focus our attention on what really matters.

As we begin to move from duplicity to a simple life with Jesus—the spiritual discipline of simplicity—we prayerfully examine the state of our hearts before we concern ourselves with how we're spending our money, what clothes we're wearing, the cars we're driving, and so on.

These issues are important and surely related to simplicity. Yet resolving our heart's allegiances—what Foster calls internal simplicity—comes first in importance. We shouldn't be surprised that as our heart's attachments are clarified and reordered, other affections and allegiances snap into place. By God's grace, internal simplicity leads to external simplicity. The ordering of our internal life ripples into our external behavior.

## Duplicity and Simplicity

So far, we've seen that duplicitous people are fundamentally divided. They tend to be worried: What are other people thinking about me? Do they like me? Would their feelings about me change if I dressed differently? Should I lose weight or add a few pounds? Why am I losing friends on Facebook?

Consider the struggles of duplicitous folks. They quickly adapt to the values of their environment; they're undecided about who they are or what they're about. If their environment changes, so do their values. They're easily swept along by the crowd, seeking its approval.

I think again of that interesting lizard, the chameleon. The chameleon's skin color literally changes with its environment as it seeks to protect itself from possible predators. It wants to blend in as completely as possible, becoming invisible to external threats.

Duplicitous people struggle similarly. They don't feel safe. They're alert to possible threats in their environment that threaten their sense of well-being. They long for acceptance and love but fear others. They want to blend in but also desire to be noticed. They tend to be dissatisfied with themselves and with life in general.

John Ortberg observes that duplicitous people often suffer from "approval addiction." Their social antennae wave constantly, searching for environmental signals guiding them to acceptable perspectives and behaviors. "Approval addiction involves not just trying to attract attention for what we do well, but also avoiding saying what we truly think if we believe speaking up could draw disapproval."[2]

A duplicitous life is exhausting. When trapped in duplicity's clutches, we expend an enormous amount of emotional energy, time, and money to present ourselves to others as worthy of acceptance, admiration, and love. We attempt to impress with our words, clothes, jewelry, cars, purchases, accomplishments, and so on.

Richella Parham has written honestly of her struggle with comparison and the sadness and dissatisfaction it injected into her life: "Comparison places us on one side of the scale and another person on the opposite side. By its very nature, comparison separates us from other people rather than connecting us to them. . . . Just when we need to feel the embrace of other people, we set ourselves apart from or even against another."[3] Here are some of the comparisons Richella struggled with:

- Not cultured enough
- Not sensitive enough
- Not spiritual enough
- Not generous enough
- Not accomplished enough
- Not independent enough.[4]

We all have comparison struggles we could readily add to Richella's list. Who has not longed to make the A-team, to be admired and accepted by others, to be noticed and have others say, "I wish I were like him" or "I wish I were like her"?

How we long to be accepted, admired, and loved by others! For me, high school in the mid-sixties was a social minefield, embedded with hidden hazards ready to blow up in my face at any time.

I discovered that maroon socks were absolutely necessary attire if I was to be "in" rather than "out." Black socks came in a close second. God help the poor soul who wore white socks with black shoes. Penny loafers were in. Laced black shoes? What could you be thinking? Cuffed pants? Yes. No cuffs? Absolutely not. Button-down collars? A social necessity. No buttons on your collar? I still hear the taunting voices: "Hall, you're going to fly away!"

We long to find a judgment-free zone. One exercise business has made millions marketing this slogan.

## A Judgment-Free Zone?

Before COVID-19 hit the United States, I exercised at Planet Fitness two or three days a week. Planet Fitness trumpets itself as a "judgment-free zone," and to some extent this is true. Older patrons are welcome and seem to feel at ease walking on the treadmill or using the weight machines. There are lots of folks of various ages and shapes. This is a good thing.

Yet there's something in the air at Planet Fitness. Eyes roam. Planet Fitness denizens slowly and surreptitiously scan the room while trying to avoid eye contact. Silent judgments float through the air: How did he put on so much weight? She's way too thin. Maybe she's anorexic. Wow, look at all those wrinkles. Few have the ideal body type, yet everyone wants one. If I've managed to lose a few pounds, I wonder, *Has anyone noticed?*

Has anybody noticed? What a telling phrase. What lies behind this simple, painful question? A desire to be loved. A desire to be accepted as

God's precious image-bearer, whether others view us as too tall or too short, too wide or too thin.

Think for a moment about the experience of many college students. Let's focus on one we'll call Hal. Hal wakes up each day anxious and fearful, but he doesn't want others to know. The day ahead looks daunting to Hal—indeed, overwhelming. Butterflies stretch their wings in Hal's stomach and soon begin to flutter. His nervous system is on alert. As Hal flips his legs over the edge of his bed, troubling questions and concerns reawaken, and disturbing emotions reignite.

Should I go to class? Will my friends be there? Why didn't I study harder for that quiz? How should I dress? Behind these basic questions, deeper ones lurk: Who are my real friends? Do they really like me? Is anyone noticing me? Does anyone care that I exist?

Hal, with these questions rumbling through his psyche like distant thunder, resumes a tough, daily construction project: transformation into the person he believes other students will like. Hal's concluded that no one could possibly be attracted to him as he really is. So each morning Hal painstakingly creates a hologram of himself that he'll project all day; surely this other Hal will be welcomed, accepted, and perhaps even loved.

The real Hal accompanies hologram Hal all day long. Some students like hologram Hal. A few don't. But Hal is convinced that no one could possibly love the real him. And so, Hal projects a self he hopes others will find attractive—a hologram—and constantly adjusts its contours and colors as the day goes by. Finally, at day's end, Hal crawls back into bed. He's exhausted and discouraged. Hal rolls over and turns off the light, and there is his companion—hologram Hal—glowing in the dark at the foot of his bed. "I don't even like you," Hal sighs. "How could anyone else?"

Finally, Hal falls asleep. Yet when he awakes the next morning, he flips the on switch, and hologram Hal lights up. It's going to be another long day.

Holograms demand lots of energy; they exhaust our mental and emotional energy supplies. We wander a dreamworld populated by others' expectations; it's grim, frightening territory and, too often, a nightmare. As Richard J. Foster comments, "How desperately and sincerely we labor to create the right impression. Instead of becoming good, we resort to all sorts of devices to make people think we are good."[5]

## Issues of Anxiety

The Lord knows most image-bearers lug a chest full of worries: money, clothing, food, our health, our appearance, our past, our future, our enemies, even our friends. Have you noticed how often in the Sermon on the Mount, Jesus encourages, even commands, us not to worry about these very things?

- "Therefore, I tell you, do not worry about your life, what you will eat or drink; or about your body, what you will wear. Is not life more than food, and the body more than clothes?" (Matt. 6:25).

- "Can any one of you by worrying add a single hour to your life?" (Matt. 6:27).
- "And why do you worry about clothes?" (Matt. 6:28).
- "So do not worry, saying, 'What shall we eat?' or 'What shall we drink?' or 'What shall we wear?'" (Matt. 6:31).
- People who don't believe in the God of Israel—or in Jesus— "run after" these things. God "knows" we need these things and will make provision for us (Matt. 6:32).
- Rather than worry, Jesus beckons us to place the kingdom of God at the center of our heart's longing and allegiance (Matt. 6:33).

When our values and allegiance drift, we assign people or things an importance and place in our lives they were never created to occupy. When we do so, life doesn't work. We end up frazzled, worried, and fundamentally divided between the values of God's kingdom and the values promoted by those who claim no allegiance to Jesus at all.

We easily drift into an unwarranted concern over how we're perceived by other people. If I dressed more carefully, if I wore an eye-catching watch or ring, if my hair was longer, or shorter, if I drove a nicer car, would folks think more highly of me? If so, are these really the kinds of people I want to impress?

I remember a Christmas morning about thirty years ago. The family was gathered around the Christmas tree slowly opening presents one at a time—a family tradition. My wife, the grand pooh-bah in charge of distributing gifts, handed me a present my dad had sent me. It was a small package. I shook the box and felt its contours under the colorful wrapping paper. *Hmm,* I thought to myself. *Maybe it's a watch. Why would Dad buy me a watch? He knows I already have one.* I opened the present, and sure enough, there it was. A Rolex. "A Rolex!" I exclaimed. "Why would he buy me a Rolex? It must have cost thousands of dollars."

I admit that the thought of having a Rolex wrapped around my wrist was appealing. Someone might notice. Someone might say, "I see you wearing a Rolex. Quite a watch."

"Yes, it is," I'd respond smugly. "It was a gift from my dad." Not only would my Rolex admirers think I was special, but they'd know I came from a wealthy family. My dad must be an impressive individual. The expensive piece of jewelry on my wrist, whose sole function was to tell me the time of day, indicated clearly how special the Hall family was. We were Rolex people.

When I regained my sanity and rose out of my Rolex reverie, I called my dad. Our Christmas conversation went something like this:

"Thanks, Dad, for the watch, but it's way too expensive. I really can't keep it. I appreciate the thought, though."

"Oh, you can keep it," he chuckled. "It's a counterfeit. I bought it in Hong Kong for twenty bucks. Maybe you can impress someone." That thought quite evidently amused him. Dad found it funny that someone might be impressed by the cost of a watch.

I think of Foster's words as I recall this conversation with my dad: "Out of fear that others might discover who we are, we create an artificial world of ostentatious display, extravagant ornamentation, and pretentious style. We call upon the beautician, the tailor, and the dressmaker to create an impression of perpetual youth. We buy clothes, cars, and houses beyond our means in a frantic attempt to *appear* successful."[6]

"Why am I so concerned about what others think of me?" Do you sometimes ask yourself that question? I do. Isn't it more likely, though, that they aren't thinking of us at all? Anthony DeMello makes me chuckle: "Before I was twenty I never worried about what other people thought of me. But after I was twenty I worried endlessly—about all the impressions I made and how people were evaluating me. Only sometime after turning fifty, did I realize that they hardly ever thought of me at all."[7]

Jesus offers *a different way.* It's called simplicity.

The person living simply with Jesus knows who she is and where her fundamental allegiance lies. She knows what she's about. She knows her yeses and noes. She's learning to live before an audience of one: the Holy Trinity. As Kierkegaard might put it, she has found purity of heart. She's embraced Jesus's exhortation to seek first the kingdom of God. As much as possible, she seeks to embody the values of Jesus's kingdom. As she learns to do so, her words and life increasingly fit together, like a key in a lock. Her life rings true. What you see is what you get, and what you get is just fine. As Clifford Williams writes, her "inner focus is unified," and her "public posture corresponds with it." She is not, "in short, divided."[8]

## The Heart of Simplicity

Simplicity is founded on trust; we trust that God has not erred in making me—and you—as the people we actually are. We trust that God can meet our deepest needs for acceptance, security, and love. We trust that Jesus was indeed correct in teaching that "life does not consist in an abundance of possessions" (Luke 12:15). We trust that we find ourselves by looking beyond ourselves to Jesus and the values of his kingdom.

Could Jesus be clearer? "Seek first his kingdom and his righteousness, and all these things will be given to you as well" (Matt. 6:33). As we learn to seek the kingdom of God above all other allegiances, values, dreams, and hopes, we experience increasing freedom.

What kind of freedom? Freedom from other people's expectations and demands. Freedom from the need to impress others. Freedom to be the precious image-bearers God has created us to be. Freedom to believe that God loves us without qualification. Freedom.

Simplicity is found in focusing our vision and desires on one person and one kingdom: Jesus and the kingdom of God.

Let's look again at Jesus's teaching in Matthew 6. Jesus is speaking to a group of Jewish people who are considering following him. There may be some Gentiles who are listening from a distance. The twelve—the apostles—have already decided to follow Jesus, and his words are particularly addressed to them. It's as though Jesus is saying, "Here's what following me on a different way looks like. If you follow me, you'll be thinking like this, speaking like this, and acting like this."

"Do not store up for yourselves treasures on earth, where moths and vermin destroy, and where thieves break in and steal" (Matt. 6:19). "Do not store up" is a single verb in Greek, and it's an imperative. That means it's a command. If we store up for ourselves treasures on earth, then, we're disobeying Jesus. Plain and simple.

Jesus comes to the heart of the matter in a few sentences. "No one can serve two masters. Either you will hate the one and love the other, or you will be devoted to the one and despise the other. You cannot serve both God and money" (Matt. 6:24).

Living simply with Jesus, then, is a matter of devotion. It is a matter of allegiance. Either we are devoted to him or devoted to money. Jesus doesn't leave a lot of middle ground on which to set up camp. Why is he so insistent?

Jesus understands that our tendency to store up stuff is related to anxiety and fear. Will we have enough to eat? Will we have clothes to wear or a roof over our heads? Will we be able to provide for our children? Who will take care of us in our old age? People living in poverty daily face these concerns, yet these anxieties trouble all God's image-bearers.

Still, Jesus is resolute. "I tell you, do not worry about your life, what you will eat or drink; or about your body, what you will wear. Is not life more than food, and the body more than clothes?" (Matt. 6:25).

"Yes, Jesus," I hear myself responding. "Life is more than food, but I still need to eat. Life is more than clothes, but I still need a shirt on my back and shoes on my feet."

God knows that we need the necessities of life. And God uses a variety of means and people to meet our basic needs for food, clothing, and shelter.

Some image-bearers have been given fine minds; they use them to create ways and means for human needs to be met. Others have been given huge hearts and strong bodies. They're healthy mentally, emotionally, and physically. So these image-bearers use what God has given to help meet needs and expand human flourishing. Still others have received or developed wealth they can use on behalf of those in need.

God wants our basic needs to be met but frowns on extravagance and self-indulgence. It's sobering to note that if human beings simply shared their resources and avoided unnecessary extravagance, every empty stomach in the world today would be full. World hunger would end.

The problem, as Jesus describes it in the Sermon on the Mount, is that we have wrapped our hearts and hands too tightly around what we possess. Why? We are anxious. We find it difficult to trust God. And, yes, we are sinful. We are *incurvatus in se*. When our ego is at the center, greed may widen its hungry maw. "For where your treasure is, there your heart will be also" (Matt. 6:21). We wrap our heart too tightly around what God has graciously given us, like a boa constrictor wrapping its coils around its prey. Why do we do this? We are afraid, and our fear fuels our self-centeredness and greed.

## Simplicity, Trust, and Security

The Scripture speaks so much about money and possessions because God knows we're prone to trust our possessions or our bank account for our sense of security, well-being, and self-worth (cf. Matt. 6:19, 24; 1 Tim. 6:6–10).

I recall a bumper sticker that was quite popular a few years ago: "He who dies with the most toys wins." Wins what? Some phrases deserve to be at the top of our "stupid" list. This bumper sticker qualifies. No, he who dies with the most toys is dead.

I learned this lesson while briefly working in the funeral business in North Hollywood when I was a student at UCLA. My job was to collect and transport the bodies of the dead, sometimes for the funeral home and sometimes for the LA Coroner's Department. My exposure to the dead taught me one lesson very quickly. Whether you're an unidentified John Doe or a world-famous Hollywood star, dead is dead. The only difference between corpses lying in a morgue is the name on a toe tag.

My mind is drawn to Jesus's parable of the rich fool in Luke 12, a story Jesus tells in response to a request to resolve a dispute about an inheritance. "Man, who appointed me a judge or an arbiter between you?" Jesus asks (Luke 12:14). Jesus turns to the listening crowd and warns, "Watch out! Be on your guard against all kinds of greed; life does not consist in an abundance of possessions." He then tells a parable to make his point as clear as possible.

The ground "of a certain rich man yielded an abundant harvest" (Luke 12:16). This man had been abundantly blessed by God. He was rich, a status that from a Jewish perspective was a sign of God's blessing. In addition, his land had been blessed. It had "yielded an abundant harvest."

How will the rich man respond to God's gracious, abundant provision? Will he thank God? Will he consider *why* God has blessed him? Perhaps God's blessing has come so the rich man can share his blessing with others.

Sadly, this possibility never enters the rich fool's mind. All the man can think to do is build bigger barns and enjoy the high life. "I will tear down my barns and build bigger ones, and there I will store my surplus grain." That's his first mistake.

His second mistake quickly follows. "And I'll say to myself, 'You have plenty of grain laid up for many years. Take life easy; eat, drink and be merry.'" God's response is not a happy one: "You fool! This very night your life will be demanded from you. Then who will get what you have prepared for yourself?" (Luke 12:20).

The rich fool thought he had many years of life ahead of him. The truth was that he had only a few hours. His riches would go to others. And his greatest mistake? He had not been "rich toward God" (Luke 12:21).

Simplicity, then, is a spiritual discipline that helps us discern, practice, and nurture genuine human flourishing, in our lives and those of others. It deepens our trust in God and frees us from needless anxiety.

## I Pledge My Allegiance

Jesus invites us to follow his different way, a better way. The heart of the matter? What am I going to seek with all my mind and heart? To whom will I bow the knee? To whom will I give my full allegiance?

Imagine a Roman soldier standing at the periphery of the crowd listening to Jesus preach his famous Sermon on the Mount. Can you imagine his surprise and concern as he heard Jesus beckon his listeners to "seek first his kingdom and his righteousness" (Matt. 6:33)? A different kingdom from that of Rome? A different king than Caesar?

Jesus's words would have challenged the values and allegiance of any Roman soldier. No doubt our Roman soldier could have arrested Jesus on the spot. What, though, if our soldier's heart was touched by Jesus's words? What if he decided to follow Jesus? Such a change of allegiance would be dramatic, disorienting, and perhaps life threatening.

For our Roman soldier's world had profoundly shaped him. For years he had perceived and interpreted his world through Roman eyes. Crucial, *largely unquestioned Roman principles* for living well were deeply ingrained in his mind and body. A faithful response to Jesus was no easier for him in his Roman world than it is for us in our modern one.

The central issue for ancient Christians—and particularly for the martyrs—was that of allegiance. Early Christians realized that their primary allegiance and loyalty must be to Christ, not to the demands of competing political and religious ideologies. The situation has not changed for us today.

In the United States the issue of ultimate allegiance always faces the Christian. American Christians experience cultural pressure to demonstrate their loyalty to American values—political, economic, and social—even when those values contradict or conflict with the values of Christ's kingdom. This is especially true in our time of global terrorism and war, with deep political polarization at home.

### Pause and Reflect

Pause for a moment and reflect on the issue of allegiance. What American values—or values of your own country—may be opposed to the values of the kingdom of God?

Try listing a few.

No human culture perfectly matches the kingdom. Now list your allegiances on a piece of paper. Do these allegiances correspond to the values of Christ's kingdom? How might Jesus want to reorient your allegiance in a more faithful kingdom direction? Try to be as specific as possible.

Ask the Lord for the insight and power to live his different way.

## Moderation, Proportion, Discretion

When I first got interested in the discipline of simplicity, I thought to myself, surely cheaper purchases best represent the values of the kingdom of God. And then I bought a Simca. A cheap red Simca. Here's what happened.

Debbie and I had moved to France in 1980 to help plant a church right across the border from Geneva in Ferney, Voltaire's hometown. We needed a car as we lived thirty-six kilometers up the road from Ferney in a beautiful little French town named Gex.

So one afternoon I set out with my best pal, Gary Edmonds, to find a car. Monds knew me well and was well aware of my impulsive streak, especially when I'm shopping. This is one of the reasons my wife starts frowning when I head off to the mall. It's rare that I'm allowed to go by myself.

Monds and I were in his car, driving past various car dealerships, when I told him to slow down. Ahead on our left was a promising place; cars were lined up in neat rows, and there, in the distance, I spotted a small, sporty-looking red car. I had to take a closer look, for I love red cars.

"Pull in here, Monds. I want to take a look at that red car." Monds gave me a skeptical look and warned, "Don't be impulsive. Take your time. There's lots of cars to look at. We don't have to buy one today."

"I know," I replied, "I know. But that red one"—I learned later it was a Simca—"looks great."

"Looks aren't everything," Monds advised.

A French car salesman spotted us across the lot and immediately noticed my interest in the Simca. It must have been the glazed look in my eyes. "*Ah, oui, oui, mon ami. Cette une super voiture, mon ami, et pas chère! Et rouge, mon ami. Rouge!*" ("Ah, yes, yes, my friend. It's a great car, my friend, and not expensive. And red, my friend. Red!")

I was close to buying the car, simply because of the color. When my new bosom buddy said "pas chère!" the deal was completed in my mind. I glanced at the car sticker, and he was right. It was a used car and around seven thousand francs, roughly a thousand bucks at that time.

And red. What could be better? And by buying cheap, I'd be practicing the discipline of simplicity. Or so I imagined.

I took the Simca for a quick test drive; it was peppy and fun. "I'm buying it, Monds."

"Why?" Monds responded grumpily. "Because it's red? Take your time. We don't need to buy a car today."

"You're wrong, pal. This is the one." Monds growled and got into his car after I'd signed the necessary papers. I seem to remember he wouldn't look at me on the way home.

Well, as things turned out, the car was indeed a disaster. I think it was possessed by an evil spirit. The door on the driver's side would fly open unexpectedly. The steering was off. In snowstorms the car delighted in swerving off the road. The engine needed constant repair. In the first six months I owned that Simca, I spent at least another seven thousand francs on repairs. I can still hear the car murmuring to me when I got in to drive, "I have something special planned for you today," and often that was exactly the case.

Suffice it to say, I finally had to admit my mistake and turn in the car for a more expensive Volvo. I had thought I was practicing simplicity, but I was actually practicing stupidity. The Volvo was much more reliable, and I ended up spending much less money in the long run than I had on the Simca. I learned the way of simplicity is not always "cheaper is better."

Less is more is a good general principle as we move into a simple life with Jesus. But let's get one thing clear. By less I don't mean not having a roof over your head, or lacking sufficient clothing or food, or access to good schools, or the opportunity to have a job that pays a fair wage.

I do mean that joy expands rather than constricts in a context of moderation, proportion, and discretion. I discovered this one evening when dinnertime with the kids and Deb had just finished.

## Häagen-Dazs!

The year was around 1992, my first year as an assistant professor of theological and biblical studies at Eastern University. I had finally finished years of graduate studies, and by God's grace Eastern hired me.

Assistant professors didn't make a lot of money at that time—they still don't—but we were happy that I was finally drawing a regular salary. Deb had also been hired as a teachers' assistant at what came to be our home church, so we were able to pay the rent, shop for groceries, and clothe ourselves and the three kids without too much strain. We weren't poor, but we weren't rich. We surely had to be careful with expenses and luxuries.

So as a general rule, we didn't have dessert with dinner. The kids learned to do without. One evening, though, when dinner had ended, I thought it was time for a treat. Suddenly, I raised my voice and arms at the table and pronounced, "Tonight we will have Häagen-Dazs!" Deb looked at me as though I'd lost my mind, but I insisted. "Tonight, Häagen-Dazs!" The kids were delighted. I'm not sure whether they knew what Häagen-Dazs was, but dessert sounded great.

As we climbed in the car, I described to everyone the delight of Häagen-Dazs ice cream bars. Silent, happy expectation filled the cabin of our Mazda hatchback as we drove down to the grocery store. We arrived and walked in a solemn procession to the frozen foods refrigerator. There, behind the frosted glass of the ice cream case, were stacked Häagen-Dazs chocolate ice cream bars sprinkled with almonds. For a moment, we paused and simply gazed.

Then I handed everyone a bar. We made our way to the checkout aisle, each carrying our treasures reverently. I paid for the ice cream bars—Deb gulped a bit when she saw how much they cost—and we headed out to the car. We settled down, opened the bars, and began munching. Glances and sighs of enjoyment were exchanged.

"They're really good," the kids murmured. And they were. Even better was the joy filling a family of image-bearers on this special occasion. Moderation (rarely did we have dessert) combined with proportion (only one bar each) and discretion (this was the right night to have a special treat) provided a wonderful occasion for joy.

Deb and I still remember that evening jaunt for Häagen-Dazs, and so do the kids—some twenty-five years later. We would have broken the bank if we made Häagen-Dazs a nightly event, but moderate scarcity increased our joy. Now, when I can afford a Häagen-Dazs bar whenever I want, the deep joy I experienced that special night has dissipated a bit. I still enjoy them, though!

## Steps into a Simple Life with Jesus

Creatures who are *incurvatus in se*—curved in on themselves—instinctively place their ego at the center. This is our fallen default position. Foster observes, "The self clamors for attention, self-recognition, applause. Through artful deception, it appears to be younger, wiser, richer, saintlier than is actually the case. The self will go to extravagant lengths to seem to belong to the intelligentsia. In meetings, it will quote authors it has never read or maintain a discreet silence in supposed superiority over so uneducated a group."[9]

Ortberg suggests the practice of *secrecy* as a helpful antidote to the incessant demands of a bent self. "Here is this practice in a nutshell: Every once in a while, do something good and try to make sure no one finds out about it. Join the club for recovering approval addicts that might be called 'Righteous Anonymous.'"[10] Foster reinforces Ortberg's point: "Nothing *disciplines* the inordinate desires of the flesh like service, and nothing *transforms* the desires of the flesh like serving in hiddenness. The flesh whines against service but screams against hidden service. It strains and pulls for honor and recognition. It will devise subtle, religiously acceptable means to call attention to the service rendered."[11]

Ortberg's and Foster's advice surely lines up well with Jesus's teaching in the Sermon on the Mount. "But when you give to the needy, do not let your left hand know what your right hand is doing, so that your giving may be in secret. Then your Father, who sees what is done in secret, will reward you" (Matt. 6:3–4).

## Pause and Reflect

**When have you tried to draw people's attention to your good deeds? What practical steps into secrecy can you take this week?**

What are some practical steps into simplicity? Try to eliminate pretending. Professors—I used to be one—pretend all the time. Because we have expertise in one area, usually quite focused and narrow, we pretend our expertise covers much broader territory. We like to be recognized for our knowledge, even in areas where we know very little! Each time image-bearers pretend, we dent our souls.

Professors are tempted to impress others with their degrees, titles, articles, or books written, or the honors they've received. It's legitimate to celebrate when we've earned a degree or been given an honor. I have a few diplomas on my home office wall. If I placed them there for other folks to see and think, *My, Chris must be really smart*, I would be trying to manage people's impression of me. If they're up there for my eyes to notice from time to time as a remembrance of God's grace and some hard work on my part, that's a different matter. Simplicity asks us to embrace the truth and not to manipulate impressions through our purchases or accomplishments.

> ### Pause and Reflect
>
> **When are you tempted to pretend? In what areas? Why are you pretending? What is the impression you're trying to create? Why do you think this impression is important? Are there particular people in your circle of acquaintances and friends you try to impress?**

I ask myself, "How can I learn to use words more simply and truly? When do I try to manipulate or exploit people with my words? What am I hoping to gain?" Foster comments, "Where simplicity abounds, words can be taken at face value: there is no hidden agenda."[12]

What about our relationship with things? I've found Foster's insights regarding the "tyranny of things" to be very helpful. Here are a few of his suggestions:

1. *Buy things for their usefulness rather than their status.* "As for your clothes, wear your clothes until they are worn out. Stop trying to impress people with your clothes and impress them with your life."[13] This quote from Foster is one of my favorites from *Celebration of Discipline*. It bridles my tendency to impress people with things that really aren't all that impressive.

2. *Reject anything that is producing an addiction in you, anything that is diverting or replacing your fundamental allegiance to the kingdom.*[14] For instance, I have to discipline myself regarding how much chocolate I eat or how much Coke Zero I drink. I sometimes break a chocolate bar in two, eat half, and am

just as satisfied. I'm reducing caffeinated drinks from my diet, and in time I hope to limit my caffeine intake to two cups of coffee in the morning. Small steps toward change work best for me. Other folks find it's best to just go cold turkey.

3. *Develop the habit of giving things away. Deaccumulate.*[15] About once a year Debbie walks through our house, looking to discard or give away any items we no longer need or desire. Though I sometimes growl, it's a helpful exercise that keeps the house from filling up with unnecessary stuff.

4. *Learn to enjoy things without owning them.*[16] We enjoyed our faculty membership at the university pool. Would I have really been happier if my fantasy of a pool in the backyard was fulfilled?

5. *Experiment with the idea of a graduated tithe.* So what's a graduated tithe? Well, try determining how much income you need to meet all your basic needs over the next year. Then add on a generous amount for savings, vacations, entertainment, and so on. Let's say you determine that $80,000 a year will meet adequately—not extravagantly—all your needs and moderate desires. You decide to tithe 10 percent on the $80,000. Then, say, your yearly income increases to $85,000 in two years' time. Rather than tithing 10 percent on the $5,000 increase, you tithe 15 percent. With each increase in income, you increase your tithe. Finally, you reach a point where you are tithing 100 percent of any increase in annual income. This is not unrealistic because you were very generous with yourself when you started tithing, for you carefully determined what yearly income you needed to meet all expenses, savings, vacation, and so on. A graduated tithe gently disciplines our tendency to think that with an increase in income we necessarily must increase our lifestyle.

I hope you find these concrete steps toward a simple life with Jesus helpful and encouraging. Jesus is clear: he calls us to seek first the kingdom of God. When we listen to his voice, when we attend to his desire for us, we realize how far we fall short of his command. I'm self-indulgent. I don't like to be pushed beyond my comfort zone. My loyalties are still divided. I surely can speak out of both sides of my mouth. Jesus is calling me to grow in simplicity in this, my eighth decade. Perhaps you feel the same way. It is never too late to respond to Christ's call to live a different way with him.

Christ calls us to honesty, openness, and receptivity, with God and others. The discipline of confession, the topic of our next chapter, provides just the opportunity.

# CHAPTER TEN

# Confess What Is in Your Heart

It is clear from the New Testament that the Lord Jesus came
as a Friend, in order to help sinners to come to Him. Our
coming to him was made possible by His first coming to us.

—Watchman Nee

To err is human; to confess one's error, wise.

—Jerome

To be gentle with oneself is to express what God does to me
daily. It is to express his mercy, his truth. We are sinners,
but don't forget the word "saved" before you call yourself
a sinner. We are saved sinners. God saved us, brought us
back to his Father, so be gentle in facing yourself.

—Catherine De Hueck Doherty

Throughout this book, the overarching narrative thread has been
keeping in step with Jesus on his different way. Why would we
desire to step into his shoes, to walk with him, to choose purposely to follow a different way with him? We want to do so because we
have heard in his words and seen in his actions an invitation to friendship, forgiveness, healing, and wholeness.

In this chapter, we explore the spiritual discipline of confession—the sacrament of confession from a Catholic perspective—a discipline Jesus never practiced, for he had no sins to confess. He led a sinless life. Yet, though Jesus never sinned, he understood the dynamics of sin very well. He experienced temptation. He saw the effect of sin on his image-bearers. He sought out sinful people to deliver them from sin's harm, pain, and sorrow.

What is especially striking is sinful folks' eagerness to be with Jesus. They sensed he would know what to do with their stuff. He would not condemn them. He would not scream at them. Yet he would not condone their sin. Instead, he taught his precious image-bearers how to deal with sin as he walked a different way with them as their friend.

## Christ—the Friend of Sinners

Jesus is the friend—not the enemy—of sinful people. If he weren't, where would we be? Not only is Jesus our friend; he knows what to do with all our stuff, all the nastiness that keeps us awake at night wondering if God could ever love someone who's done the things we've done and thought the things we've thought. Thank God, Jesus is the greatest expert in dealing with human sin that has ever lived. He is the great physician of the soul. Jesus is our friend, not our enemy. The first step we take, then, in confessing our sin is always toward Jesus. Every time we're honest with Jesus in confession, our friendship with him deepens.

Sometimes, though, I have a conversation like this with Jesus: "Lord, aren't you tired of me? I've done it again. I told you the last time we had this conversation that I would never do this again. And I've done the very thing I said I wouldn't do. I'm tired of myself, Lord. I'm tired of letting you down. I'm tired of confessing the same thing again and again. Aren't you tired of me?"

Have you ever felt this way? Have you ever felt you've sinned one too many times, that Jesus is simply tired of dealing with you?

The wonder and beauty are that Jesus never tires of us, for we are his precious image-bearers. There is not a single story in the Bible where a sinful person comes to Jesus and honestly confesses he has sinned, and Jesus turns away in anger or disgust. Not one. Jesus has no desire to discourage sinners, for he wants to help us change and learn a different way to live. He knows scolding doesn't help. Nagging doesn't help. Condemnation doesn't help. He doesn't yell at folks who want to change. He saves his yelling for the self-righteous.

The folks who drive Jesus crazy are those who don't recognize or acknowledge their sin. These blind souls are the finger-pointers, the courtroom prosecutors, the screamers. They point their fingers at others and shout, "You are the one!"—shockingly oblivious to their own sin.

Jesus consistently teaches that God loves lost people and welcomes them home with open arms. This idea drove crazy many Pharisees and teachers of the law. "This man welcomes sinners and eats with them," they complained. Did you hear the operative word? Jesus "welcomes" sinners. His enemies knew this, and it infuriated them (Luke 15:2). *God would never act like that,* they thought. Yet Jesus didn't back down. He knew what God is like.

In Luke 15, Luke gathers a group of Jesus's parables, each story describing God's concern for folks who are lost. In each parable Jesus teaches that God delights in finding what is lost. God is like a shepherd who loses a sheep, leaves "the ninety-nine in the open country," and finds the lost, wandering sheep. God is like a woman who loses a coin and searches high and low until she has found it. God is like the father of a wandering, dissipated son who welcomes the wanderer home with open arms (Luke 15:1–32). Not only is the dissolute son welcomed home; his father throws a party for him upon his return.

"It's too good to be true," we say to ourselves. "No, it's not," Jesus replies. "You're lost. You've wandered. I just want you to come home. The door is open. The lights are on. The table is set. It's time we talked and had a nice meal together."

In each parable, Jesus relentlessly drives home the same point: "I tell you that in the same way there will be more rejoicing in heaven over one sinner who repents than over ninety-nine righteous persons who do not need to repent" (Luke 15:7). "In the same way, I tell you, there is rejoicing in the presence of the angels of God over one sinner who repents" (Luke 15:10). "But we had to celebrate and be glad, because this brother of yours was dead and is alive again; he was lost and is found" (Luke 15:32).

## Pause and Reflect

Here's an exercise you might engage in for the next six months or year. Repeatedly read all four Gospels. Read slowly. Take time to meditate on stories where Jesus helps people deal with their sin. What themes are repeatedly emphasized? What surprises and encourages you?

As you read, slow down when you find Jesus talking about specific sins or helping individual image-bearers who are struggling with sin. In John's Gospel, for instance, I think of the conversation Jesus had with a Samaritan woman (John 4) and the situation with the woman caught in adultery (John 8). Jesus's encounter with Zacchaeus the tax gatherer, a well-known sinner, also comes to mind (Luke 19:1–10). The Gospels are filled with stories like these. Just think of all the times Jesus helps the disciples fess up to their own sin (cf. Mark 10:13–16; 2:13–17). They, too, had lots of stuff to deal with.

As you meditate, ask yourself questions like these: What in the words and actions of Jesus is God offering me? What does Jesus want me to learn? How is Jesus loving me through his earthly ministry? How is he helping me change and move to a new place in my relationship with God? How is Jesus helping me deal with all my stuff? Jesus

**taught and acted with you in mind. And me. I think you'll walk away from this exercise encouraged.**

## Living Beneath the Cross

Ponder with me Dietrich Bonhoeffer's perspective on learning to live beneath the cross of Jesus. Bonhoeffer's words are worth quoting in full: "Anybody who lives beneath the Cross and who has discerned in the Cross of Jesus the utter wickedness of all men and of his own heart will find there is no sin that can ever be alien to him. Anybody who has once been horrified by the dreadfulness of his own sin that nailed Jesus to the Cross will no longer be horrified by even the rankest sins of a brother."[1]

As we live beneath the cross we learn to welcome confession as a gift. By God's grace and power, a cruciform self-awareness slowly develops in our minds and hearts. We see who we are. We confess who we are and what we have done. And our love and compassion for other sinful image-bearers grows. Healing from the cross flows into our veins, and through the power of the Holy Spirit we offer the healing we have received to others.

If I live beneath the cross, how could I ever scold, manipulate, exploit, reject, or condemn a struggling image-bearer who comes to me and asks, "Can you help me? I'm stuck. I've got so much stuff in my life, and it's killing me. I need to talk to somebody about it. I want to get to a new place." For, as Richard J. Foster writes, those who live under the cross of Jesus "are delivered from the danger of spiritual domination. We have stood where our brother now stands and so the desire to use his confession against him is gone. Nor do we feel any need to control him or to straighten him out. All we feel is acceptance and understanding."[2]

What characterizes wise, compassionate image-bearers who live beneath the cross? The incarnate love embodied in Jesus on the cross teaches us it's safe—indeed life-giving—to confess our sin to Christ and to name it for what it is. Jesus will know what to do with the stuff we bring to him.

## Come Home

Jesus asks us to come to our senses. "Admit that life's not working," Jesus urges. "You've lost your way. You're hurting others. You're hurting yourself. It's time to head home. It's time for new beginnings. It's time to follow a different way."

Maybe all we're able to do initially is ask for the grace to go no farther into our sin. We acknowledge to God that our disordered desires run deep. "I'll never do this again, Lord" hasn't worked. We humbly and honestly ask God to change our desires. "Lord, I love doing this. Yet I know it's killing me. I know it's wrong. And I'm hurting those around me. Help me develop new habits of love to replace my disordered loves. I need mercy, Lord. Lots of it. And I need to learn a different way for dealing with my sin and living a different way. The old ways aren't working. I need your friendship and help to get to a new place."

So we start by fessing up. Yet because the sinful patterns in our lives are often deeply habituated, we shouldn't be surprised if our sins don't magically disappear when we confess them. This rarely happens. After all, we've spent years developing our anger, or greed, or lust, or whatever the sin may be. It's been part of the landscape of our lives for a long time. Don't despair, John Chrysostom encourages. Try for two days. If you can make it for two days, "you will keep off on the third day more easily; and after three days you will add ten, then twenty, then a hundred, than your whole life."[3]

Try small, slow, Spirit-empowered steps in the right direction. And when we stumble—which we surely will—we confess our sin, rejoice in our forgiveness, and keep moving in the same direction. Rarely if ever can we do this on our own. We've tried on our own for too long, and we've failed. We link arms with Jesus and other trusted friends and begin to learn a different way.

## Pause and Reflect

Is Jesus inviting you to come home? Why are you reluctant to begin the journey home with him? What are you loving that Jesus is asking you not to love? Which sins of yours have become habitual? List them on a piece of paper.

What concrete steps in the power of the Spirit can you take in a new direction? Who do you know who can help you with these habitual sins?

## Keep Your Eyes on Yourself

Keep your attention focused on Jesus and on yourself. Avoid comparing yourself to others; we all have enough stuff to work on. When we compare ourselves to others, we invariably get it wrong. Comparison is the path of the proud; it is the path of the blind. It feeds dissatisfaction with others—and with ourselves.

Jesus often describes self-righteous people as being blind. In Matthew 23 he turns up the volume as he scolds the teachers of the law and Pharisees for their hypocrisy and the heavy burdens they lay on other people: "Woe to you, blind guides!" (Matt. 23:16); "You blind men!" (Matt. 23:19).

Blind people, by definition, can't see. And yet self-righteous folks—people apt to condemn themselves with others—claim to possess eyesight so clear they can judge another person's thoughts and life. They focus on others rather than themselves but do so with blind eyes. They are blind as bats.

"Look at what you're doing!" is a favorite phrase of the self-righteous. "Thank God I can see what's really going on." The self-righteous resemble the Pharisee Jesus describes in Luke 18:11: "The Pharisee stood by himself and prayed: 'God, I thank you that I am not like other people—robbers, evildoers, adulterers—or even like this tax collector.'"

The tax collector, unlike the Pharisee, begged for God's mercy. He knew he was a sinner. "But the tax collector stood at a distance. He would not even look up to heaven, but beat his breast and said, 'God, have mercy on me, a sinner'" (Luke 18:13).

Jesus warns against self-righteousness and moral judgmentalism in his Sermon on the Mount (Matt. 7:1–5). He cautions against judging another person's sin. How, Jesus asks, could we ever imagine we see clearly enough to judge another? Though our neighbor may have a spot of dust in his eye, we have a whopping plank in our own.[4]

Pause for a moment and imagine a board covering your eyes. Your field of vision is entirely blocked. All you see is wood. Still, despite our blindness, do we not have a penchant for judging others? How quick we are to point our finger at someone else! Instead, Jesus teaches, we should be thumping our own chests.

## Projection

In the early 1980s, I attended a conference in London led by John Stott. You may have been helped by John's writings. He was a wonderful Bible teacher. One evening John graciously invited several conference attendees over to his apartment for dinner. Somehow, I was on the invitation list. During dinner conversation we discussed the dynamics of sin and our tendency to project our sin onto others and condemn it in them.

John told the story of traveling with a pastor friend. They were going to their destination by way of the London Tube. As they descended into the Tube on the downward escalator, the advertising covering the walls caught the attention of John's friend. Much of it was sexually charged. Photographs of attractive models, most scantily clad, predominated. I think they were selling lingerie, perfumes, and liquor. Few of the models were wearing overalls!

Suddenly John's friend started talking loudly about the moral decline of the English, the rampant immorality that surrounded travelers, and how advertising had sunk to new lows. His companion's voice grew louder and louder.

John stepped off the escalator and began to walk toward the underground train; suddenly he realized his companion wasn't with him. He turned to see his pastor friend back on the escalator, heading up! He was still ranting but now to an audience of one.

John wasn't surprised to later learn that his friend and fellow traveler was addicted to pornography. This poor image-bearer, subconsciously horrified by his own sin, had projected it onto the advertisers and models and was judging it in them.

## Help from the Desert Dwellers

The desert dwellers warned against judging others and were well aware of the danger of projection, though they wouldn't have known the precise term. Judging others was at the top of their "avoid this at all costs" list. How might their insights help us think and live a different way with Jesus as our guide?

These ancient sisters and brothers of ours took very seriously Jesus's warning that we will be judged by God with the same measure or standard we have used in judging others (Matt. 7:1–5). Though the desert dwellers weren't averse to making moral judgments concerning right and wrong, they warned against judging and condemning people who appeared to be guilty of sin. Desert mothers or fathers were much more likely to condemn themselves than another.

Abba Moses is a helpful example. Moses was a tall African who in his younger days was notorious in Egypt as a very cruel man, a murderer and thief. Occasionally, Moses would swim across the Nile and slaughter the sheep and goats of local shepherds, not because he was hungry but simply for the joy of killing.

There was a lot of blood on Moses's hands when he entered the kingdom of God. He never forgot this. Moses had been forgiven much. Over the course of his life as a monastic leader in the Egyptian desert Abba Moses came to be known, admired, and loved for his wisdom, profound self-awareness, and gentleness. The following story from Abba Moses's life illustrates how much his faith in Christ changed him. He had indeed chosen to follow a different way.

"In Scete [an area in Northern Egypt where desert dwellers lived in community], a brother was once found guilty. They assembled the elders, and sent a message to Abba Moses telling him to come. Then the presbyter sent, saying, 'Come, for a meeting of monks is waiting for you.' Moses rose up and went. He took with him an old basket which he filled with sand and carried on his back. The people who went to meet him said: 'What is this, Father?' The old man said to them: 'My sins are chasing me, and I do not see them—have I come today to judge the sins of someone else?' They listened to him, and said nothing to the erring brother, but pardoned him."[5]

This story was well known among the desert dwellers and occurs in more than one form in ancient desert literature. In one story, Abba Moses's basket is filled with sand. In another, he places a cask filled with water on his back. I imagine the brothers' nervousness when the large ex-murderer pulled out a knife and started poking holes in the cask! As Abba Moses walked to the meeting, his sins leaked out behind him. The point of both versions is identical and still applicable to us today: Don't play the judge! We don't see our own sins. We're too blind to do so.

Abba Moses had been called to judge a brother's sin, and all the while his own sins trailed behind him. Abba Moses explicitly says, "I do not see them." Isn't this Jesus's very point in his teaching in Matthew 7? Our moral sight tends to be blurred, foggy, cloudy. Still, rather than focusing on our own sins, we somehow consider ourselves qualified to judge those of another.

Does this mean that we shouldn't be concerned about sin? No. The desert dwellers are much more interested, though, in helping precious image-bearers stop sinning than in condemning them. The wounds of a friend are one thing, the condemnation of the self-righteous another. One leads to life, the other death.

Our next story from the desert illustrates the danger of projection: "A brother, being tempted by a demon, went to an old man and said: 'Those two monks over there who live together, live wickedly.' But the old man knew that a demon was playing with him, and he sent and called them to him. And at evening he put a mat for them, and covered them with a single blanket, and said: 'They are sons of God, and holy persons.' But he said to his disciple: 'Shut this slandering brother up in a room by himself: he is suffering from the passions of which he accuses them.'"[6]

One brother—the slanderer—is absolutely convinced the other two brothers are sinning sexually with each other. Thankfully, the older, wiser abba discerns what's genuinely going on. A demon is playing with the slanderer. One blanket will suffice for the two accused brothers, for they are sons of God and holy persons. The accusing brother is suffering from the very sin he is so quick to condemn. A long time-out for the judgmental brother is the medicine recommended.

Self-righteous, judgmental people tend to be harsh, self-deceived, angry, and sad. In all likelihood, they were once treated harshly by others. Did they once confess their sin to another, only to be scolded or even condemned? Perhaps the self-righteous folks we sometimes encounter have concluded it's not safe to be honest about sin. Or sadly, maybe the only examples they've seen of someone addressing another's sin were harsh, angry, condemning ones. Surely there's a different way, a better way, to help one another grow into holiness and love and leave an unhappy life of sin behind.

How we long for gentle, wise, compassionate people to come alongside, link arms with us, and walk with us on our journey through this present evil age. Robert Wicks describes the desert dwellers as just this kind of people. "There is nothing so strong as gentleness and nothing so gentle as real strength. Having a better sense of themselves and God enabled them to be compassionate in a freer, more natural, and kinder way. It wasn't that there was never a time for being firm. But their self-knowledge and awareness of their own frailties gave rise to a special sensitivity to individual situations and an appreciation of the value of pacing with respect to spiritual growth."[7]

Reflect with me on another desert story, one Wicks believes captures well the wisdom, gentleness, and compassion of the desert dwellers. It's one of my favorites.

"A few of the brothers came to see Abba Poemen. They said to him, 'Tell us what to do when we see brothers dozing during prayer. Should we pinch them to help them stay awake?' The elder said to them, 'Actually what I would do if I saw a brother sleeping is to put his head on my knees and let him rest.'"[8]

Don't you long to be in relationship with someone like that? Someone who knew your heated temptations and great sins, and simply allowed you to rest your head on his lap? You can trust people like that. You know that they have struggled themselves and that your sins are not foreign to them. They will never harshly scold or scream. And in all likelihood, they'll be expert guides on a different way to holiness and love. For they have walked in Jesus's steps and are his friends.

A fourth story from the desert dwellers again shows a different way—a better way—to deal with sin than anger and condemnation: "A certain brother was incited by lust. He rose up in the night and went to tell his temptations to an old man—an abba—and the old man consoled him. So, the younger brother returned to his room, comforted. Again, he was tempted by the spirit of lust. And a second time he went to the old man. This happened several times. The old man did not reproach him, but spoke words that helped. 'Don't yield to the devil. Guard your soul. Whenever the demon comes to tempt you, come to me, rebuke him, and he will go away. Nothing troubles the demon of lust more than for his tactics to be disclosed. Nothing pleases him more than for the temptation to be concealed.' Eleven times the brother went to the old man, and blamed himself for his imaginings. 'Please, Abba, speak to me a word.' The old man said to him, 'Believe me, my son, if God allowed the imaginings that goad me to be passed to you, you could not bear them. They would destroy you.' And so, by his words and deep humility, that brother found rest from the stimulation of lust."[9]

Let's break the story down. A young man—in this case a fledgling monk—is struggling with a heated temptation to lust; in all likelihood if the temptation continues, he will seek relief by finding someone to sleep with. Yet he has the courage to share his struggle with a wise, gentle abba, perhaps the leader of the young man's community.

The temptation doesn't immediately disappear. In fact, the young man comes many times the same night to confess his struggle and seek relief. He has not yet sinned with his body but is sorely tempted. So how does the older monk respond? He receives the young monk patiently, refuses to scold him for having such thoughts, and encourages him to rebuke the devil, who in this case, the abba discerns, is the source of the temptation.

The battle is long and hard. Finally, the power of the temptation dissipates as the abba shares that he, too, struggles with sexual temptation. In fact, the old man's temptations are more intense and severe than what the young man is experiencing. The young monk discovers he is not isolated in his temptation. Even holy people, like this abba whom he deeply admires, experience temptation. The abba's humble and grace-filled words strengthen the young man, and finally the power of his temptation crumbles.

## The Cycle of Sin

Let's further ponder the dynamics of temptation, sin, and confession. I've noticed that temptation and sin often occur in cycles. The cycle begins with temptation: a thought arises or there is an impulse in our body, sometimes in response to a cue of some kind in our environment.

Suddenly, out of the blue, a heated temptation envelops us. And sometimes—not always—we succumb to the temptation. We sin. Our sin is quickly followed by another temptation: the temptation to keep our sin to ourselves. "Nobody's going to find out about this," we say to ourselves, as shame and remorse engulf us. Our isolation and loneliness in our sin deepen.

There we are alone with our sin, isolated in our guilt and shame, and paralyzed as to what we should do. We want to stop the sinful behavior, but the roadblocks of shame, guilt, isolation, and habituation prevent us from discerning the way to freedom. Self-loathing swells. Terrible thoughts swirl within:

- *What's wrong with me?*
- *What kind of a person would do something like this?*
- *I'm worthless.*
- *I'm a horrible person.*
- *If other people found out, they'd desert me.*
- *How can I hide what I've done? What am I going to do?*

Hopelessness attacks us in our isolation. *I'll never change. I'm trapped. I'll never get beyond this. Never. I might as well do it again.* And so, the cycle repeats itself: temptation, sin, shame and guilt, isolation, self-loathing, hopelessness, temptation, sin.

Can the cycle be broken? Yes, but not on our own.

Thankfully, I've been blessed with mentors and friends who've helped me with my own sins. Hopefully, you have, too. I've learned from them. Some lived long before my time. I think of the desert dwellers. Others are still alive. I think of a mentor at the first Bible school I ever attended, a wise soul whose gentle severity helped me reset my moral compass in the direction of the kingdom of God.

## Gentle Severity

If I choose to live in a manner diametrically opposed to Jesus's teaching and the values of his kingdom, I'll inevitably experience misery. Why? I'm living against the grain of the universe. I'm spitting into the wind. I'm butting my head against the wall of reality. That hurts.

I've shared with you my struggle with God over the divorce of my parents. My anger toward God combined with my natural penchant for self-indulgence—I'm a seven on the enneagram—led to a stretch of overdrinking.

I had just graduated from UCLA and was living and studying at a new, unaccredited Bible school next to campus.

One night I got drunk, climbed into a shopping cart, and rolled down a hill in Westwood at three in the morning. All the while I shouted, "Woo-hah! Woo-hah!" at the top of my lungs. It seemed like a good idea. It wasn't.

Neighbors of the Bible school didn't appreciate my late-night serenade and reported it to the teachers I had come to admire.

The morning after my escapade I had a conversation with a kind, gentle teacher who became a formative influence in my life, a life coach of sorts. After morning class ended, he asked if we might have a talk. I said sure.

"Chris, did you drink too much last night?"

"Yep." I was still feeling some of the effects. *What's the problem?* I thought to myself.

"Did you get into a shopping cart and head off down the hill into Westwood, shouting, 'Woo-hah' at the top of your lungs?"

"Yep." Seemed like acceptable behavior to me.

"So, Chris, let me explain something to you. If you ever do that again, you'll be out of this school before you can blink an eye."

He caught my attention. "Really?"

"Yes," my wise teacher gently but firmly responded. He didn't yell. He didn't shame. He simply explained why my behavior was a bad idea and wouldn't be tolerated.

I listened. And I experienced his gentle severity. His words stung, but I knew he wasn't speaking in anger. I knew he wasn't giving up on me. He ended our time with wise, kind words of forgiveness. I experienced a "good misery" that God gracefully used to help me reset my moral compass, which for too long had been spinning wildly.

## The Temptation to Euphemize

In a nutshell, confession is honesty and openness before God concerning our sin. When we confess our sins, we come to God and name our sin for what it is. If we've been greedy, we say, "Lord, I have been greedy, and here's how, when, and where." If we've been envious, we name our envy for what it is. Or our lust. Or our greed. Or our pride. As George Buttrick encourages, "Confession, like thanksgiving, should be specific. It should not be ruthless, but it should not excuse; it should set hooks into the facts. 'I confess this sharp judgment, this jealousy, this cowardice, this bondage to dark habit, this part in the world's evil.'"[10]

As we confess, we may be tempted to euphemize. We euphemize when we use words or phrases to lessen the seriousness or severity of what we've done. As one dictionary puts it, to euphemize is to "cushion the blow of reality, allowing us to avoid an unpleasant word or topic." For instance, German SS troops consistently euphemized in their recordkeeping at concentration camps such as Auschwitz or Dachau. "We processed 17,000 units today." No. Absolutely not. You didn't "process 17,000 units." You killed 17,000 innocent people, 17,000 precious image-bearers.

In light of our tendency to euphemize, I'd encourage you to be as specific as possible in your times of confession. Name something for what it is. If you've committed adultery, name it for what it is. "Lord, I committed adultery with . . . ; I confess my sin. I name it for what it is." If you've envied your colleague's promotion, name it for what it is. "Lord, I was envious of . . . when she was promoted, and I was passed over. I name my envy for what it is." Our willingness to be specific with our sin weakens its power over us in a way that broad generalities don't.

## Pause and Reflect

Here's an exercise you might find helpful. Pray through your life decade by decade. Ask the Lord to bring to your awareness particular instances of sin that you sense were never adequately acknowledged. Confess your way through the years. You might engage in this exercise with a trusted friend, pastor, or priest.

Although this exercise may initially sound frightening and discouraging, I don't think it will be. You're inviting Christ's light and love into darkness that overshadowed your life at specific times and places, and sometimes with specific people. When you've finished the exercise—you can spread it out over a few months—you'll feel refreshed, renewed, and cleansed.

Be sure to immerse this exercise in the grace of God. Remember that nothing you recall is a surprise to God. Christ is always pleased when we come to him honestly and transparently. Deeper healing occurs as Christ's light invades the hidden crevasses and ravines in our personality and life experiences.

What do we do after we confess our sins? We start again. We get back on our feet. If we fall in the future, we get back up. Each time we get back up, relying on God's strength to help us, we're a little bit stronger, a little bit less apt to sin again in the same way. Our spiritual muscles, once atrophied in a particular area of struggle, are now breathing in the healing oxygen of God.

Perhaps most importantly, with Jesus and hopefully a trusted friend or pastor, we form a strategy for avoiding sin in the future. We ponder questions like these: When does this particular sin tend to occur? Are there times, people, influences, or cues that trigger it? What legitimate need is this sin illegitimately meeting in my life? How can I develop a different way to meet this need? How can my friends or church community help me bring this dead zone in my soul back to life?

## Confession as an Act of Trust

Confession is fundamentally an act of trust.

When I confess my sin, naming it for what it is, I trust that God loves me. I trust that God will not turn away when I confess but rather will embrace me with the loving arms of Jesus, the very one who died for my sin and rose from the dead on my behalf (1 John 1:9). Yes, I trust that God loves me.

When I confess my sin, naming it for what it is, I trust that God has forgiven me. I trust that faith in Christ's sacrifice for me is all I need to receive the forgiveness of God for all my transgressions. All of them. Yes, I trust that God has forgiven me. I invite you to enjoy a nice, long swim in the ocean of God's forgiveness.

When I confess my sin, naming it for what it is, I trust that God, not my sin, gets the last word. God gets the last word, and the last word is "I love you and I forgive you. Let's learn a different way to live together."

When I confess my sin, I trust that new beginnings are possible. I have been reborn. I have been baptized. I have been re-created. I have been renewed. I am God's precious image-bearer. Yes, I trust that new beginnings are possible.

## Pause and Reflect

As I draw this chapter to a close, let's pause and reflect together. Reflect with me on confession as an act of trust. Which of the following questions resonates with your personality and life experience? Some readers may want to journal through these questions. Others will simply want to ponder and pray.

Do you struggle with trusting that God loves you? Why might this be? How might you develop deeper trust in God's love for you?

Do you struggle with trusting that God has forgiven you? Why might this be? How can you deepen your trust in God's forgiveness?

Do you struggle with trusting that God gets the last word regarding your sin, rather than you? Or Satan? What are the words you're tempted to say about your sin that discourage you and push you toward despair and disillusionment? What are the words that God desires to speak to you, perhaps at this very moment? Words of love? Words of encouragement?

Do you struggle with trusting that new beginnings are possible? Why? With renewed hope in the wonder and beauty of God and God's provision on your behalf in Christ, invite Jesus to initiate the new beginnings you long for. Keep your eyes open. God will answer your prayer.

# CHAPTER ELEVEN

# Count It All Joy

It is critical for us to understand that the Spiritual Disciplines
possess no moral rectitude or righteousness in and of themselves.
They are, most definitely, not "works righteousness," as it is
sometimes said. They place us—body, mind, and spirit—before
God. That is all. The results of this process are all of God, all of grace.

—Richard J. Foster

"Spirituality" wrongly understood or pursued is a great
source of human misery and rebellion against God.

—Dallas Willard

We have spent hours together learning how to practice a different way with Jesus. By God's grace, in the future we will continue to trace his footsteps, keeping in step with him, no faster and no slower. Jesus graciously offers his shoes to us.

Now, picture yourself walking with Jesus; he is at your side. As you travel you begin to notice warning signs along the path. Jesus points to these markers, each one warning of misery if followed.

Screwy ideas and wacky practices in spiritual formation cause immense misery. We've seen, for instance, that distorted views of God disrupt and distort our spiritual formation. Dysfunctional views of

God birth a spiritual life from hell, not heaven. They are key misery markers.

Ponder with me other misery markers of sick spiritual formation.

- Sick spiritual formation lacks joy.
- Sick spiritual formation is fueled by effort, rather than the grace of God.
- Sick spiritual formation is self-centered, rather than God-centered.
- Sick spiritual formation relies on technique, rather than relationship.
- Sick spiritual formation constantly takes its own temperature: How am I doing? How am I measuring up?
- Sick spiritual formation concentrates on tasks rather than gifts, doing rather than receiving.
- Sick spiritual formation pictures the spiritual life as duty to God rather than delight in God.
- Sick spiritual formation is exhausting. It tires us out.
- Sick spiritual formation tries and tries but always falls short.
- Sick spiritual formation is shaped by distorted images of God and of ourselves.
- Sick spiritual formation is apt to judge others for their sins and shortcomings.

Wow. That's a lot of misery.

## Counterfeit Spirituality

Counterfeit spirituality discourages, drains, and dries us out. It withers us. We grow old and withered before our time. It characterizes people whom Dallas Willard describes as "unfeeling, stiff, unapproachable, boringly lifeless, obsessive, and dissatisfied."[1] Now think of Jesus. Not one of these words fits him. Jesus unapproachable? Boringly lifeless? Hardly.

A counterfeit looks like the real thing. This is the reason we have trouble distinguishing a sick spiritual life from a healthy one.

Francis de Sales, a kind, direct, sensible coach on the spiritual life, encourages us to set a firm, wise foundation for our life with Christ. Get things right at the beginning, Francis encourages. "Since little faults committed in the beginning of a project grow infinitely greater in its course and finally are almost irreparable, above all else you must know what the virtue of devotion is."[2] If we know what genuine devotion is, we'll be much better prepared to pursue it wisely and safely, and more skilled in identifying its counterfeits.

What is devotion? Francis's answer is simple and clear: "Genuine, living devotion . . . presupposes love of God, and hence it is simply true love of God."[3] Love for God and love for neighbor are the means and the goal of healthy spiritual formation. Every spiritual discipline in some fashion develops love in our lives. If it doesn't, we're practicing it poorly or may need to set it aside for a while.

We don't pursue a different way with Jesus to become experts in spiritual disciplines. We don't pursue a different way to become theologically well informed. We don't pursue a different way to practice silence, solitude, or simplicity for its own sake. We don't pursue a different way to learn how to pray. We pursue a different way with Jesus to develop and nurture love for God and our neighbor.

Each spiritual discipline we've studied in this book trains us in how to love well. The spiritual disciplines are a means of grace God uses to grow our ability to love. Think of the disciplines, then, as the trellis or scaffolding for supporting and facilitating love's growth in our lives.

Francis witnessed plenty of counterfeit spirituality in his day. He worried that "everyone paints devotion according to his own passions and fancies."[4] Some folks are quite disciplined, but their discipline is fruitless. Their character remains barren and loveless.

One person, Francis comments, is very strict in her fasting while her heart "may be filled with hatred." Another is scrupulous about his drinking habits, "but won't hesitate to drink deep of his neighbor's blood by detraction and gossip." Still another "thinks himself devout because he daily recites a vast number of prayers, but after saying them he utters the most disagreeable, arrogant, and harmful words at home and among the neighbors. Another gladly takes a coin out of his purse and gives it to the poor, but he cannot extract kindness from his heart to forgive his enemies."[5]

Spiritual phoniness marks the people Francis describes. Isn't spiritual counterfeiting a skill we all have learned? We detect its presence when the gold of our lives fails to support the currency of our words: "Many persons clothe themselves with certain outward actions connected with holy devotion, and the world believes they are truly devout and spiritual, whereas they are in fact nothing but copies and phantoms of devotion."[6]

## No Tricks or Techniques

Do you recall Thomas Merton's advice on the slow pace of spiritual growth and our tendency to try to speed things up? A good coach will slow us down if we're willing to listen. "Anyone who is trying to deepen his or her life of prayer" will need a good dose of "humility and docile acceptance of sound advice," Merton writes.[7]

A spiritual director can help us navigate our way with Jesus. If we can't find a director, good friends who know Jesus well are indispensable. They help us "recognize God's grace and his will, how to be humble and patient, how to develop insight into our own difficulties, and how to remove the main obstacles keeping us from becoming people of prayer."[8]

For in the spiritual life "there are no tricks and no shortcuts. Those who imagine that they can discover spiritual gimmicks and put them to work for themselves usually ignore God's will and his grace." The last thing we want to do, Merton counsels, is to place our confidence in ourselves and whatever natural abilities God may have given us.

One cannot begin to face the real difficulties of the life of prayer and meditation unless one is first perfectly content to be a beginner and really experience himself as one who knows little or nothing and has a desperate need to learn the bare rudiments. Those who think they "know" from the beginning will never, in fact, come to know anything.[9]

So, in our slow journey traveling with Jesus on a different way, gladly assume the posture of a beginner. We don't want to get ahead of ourselves or Jesus. Know that we're all apt to overestimate our capabilities. Let's grow our self-awareness and become more attuned to where we're apt to be self-deceived. The last place we want to get imprisoned is in ourselves. "We do not want to be beginners," Merton writes. "But let us be convinced of the fact that we will never be anything else but beginners." And that's absolutely fine.[10]

## Coaching from Antony

Antony the Great, perhaps the greatest of the desert dwellers—the monastic friends we've spent time with in this book—was well aware of our tendency to try to speed up our spiritual growth, to bite off more than we can chew.[11]

Antony understood that God's precious image-bearers will experience stiff opposition, both within themselves and from external forces.

He speaks freely of the devil's attempts to run Christ's image-bearers off the road of sensible spiritual perspective and practice, sometimes by tempting us to practice an extreme, oppressive, exaggerated spirituality.

"Therefore, let us pay them [the demons] no heed," Antony exhorts. Treat "them as strangers to us, and let us not obey them, even in the event that they arouse us for prayer, or talk to us about fasting. Rather, let us devote ourselves to our own purpose in the discipline, and not be led astray by them, though they do all things with cunning."[12]

Satan tempted some desert dwellers to live their lives with God in a punitive, unreasonably harsh way. Some monks, for instance, were tempted to spiritual competitiveness. If word got out that one monk was sleeping only four hours a night, neighboring monks might try to make it through the night on three.

How surprising and counterintuitive to discover that Satan might tempt us to pray, fast, or work beyond our capabilities. The demons' tactics are subtle and relentless. "They do not do these things," Antony teaches, "for the sake of piety or truth, but so that they might bring the simple to despair, and declare the discipline useless."[13]

Imagine a young monk who has recently joined the community and is just beginning his journey with God. He looks around at his brothers and is impressed. Some, he observes, are able to pray for hours on end. Others go without food for extended periods of time. Then there are the monastic masters like Antony, whom many call "the great."

So what does our young, immature monk do? He tries to pray or fast or work beyond his ability. When he comes to his senses, he realizes he needs rest, sleep, food. Then the demons attack. "Oh, no. God wants you to pray. God wants you to fast. How can you think of stopping? Don't disappoint God. Don't disappoint yourself. And what would others think if they saw you resting or eating? Keep up the good work. You can pray for another hour, at least."

If our young monk heeds these demonic voices, he'll end up discouraged and disillusioned with himself and with God. The devils know this. Exaggerated, harsh, competitive practices harm rather than help. A good end pursued in a foolish way gets us nowhere.

## Pause and Reflect

**When have you been spiritually discouraged because you've bitten off too much to chew in your relationship with God? We may hear of folks who pray for two or three hours and set the same standard for ourselves, though we've rarely prayed for longer than five or ten minutes. The unhappy but predictable result? Discouragement. Frustration. Anger at ourselves and perhaps at God. "I'll never learn to pray. I might as well give up." Have there been times when you've tried to do too much?**

Antony coaches us to walk before we try to run. Small, consistent steps add up. Know yourself, and acknowledge your weaknesses. God is patient. He does not ask us for more than we can give. Instead, Jesus slowly and gracefully increases our ability to give to him and to others. And by his grace, there comes a time when we can give much more. We will grow, but genuine growth can't be rushed.

John Chrysostom, archbishop of Constantinople, learned this lesson the hard way. John permanently damaged his digestive health by practicing a harsh spiritual discipline. As a young man, John joined a community of monks in the hills above Antioch and set the goal of memorizing much of the Bible. This was an admirable goal, but he pursued it in a foolish way.

John tried to sleep as little as possible. To do so he braced himself against the wall of his cave to stay awake for days on end. Not only this, but Chrysostom started this discipline without consulting his elders. When John's bishop heard what he was up to, he commanded Chrysostom to return to Antioch. Yet the damage to John's health proved permanent. A misguided zeal—and probably a good dose of spiritual pride—caused lasting damage to John's digestive system. He suffered from poor digestion for the rest of his life.

It's better to get a good night's sleep, Antony advises, than to remain awake, if nighttime vigilance and prayer lead to physical, emotional, and spiritual exhaustion. Oppressive spirituality engenders lots of nastiness and misery: discouragement, disillusionment, pride, self-righteousness, a judgmental spirit, and self-deception. The list goes on and on.

## Pause and Reflect

Have you adopted misguided practices in your desire to be formed in Christ's image? Are these practices harming rather than helping you? Are you tempted to impress others with your spiritual performance? Do you imagine that God loves you more if you're spiritually disciplined, and less when you're not? Do you tend to judge others when they fail to meet your standards for faithfulness or obedience, ideals you often fail to reach yourself? Do you find your life with God frustrating and oppressive? Is love growing in your life—or not?

## The Danger of Distraction

Richard J. Foster published a revised edition of *Celebration of Discipline* in 2018. Has Foster's perspective changed since the first publication of his book in 1978? Yes, in one important way: "There is one major difference that has occurred in the past forty years that does indeed impinge upon the spiritual life. I can state it in one word: distraction. Distraction is the primary spiritual problem in contemporary culture. . . . Oh, for the day when all we had to do was turn off the television if we wanted solitude and silence! Now, we click through an endless stream of internet links, write daily blogs, read tweets from God knows who, check our emails constantly, text family and others, and mindlessly scroll through Facebook."[14]

Distracted people have a difficult time identifying and attending to what's genuinely important; they are habitually diverted to less important things. Our distractions can gobble up hours before we know it.

Serious research has been conducted on "the most distracted generation in human history." The attention span of children growing up in our media-saturated environment is decreasing significantly. A Pew Research Center study reports that 90 percent of 2,462 teachers believed digital technologies were creating "an easily distracted generation with short attention spans."[15]

Attentiveness, the opposite of distraction, broadens our field of vision to what matters. Who or what is worthy of our attention? To develop attentiveness and disperse distraction, though, requires an environment that sifts out influences that deflect our attention from what really counts. If our media-saturated environment is fomenting distraction on an unprecedented scale, an occasional media fast might be just the remedy to refocus our attention.[16]

## A Media Fast

I remember the day well. We were not yet halfway through the semester, and the students in Foundations of Christian Spirituality had not done well on their midterm. As I walked down the auditorium aisle to the front of the class, I looked out at 230 sleepy students beginning their day at 8:30 in the morning with me. "How can I help them?" I asked myself. Some seniors were in danger of not graduating in nine weeks. I had no desire to prolong their stay at Eastern.

Then an idea came to me. What if I offered a media fast to students who wished to improve their semester grade? By the time I reached the front of the auditorium I knew what to do.

"Well, some of you haven't done very well on the midterm. Here's what I'm going to do. I'm going to offer you a chance to increase your end-of-semester grade by 5 percent." Sleepy students suddenly started waking up. A 5 percent increase on a grade is very significant. A B (85 percent) is raised to an A- (90 percent). A C (75 percent) is transformed into a B- (80 percent). And a D (65 percent) rises to a C- (70 percent).

I offered the class the possibility of a media fast. When I mentioned the media fast, I heard audible groans from some students, but everyone was listening. Each student could decide whether to take me up on the offer or not. Their participation in the fast was completely voluntary.

"Here's what you have to do. Starting this afternoon, the fast begins. No radio, no TV, no film, no CDs, no music, no Facebook, no Twitter, no Instagram—and only five minutes a day for cell phone use and email." The groans grew louder.

One sweet young woman raised her hand and asked, "Well, Dr. Hall, on Easter afternoon I always listen to two favorite praise songs."

"Nope," I replied.

Other students raised further questions about what was allowed, and I kept saying the same word: "Nope." If they were going to receive the 5 percent increase in their semester grade, they had to enter a very quiet, unfamiliar world—for nine weeks.

One student asked, "Well, Dr. Hall, how am I going to talk to my friends?"

"Like most human beings over the course of human history. You'll use your legs and your mouth." She wasn't pleased with my response. I seem to remember her rolling her eyes.

Students raised question after question, but finally we reached an agreement. Those students who maintained the media fast for nine weeks would receive a 5 percent increase on their final grade. I would rely on students' honesty but told them they would have to journal about their experience.

I didn't know what to expect. I thought maybe four or five of the 230 students might take me up on the offer. After all, nine weeks is a very long time to disengage from all social media. At the end of the semester, I discovered that forty-two students, close to 20 percent of the class, had engaged in the media fast. I was surprised and pleased.

What did they experience? Most said the first week or so was very hard. Some experienced periodic anxiety. Their world had become very quiet. Time seemed to expand.

Once two weeks had passed, most students adjusted to the fast, and the rhythms of their day significantly changed. Some students said they enjoyed it. Some said they experienced bouts of boredom. Overall, though, students reported that the fast was a positive experience.

Here are some of the outcomes I gleaned from their journaling: better sleep patterns, lower levels of anxiety, increased spiritual sensitivity, and more face-to-face time with other students. Students reported greater attentiveness to God and to their environment. Some commented that they never realized they had so much time to study!

Not all students who began the fast completed it. For some, the silence was just too difficult. Others simply missed their social media too much. But most students, even those who only fasted for a few days, felt their fast was a positive experience. I remember one student said at the end of the semester, "Dr. Hall, I'm not going to continue the fast. But I plan on occasional media fasts in the future. It really changed my life. I never realized how quiet the world can be."

Over my last few years at Eastern, we continued the media fast in Foundations of Christian Spirituality. Some students told me they took the class because they wanted to try the fast! Who would have thought? I was surprised—and pleased—to pick up a copy of the student newspaper one spring and read in large block letters on the front page: "It's that time of year again!"—a reference to the media fast that would soon begin in Foundations.

We've looked at misery markers of sick spirituality. You might be able to supply a few more from your own life experience. Let's now trace the beams of the beacon lights of healthy spiritual formation; they illuminate the path of a different way as we keep in step with Jesus.

## Beacon Lights on a Different Way

Healthy spiritual formation increases and nourishes joy and human flourishing.

Healthy spiritual formation burns grace, in Dallas Willard's wonderful phrase, "like a 747 burns fuel on take-off."[17]

Healthy spiritual formation is God-centered, not self-centered.

Healthy spiritual formation focuses its attention on the beauty and wonder of God revealed to us in Jesus.

Healthy spiritual formation assumes a posture of open hands and open heart, eager to receive the abundance God longs to give.

Healthy spiritual formation refreshes and exhilarates.

Healthy spiritual formation focuses on training, not trying.[18]

Healthy spiritual formation links arms with Jesus, the image of the invisible God, the firstborn over all creation (cf. Col. 1:15–20), and joyfully keeps step with him into the future in the power of the Spirit.

Healthy spiritual formation never judges others and refuses to condemn.

## Truckloads of Grace

All spiritual growth begins with grace, is nurtured by grace, and reaches maturity through grace. Spiritual formation is not a self-help program for change. Indeed, the spiritually formed image-bearer has already admitted that she needs truckloads of grace from outside the self if lasting change is ever to occur. Or, to change metaphors, if we ever switch off the grace switch, we're in trouble. We'll quickly run out of power.

Understanding the dynamics of grace is tricky business. Why? Image-bearers, especially Protestant ones, tend to equate exertion in our spiritual lives with "works righteousness." We're quick to affirm that we are saved by grace alone. Yet to practice a spiritual discipline—each one a means of grace God uses to grow us in love—involves determination, engagement, and effort. None are practiced passively. "Let go and let God" is a poor descriptor of a healthy spiritual life. Yet we earn nothing from God when we practice a spiritual discipline. We're simply growing in grace.

Henri Nouwen encourages us to view our lives with God as both a gift and a responsibility. I think he's right. "The spiritual life is a gift," Nouwen writes. "It is the gift of the Holy Spirit, who lifts us up into the kingdom of God's love. But to say that being lifted up into the kingdom of love is a divine gift does not mean that we wait passively until the gift is offered to us."[19]

Rather, Nouwen explains, Jesus encourages us "to set our hearts on the kingdom. Setting our hearts on something involves not only serious aspiration but also strong determination. A spiritual life requires human effort. The forces that keep pulling us back into a worry-filled life are far from easy to overcome."[20]

Effort in spiritual formation, though, is never divorced from grace. Healthy exertion is empowered by grace. Healthy, wise, paced effort is not the legalistic grind to gain God's approval and acceptance. Instead, it is more like the effort—and exhilaration—athletes experience as they train to run a race or play a game well.

Strong effort, immersion in grace, and wise training in our life with God generate freedom, fulfillment, exhilaration, and joy. We progressively experience lives that make sense, lives aligned with and empowered by Jesus's life and the values of his kingdom. We are keeping in step with Jesus. Exertion divorced from grace spawns frustration, discouragement, guilt, and sadness.

## An Invitation to Play in the Field of God's Grace

I've sometimes heard Christians refer to what is spiritual and what is worldly. I'm sure you have, too. Spiritual people do spiritual things and avoid worldly things. In the late nineteenth century and up through the 1950s, many Christians believed that playing cards, smoking, drinking, and going to movies were worldly activities. Today, many Christians would not consider these activities worldly, though most would agree that smoking and overdrinking can surely harm our health.

My concern is that we may mislabel perspectives and practices as worldly that actually are spiritual, and by doing so set up misery markers that do no one any good.

### Pause and Reflect

Draw a line down the center of a sheet of paper. Label the left-hand side of the line "unspiritual" and the right-hand side "spiritual." Now list perspectives and behaviors you understand to be spiritual and unspiritual in each column.

Should we be surprised that distorted and dysfunctional views

**of God affect our choices for each column? Consider the words *fun*
and *play*. Which column would you place them in? Can you imagine God having fun? Enjoying play?**

God might well love fun and play more than some spiritual people
do. Consider the millions of creatures God has created, all of them
described as "good" in the Genesis creation accounts (Gen. 1:22, 25).
A recent study estimates that the world contains 8.7 million species.
Cataloging them all would take more than a thousand years. All of
these creatures—reptiles, bugs, birds, mammals, amphibians, single-
cell creatures—are God's creation, God's delight.

God enjoys variety. God evidently likes wild things, color, teeth,
bones, blood, wings, feathers, fins, roaring, buzzing—the list of things
God enjoys seems endless. What was God thinking when he created a
zebra? A giraffe? A volcano? A star? An albatross? A lion? A cobra? A
butterfly? An ostrich? An amoeba? A platypus?

Just yesterday I enjoyed a film of dolphins frolicking with humpback
whales off the coast of Australia. By all appearances, these wondrous
creatures were simply having fun. The whales were trying to whack the
dolphins with their tails as the dolphins dodged effortlessly. Both whales
and dolphins continued the dodge-and-miss game a long time; each attempt and each miss seemed to bring delight to all. If whales can chuckle,
I'm sure they were doing so. I could hear the dolphins clicking to each
other. Were they laughing? Or cheering each other on? Why should this
surprise us? What might these frolicking creatures teach us about God?
About what God enjoys? About what God offers us to enrich our spiritual
lives and our relationship with Father, Son, and Holy Spirit?

Sadly, by circumscribing spiritual activities in too narrow a way,
we weaken, not strengthen, ourselves. I think of the many pastors and
priests who are spiritually, emotionally, and physically exhausted. They

are burning out at an unprecedented rate. Might a trip to the zoo help to reenergize them? Or a trip to the ballpark?

Fatigue weakens our resistance to temptation and other hazards of the spiritual life. Agnes Sanford writes of the pastor who fell into adultery, when all he really wanted to do was to play golf.[21] Might not God enjoy accompanying this pastor for a round of golf? Hardly, this pastor must have thought. The result? A desire to stroll down a fairway whacking a little white ball mutates into an adulterous affair, with all its accompanying carnage.

Willard warns, "To cut off the joys and pleasures associated with our bodily and social existence as 'unspiritual,' then, can actually have the effect of weakening us in our efforts to do what is right. It makes it impossible for us to see and draw strength from the goodness of rightness."[22]

## The Blessing of Childlikeness

Children—God's precious young image-bearers—love to play. A child, G. K. Chesterton comments, "kicks his legs rhythmically through excess, not absence, of life."[23] Children love to do the same thing again and again. Didn't you?

Chesterton describes children's playfulness as an inner strength given them by God. "Because children have abounding vitality, because they are in spirit fierce and free, therefore they want things repeated and unchanged. They always say, 'Do it again'; and the grown-up person does it again until he is nearly dead. For grown-up people are not strong enough to exult in monotony."[24]

Our imaginations, affections, and appetites, so lively in us as children, too often shrivel as we grow older. "I've matured," we say to ourselves. "I'm more focused on important things. I don't have time for fun and play."

Happily, such is not the case with God. I simply offer the zoo, wildflowers, or a clear night sky as empirical proof. God's idea of what is important, delightful, or fun is constantly displayed before us, if only we have eyes to see.

"It is possible," Chesterton writes, "that God says every morning, 'Do it again' to the sun; and every evening, 'Do it again' to the moon. It may not be automatic necessity that makes all daisies alike; it may be that God makes every daisy separately, but has never got tired of making them. It may be that He has the eternal appetite of infancy; for we have sinned and grown old, and our Father is younger than we."[25] Sadly, as we grow older, we learn to hide, our faces disguising the true state of affairs within us.

Not so with children. Willard comments that a "child's face is a constant epiphany," because a child has not yet learned to hide. "It cannot manage its face." Willard comments that those "who have attained considerable spiritual stature are frequently noted for their 'childlikeness.' What this really means is that they do not use their face and body to hide their spiritual reality. In their body they are genuinely present to those around them. That is a great spiritual attainment or gift."[26]

### Pause and Reflect

**What do you like to do simply because it's fun? What brings you joy? In what ways have you grown too old? What steps can you take toward fun and play with God as your friend, your playmate? How might God be offering you "the eternal appetite of infancy"?**

## A Relationship, Not a Task

Healthy spiritual formation is deeply relational in character. As we learn to love, we're engaging in a process of maturation that feeds off the life and love of God, the communion of love that is the Trinity: Father, Son, and Holy Spirit. "God is love," the apostle John writes. "Whoever lives in love lives in God, and God in them" (1 John 4:16). Every characteristic of God—from God's righteousness to God's wrath—manifests God's love as the facets of a diamond reflect light.

God's essence as Father, Son, and Holy Spirit is immensely, unimaginably, incomprehensibly relational. Why should we be surprised, then, that spiritual growth into the image of the incarnate Son is fundamentally relational in nature? Hence, the spiritual disciplines— the means of grace God uses to grow us into Christ's image—are also deeply relational in character.

Think of the five disciplines we have studied together in this book: prayer, meditation on Scripture, silence and solitude, simplicity, and confession. Each is relational in nature.

In petitionary and intercessory prayer, I'm loving other precious image-bearers through my prayers.

I meditate on the Scripture to deepen my relationship with God and others, some who lived hundreds of years before me. Gradually I get to know Abraham, Ruth, Mary, Peter, John, Paul, or other biblical characters. As I do so my relationship with Jesus matures. And I bring what I learn in meditation into my modern context and the relationships I experience there.

In silence and solitude, I am with God, not away from God. And what I learn in silence and solitude I bring back into my relationships with others.

In simplicity, I learn to live in a manner that brings health and safety, wisdom and love, to others. My relationship to the earth, to the poor, and to my neighbor deepens as I practice simplicity.

In confession, I name my sin against God and others for what it is. I seek to make restitution to those I may have harmed. I begin anew to learn to love.

In a word, my spiritual formation is related to yours, and yours to mine, and ours to the relational communion of the Holy Trinity. Spiritual formation is always deeply relational.

## The Slowest of All Human Movements

Some things just take time, and spiritual formation is one of them. It can't be rushed. Imagine a five-year-old child wishing she was fifteen. Wish though she might, fifteen is still ten years away. A thirty-year-old baby Christian, just starting out in his relationship with Christ, might long to have the depth and wisdom of someone who's been walking with Jesus on a different way for forty years, but the wish is no more realistic than that of our five-year-old child. As a wise mentor told me some thirty-five years ago, "Chris, spiritual formation is the slowest of all human movements."

I remember how relieved I was to hear this wise word, for things were taking so long! Was there something wrong with me? *Surely*, I remember thinking, *I should be beyond this sinful habit or character flaw by now. After all, I've been working on this for three months!* When I learned that spiritual formation is a very, very slow process, I embraced the freedom to be patient with myself—and with others.

Just as there are specific times, seasons, and rhythms for physical growth, the same is true for spiritual growth. Almost every character we encounter in the pages of the Bible grows over years, not over days or months, and many seem unaware that any growth is occurring.

Think of Abraham, Jacob, or David. The growth they experienced occurred over long stretches of time—lengthy periods peppered with extremely difficult circumstances and challenges. Abraham learns to wait for a promised child, a waiting that stretches and deepens his character. Jacob starts out as a pampered deceiver and spends years away from home growing up. Only after a very long time does Jacob grow into his new name, Israel. David triumphs over Goliath as a very young man, then spends the rest of his life learning about God—and himself. At the end of David's life there is still much growth that needs to occur. All three of these men grew in their lifelong relationship with God, but the pattern of growth was slow, arduous, painful, and sometimes discouraging.

This pattern remains true for us. The Lord knows us better than we know ourselves. He knows the weak spots, the recurring temptations, the sinful habits, the roadblocks to love. He perceives a destination and a transformation for each of us that we rarely discern clearly. Because we're so directly involved, it's hard for us to spot where and when the growing is happening. Thus the importance of patience, with ourselves and with God.

I remember a conversation I had with a friend who had not seen me for a long stretch. She had known me with I first started my relationship with Jesus, and when we crossed paths a few years later, she spotted growth I had never noticed.

"You've changed," she said in the course of our conversation.

"Really?" I asked somewhat skeptically.

"Oh, yes. Now you can love. When I first met you, you couldn't." Her words encouraged me and gave me hope.

So, as you keep in step with Christ on a different way, be patient with yourself. Small, slow steps with Jesus do add up.

## Love as the Means, the Way, and the Goal

Our journey together on a different way has drawn to a close, at least in the pages of this book. As I say good-bye, one last reminder that love is the principal means of spiritual growth, the mark of a maturing Christian, and the goal toward which we are called by the Holy Trinity.

We grow by loving, and every spiritual discipline helps us to love more deeply. As we keep in step with Jesus, we look more and more like him, think more and more like him, and act more and more like him, for we are his precious image-bearers. Our footsteps match his ever more faithfully. We stumble fewer times. By God's grace, people see him in us, and are blessed in the seeing. For Jesus is the greatest lover in the universe.

As we continue our pilgrimage with Christ into the future, our love grows and matures. For we are finite creatures, and our traveling companion is both human and divine. Jesus's love, like that of the Father and the Spirit, is boundless; it is infinite. When a finite image-bearer travels with the incarnate Son, our capacity to give and receive love continues to expand. This is what the future holds for us—each moment a new taste of God's immense, intense love—and the pathway to this wonder and beauty is a different way.

# Acknowledgments

In *A Different Way*, I emphasize that spiritual formation is deeply relational, and with the book's completion, I want to acknowledge the
relationships that formed me, grew me, nourished me, and stretched me.

I look back over seventy-two years and am thankful for the many
people who not only prayed for me when I was a young man, but those
many folks who served as mentors across the years. I think of my dad—
not a deeply spiritual man—but whose influence is plain in *A Different
Way*. My mom, a troubled soul in some ways, prayed for me and taught
me about God as best as she could. There is Uncle Bob, Aunt Ern, and
Aunt Helen, tremendous models of love and care. Uncle Bob's mentor-
ing steered me straight when I was prone to wander. My hope is that all
five of these folks—four of whom have left this earth—will somehow
be aware of what I've written.

Special mentors and friends come to mind from my school days at
UCLA and for years afterward: Bill Counts, Linus Morris, and Gary
Edmonds. How I miss you, Monds. Your death left a hole in my heart.
Thanks to Vince Leong for being my pal, and to Rod Stiling, Ralph
McCall, Randy Beck, and Jeff Farrar. Linus and Sharon Morris, Gary
and Tricia Edmonds, and Debbie and I traveled to France to plant a
church, an experience that left an indelible mark on my soul.

Other friends from our years in France come to mind, all of whom helped to form me spiritually: Daphne and Merlin Skredvedt, George and Alison Mills, Daphne and Richard Minchin, Trevor and Dorothy Davies, and Margine and Joe Smolik. Sadly, some have passed into eternity. How hard these partings are. I look forward to happy reunions.

I think, too, of Ward and Laurel Gasque, Jim Packer, and Jim Houston, who all took me under their wings at Regent College. It was Jim who said to me, "It's impossible to grow spiritually without friends." When I travel to Vancouver, I think of them. Other Canadian friends come to mind: Nancy and Ken Morrison have been dear mentors and friends. Dan and Tim MacIntosh are valued pals and continue to speak love and wisdom into my life. Dan and Tim's dad and mom, Cam and Kay MacIntosh, offered deep fellowship over many a meal.

At Drew University I met Tom Oden. He has had a tremendous effect on my life, both as a mentor and a friend. It was Tom who said to me, "Chris, a spiritual life without some form of asceticism is impossible." A group of other friends coalesced around Tom's life at Drew University and later in Oklahoma City. I'm thankful for them all: Roberta and Howard Ahmanson, Steve Ferguson, Mike Glerup, and Joel Elowsky. Thanks to each of you. You all have formed and encouraged me. Lamin Sanneh and Tite Tienou bring a smile to my face. We miss you, Lamin.

During my Drew University years I met fellow graduate student Joe Modica, who went on to become the chaplain at Eastern University. Our friendship has lasted many years, and I'm glad.

Of course, there is the Renovaré crew and folks from the Dallas Willard Center at Westmont. Dallas Willard's writing helped me immensely. Unfortunately, he died before I could know him personally. Thankfully, Jane Willard, Becky Heatley, Gayle Beebe, and Gary Moon have been able to fill the gap. In other ways Gary's counsel and friendship, along with that of Regina, Gary's wife, has been invaluable. Richard J. Foster's writings, life, and friendship have meant much to me. John Ortberg's writing has helped me profoundly. It has been a joy getting to know John over the past few years. Rebecca de Young's mind and heart are a gift to me. She is a model of courage and perseverance. James Catford has offered wise counsel and generous prayers. Juanita and Rudy Rasmus and Richella Parham have helped me in many ways. Tina Dyer, Siang-Yang Tan, Ted Harro, Brian Kang, Margaret and Justin Campbell, Glandion and Marian Carney, Linda Christians, Rhonda Ward and the Houston group, and Donn and Lavaughn Thomas have been folks who have prayed for me for a long time. Mimi Dixon has been a wise counselor and dear friend. Lacy Borgo has a special place in my heart, as does Trevor Hudson. And then there is the Renovaré staff, with whom I had the privilege of working for seven years. I gladly dedicated this book to them.

I think, too, of my friends at Eastern University over twenty-four years. Time spent with presidents Roberta Hestenes, David Black, Bob Duffett, and Ron Matthews was invaluable in my spiritual formation. Other names come to mind: Kent Sparks, Margaret and Dwight Peterson, Derek Ritchie, Chip Olson, Mark Wagner, and Ron Evans. Dinners with Duffy and Maggy Robbins and Joe and Marianne Modica continue to feed my tummy, and my soul. Steve Boyer was and is a valued counselor and gifted theologian. My friendships with Shane Claiborne and Jonathan Wilson-Hartgrove began at Eastern and continue strong today.

Special thanks to Mickey Maudlin at HarperOne for encouraging me to write this book and shepherding it home. I'm grateful.

All these precious image-bearers have been the scaffolding for the Holy Spirit's work in my life. The scaffolding is built on a strong foundation, my family. Where would I be without Debbie? We are now in our forty-eighth year of marriage. She keeps me centered and on course along with my kids and kids-in-law: Nathan, Michelle, and Vinny;

Nathalie, Sean, and Stella; and Josh. They are the compass that guides me on a different way with Jesus. I love them very much.

Each person I've mentioned has played a role in my spiritual formation. They have all journeyed with me on *A Different Way* with Jesus, and I'm glad.

# Notes

## Introduction

1. Dan White Jr. writes that "experts call the era we are experiencing VUCA; one that is volatile, uncertain, complex, and ambiguous. These four conditions combine to create a situation of mass anxiety, the kind of which we (at least for those of us living in the West) have not experienced for a long, long time. The last time we experienced significant levels of VUCA was probably between the two world wars, and it accelerated the ideologically driven search for a stable moral and social order. The net result was World War II. There are real similarities to our current times; we are now living in instability because everything is now wired and connected, and now fear can go viral." *Love over Fear: Facing Monsters, Befriending Enemies, and Healing Our Polarized World* (Chicago: Moody, 2019), 9.

## Chapter One: Reject Distorted Views of God

1. David Bentley Hart, *That All Shall Be Saved: Heaven, Hell, and Universal Salvation* (New Haven, CT: Yale Univ. Press, 2019), 40–41.

2. Trevor Hudson, *Discovering Our Spiritual Identity* (Downers Grove, IL: InterVarsity Press, 2010), 14.

3. *Foundations of Christian Spirituality* was filmed in 2008 and is available for viewing on the Renovaré website (renovare.org) and on YouTube. It was filmed by Gorilla Films, the same company known for its films of the gorillas of Rwanda.

4. Hudson, *Discovering Our Spiritual Identity*, 14.

5. Hudson, *Discovering Our Spiritual Identity*, 14.

6. All biblical quotations are from the New International Version. Any italics are mine.

7. This rewriting of the parable of the prodigal son can be found in Philip Yancey's wonderful book *What's So Amazing about Grace* (Grand Rapids, MI: Zondervan, 1997), 49–51. Used by permission of Harper-Collins Christian Publishing.

## Chapter Two: Learn to Live in an In-Between Time

1. Gordon Fee and Douglas Stuart, *How to Read the Bible for All Its Worth*, 4th ed. (Grand Rapids, MI: Zondervan, 2014), 161.

2. Fee and Stuart, *How to Read*, 150. Fee and Stuart's explanation of the dynamic of the kingdom is extremely helpful, and I will be drawing on their insights.

3. Fee and Stuart, *How to Read*, 151. My emphasis.

4. Fee and Stuart, *How to Read*, 151. My emphasis.

5. Fee and Stuart, *How to Read*, 151.

6. N. T. Wright, *How God Became King* (San Francisco: HarperOne, 2012), 223.

7. Stanley Hauerwas, *Matthew* (Grand Rapids, MI: Brazos Press, 2006), 56.

8. This quotation is found in Richard J. Foster, *Celebration of Discipline: The Path to Spiritual Growth* (San Francisco: HarperOne, 2018), 126. The original reference is not given.

9. Foster, *Celebration of Discipline*, 127–28.

10. Fee and Stuart, *How to Read*, 151.

11. Fee and Stuart, *How to Read*, 152.

12. Fee and Stuart, *How to Read*, 153.

13. Fee and Stuart, *How to Read*, 153.

## Chapter Three: Live Well amid a Cosmic Struggle

1. The phrase "We are not what we were meant to be" comes from Plantinga. Cornelius Plantinga Jr., *Not the Way It's Supposed to Be: A Breviary of Sin* (Grand Rapids, MI: Eerdmans, 1995), 30–31, 33.

2. Ashley Cocksworth, "Sabbatical Contemplation," in John H. Coe and Kyle C. Strobel, eds., *Embracing Contemplation* (Downers Grove, IL: IVP Academic, 2019), 90.

3. The phrase "negative force field" is Lovelace's. Richard Lovelace, *Dynamics of Spiritual Life: An Evangelical Theology of Renewal* (Downers Grove, IL: InterVarsity Press, 1979), 94.

4. Lovelace, *Dynamics of Spiritual Life*, 93.

5. Lovelace, *Dynamics of Spiritual Life*, 93.

6. Quoted in Pete Greig, *How to Pray: A Simple Guide for Normal People* (Colorado Springs, CO: NavPress, 2019), 192. Cf. Helmut Thielicke, "Deliver Us from Evil," *The Prayer that Spans the World: Sermons on the Lord's Prayer* (Cambridge: Lutterworth, 2016), 84–94.

7. Francis MacNutt, *Deliverance from Evil Spirits: A Practical Manual* (Grand Rapids, MI: Chosen Books, 1995), 260.

8. Charles de Foucauld, *Writings Selected with an Introduction by Robert Ellsberg* (Maryknoll, NY: Orbis Books, 1999), 81.

9. Lovelace, *Dynamics of Spiritual Life*, 94.

10. I am here drawing on material from Christopher A. Hall, *Living Wisely with the Church Fathers* (Downers Grove, IL: IVP Academic, 2017), 56–57. Used by permission of IVP.

11. Walter Wink quoted in MacNutt, *Deliverance from Evil Spirits*, 9.

12. C. S. Lewis, *The Screwtape Letters* (San Francisco: HarperSanFrancisco, 2001), ix.

13. Michael Casey, *Fully Human, Fully Divine: An Interactive Christology* (Liguori, MO: Liguori/Triumph, 2004), 66.

14. Greig, *How to Pray,* 202.

15. Book of Common Prayer, Collect for November 16, 236.

## Chapter Four: Work at What You're Not Good At

1.  Dallas Willard, *The Spirit of the Disciplines: Understanding How God Changes Lives* (San Francisco: Harper & Row, 1988), 63.

2.  The English noun *Docetism* is related to the Greek verb *dokeo,* "to seem."

3.  Gregory of Nazianzus, "Letter to Cledonius Against Apollinaris," Epistle 101, in *Christology of the Later Fathers,* ed. Edward R. Hardy (Philadelphia: Westminster Press, 1954), 218.

4.  This is a major point Dallas Willard made again and again.

5.  Willard, *Spirit of the Disciplines,* 29.

6.  Willard, *Spirit of the Disciplines,* 168.

7.  I am drawing on the excerpts from Chrysostom's sermon found in *Devotional Classics.* John Chrysostom, "Sermon on Dying to Sin," in Richard J. Foster and James Bryan Smith, eds., *Devotional Classics,* rev. ed. (San Francisco: HarperSanFrancisco, 2005), 309–12.

8.  Chrysostom, "Sermon on Dying to Sin," in Foster and Smith, *Devotional Classics,* 310.

9.  Chrysostom, "Sermon on Dying to Sin," in Foster and Smith, *Devotional Classics,* 309–12

10. Thomas Merton, "Excerpts from *Contemplative Prayer,*" in Foster and Smith, *Devotional Classics,* 67–68.

## Chapter Five: Keep in Step with Jesus in Your Gift of Years

1.  Dallas Willard, *The Great Omission* (HarperOne: San Francisco, 2006), 215.

2. Chrysostom, quoted in Joel C. Elowsky, ed., *John 11–21*, Ancient Christian Commentary on Scripture, New Testament (Downers Grove, IL: InterVarsity Press, 2007), 4b:386.

3. Ambrose, quoted in Elowsky, John 11–21, 4b:386.

4. Cyril of Alexandria quote in Elowsky, *John 11–21*, 4b:389.

5. Theodore of Mopsuestia quoted in Elowsky, *John 11–21*, 4b:387.

6. Romanus Melodus quoted in Elowsky, *John 11–21*, 4b:388.

7. Jerome quoted in Elowsky, *John 11–21*, 4b:391.

8. Augustine quoted in Elowsky, *John 11–21*, 4b:391.

9. Genevieve Carlton, "Legendary Pastors Who Fell from Grace," Ranker, September 12, 2021, https://www.ranker.com/list/pastors -that-fell-from-grace/genevieve-carlton.

10. Richard J. Foster, *Money, Sex, and Power: The Challenge of the Disciplined Life* (London: Hodder & Stoughton Ltd, 2009), 1.

## Chapter Six: Read Christ into Your Heart

1. The title of this chapter is taken from my essay "Reading Christ into the Heart," found in *Life in the Spirit: Spiritual Formation in Theological Perspective*, ed. Jeffrey P. Greenman and George Kalantzis (Downers Grove, IL: IVP Academic, 2010), 141–59. This chapter builds upon ideas found in that essay. I've also added significant new material.

2. Jean Leclercq, *The Love of Learning and the Desire for God* (New York: Fordham Univ. Press, 1982), 17.

3. Eugene Peterson, *Eat This Book: A Conversation in the Art of Spiritual Reading* (Grand Rapids, MI: Eerdmans, 2006), 90. The quote is from Hebrews 12:1.

4. The von Hügel and Rilke examples come from Peterson, *Eat This Book*, 3–4.

5. Peterson, *Eat This Book*, 1–2.

6. Peterson, *Eat This Book*, 2.

7. Leclercq, *Love of Learning*, 15.

8. Michael Casey, *Sacred Reading: The Ancient Art of Lectio Divina* (Liguori, MO: Triumph, 1995), 4.

9. Henri J. M. Nouwen, excerpted in Richard J. Foster and James Bryan Smith, eds., *Devotional Classics*, rev. ed. (San Francisco: Harper-SanFrancisco, 2005), 81.

10. John Ortberg, *The Life You Always Wanted: Spiritual Disciplines for Ordinary People* (Grand Rapids, MI: Zondervan, 2002), 188. John's thoughts and writing have helped me in many ways across the years. He is a blessing.

11. Nouwen, excerpted in Foster and Smith, *Devotional Classics*, 81.

12. Peterson, *Eat This Book*, 90.

13. Casey, *Sacred Reading*, 39.

14. A comment from Bishop Robert Barron I heard on the app Hallow as Barron explained the dynamics of the rosary.

15. Gary Haugen, for instance, and folks at the International Justice Mission have regular times of prayer throughout the day, much like the monastic hours. The welding of a rich inner life and social justice led to the insights and actions you'll find in this limited bibliography. Bryan Stevenson, *Just Mercy: A Story of Justice and Redemption* (New York: Spiegel and Grau, 2015); Gary Haugen, *Just Courage: God's Great Expedition for the Restless Christian* (Downers Grove, IL: InterVarsity Press, 2008); Ronald J. Sider, *Rich Christians in an Age of Hunger: A Biblical Study* (Downers Grove, IL: InterVarsity Press, 1978); Justin Welby, *Dethroning Mammon: Making Money Serve Grace—The Archbishop of Canterbury's Lent Book—2017* (London: Bloomsbury, 2016); Jonathan Wilson-Hartgrove, *New Monasticism: What It Has to Say to Today's Church* (Grand Rapids, MI: Brazos Press, 2008); Jonathan Wilson-Hartgrove, *The Wisdom of Stability: Rooting Faith in a Mobile Culture* (Brewster, MA: Paraclete Press, 2010); Lisa Sharon Harper, *Fortune: How Race Broke My Family and the World—and How to Repair It All* (Grand Rapids, MI: Brazos Press, 2022); Rutba House, ed., *School(s) for Conversion: Twelve Marks of a New Monasticism* (Eugene, OR: Cascade Books, 2005); Shane Claiborne and Chris Haw, *Jesus for President* (Grand Rapids, MI: Zondervan, 2008); Shane Claiborne and Jonathan Wilson-Hartgrove, *Becoming the Answer to Our Prayers: Prayer for Ordinary Radicals* (Downers Grove, IL: Inter-

Varsity Press, 2008); Jonathan Wilson-Hartgrove, *God's Economy: Redefining the Health and Wealth Gospel* (Grand Rapids, MI: Zondervan, 2009); Shane Claiborne, *Executing Grace: How the Death Penalty Killed Jesus and Why It's Killing Us* (San Francisco: HarperOne, 2016); Shane Claiborne, Jonathan Wilson-Hartgrove, and Enuma Okoro, *Common Prayer: A Liturgy for Ordinary Radicals* (Grand Rapids, MI: Zondervan, 2010).

16. John Perkins, *Parting Words to the Church on Race* (Chicago: Moody Press, 2018); Shane Claiborne and John M. Perkins, *Follow Me to Freedom: Leading and Following as an Ordinary Radical* (Ventura, CA: Regal, 2009); Martin Luther King Jr., *Strength to Love* (Philadelphia: Fortress Press, 1981); Christena Cleveland, *Disunity in Christ* (Downers Grove, IL: InterVarsity Press, 2013); Barbara L. Peacock, *Soul Care in African American Practice* (Downers Grove, IL: InterVarsity Press, 2020); Willie Jennings, *The Christian Imagination: Theology and the Origins of Race* (New Haven, CT: Yale Univ. Press, 2010); Dorothy Day, *Selected Writings,* ed. Robert Ellsberg (Maryknoll, NY: Orbis Books, 2005); Natasha Sistrunk Robinson, *A Sojourner's Truth: Choosing Freedom and Courage in a Divided World* (Downers Grove, IL: InterVarsity Press, 2018); Elizabeth Conde-Frazier, S. Steve Kang, and Gary A. Parrett, *A Multi-Colored Kingdom: Multicultural Dynamics for Spiritual Formation* (Grand Rapids, MI: Baker Academic, 2004); Samuel Escobar, *The New Global Mission: The Gospel from Everywhere to Everyone* (Downers Grove, IL: InterVarsity Press, 2003); Orlando Costas, *Christ Outside the Gate: Mission and Christendom* (Eugene: Wipf & Stock, 2005).

17. Casey, *Sacred Reading*, 39.

18. Casey, *Sacred Reading*, 17.

19. *Homilies on Acts* 9.1, 4.3, quoted in Margaret Mitchell, *The Heavenly Trumpet: John Chrysostom and the Art of Pauline Interpretation* (Louisville, KY: Westminster John Knox Press, 2002), 71. My emphasis.

20. Mitchell, *The Heavenly Trumpet*, 71.

21. Peterson, *Eat This Book*, 99.

22. Leclercq, *Love of Learning*, 16–17.

23. I've found this phrase to be very helpful. I first ran across it in Joyce Huggett's book *Learning to Listen to God* (Downers Grove, IL: InterVarsity Press, 1986), 171–72.

24. A prayer I learned from Mimi Dixon, a Renovaré ministry team member.

## Chapter Seven: Commune and Communicate with God

1. Merton quotes in Richard J. Foster and James Bryan Smith, eds., *Devotional Classics* (San Francisco: HarperSanFrancisco, 1993), 68.

2. Brian Doyle, "The Long of Our Legs," in *So Very Much the Best of Us: Songs of Praise in Prose* (Chicago: ACTA Publications, 2015), 220–21.

3. The story comes from Anthony Bloom, *Beginning to Pray* (New York/Mahwah, NJ: Paulist Press, 1970), 48–49. I have paraphrased from Bloom's story.

4. Richard J. Foster, *Prayer: Finding the Heart's True Home* (San Francisco: HarperSanFrancisco, 1992), 180.

5. Here I am drawing on ideas the reader can find further developed in my book *The Mystery of God*. Steven D. Boyer and Christopher A. Hall, *The Mystery of God: Theology for Knowing the Unable* (Grand Rapids, MI: Baker Academic, 2012), 71–75.

6. Foster, *Prayer*, 181.

7. C. S. Lewis, *Letters to Malcolm: Chiefly on Prayer* (New York: Harcourt Brace Javanovich, 1964), 23.

8. Lewis, *Letters to Malcolm*, 40.

9. Lewis, *Letters to Malcolm*, 58.

10. Forsythe is quoted by Foster in *Prayer*, 182.

11. You can also find Reba's story in Christopher A. Hall, *Worshiping with the Church Fathers* (Downers Grove, IL: IVP Academic, 2009), 162–65. Used with permission from IVP Academic.

12. Lewis, *Letters to Malcolm*, 28.

13. I have also told the story of Nathalie and the snowstorm in Hall, *Worshiping with the Church Fathers*, 160. Used with permission from IVP Academic.

14. I also tell the story of Rachel—not her real name—in Hall, *Worshiping with the Church Fathers,* 166–69. Used with permission from IVP Academic.

15. I also share this experience in France in Hall, *Worshiping with the Church Fathers,* 160–62. Used with permission from IVP Academic.

16. Abba Agathon is quoted in Everett Ferguson, *Inheriting Wisdom: Readings for Today from Ancient Christian Writers* (Peabody, MA: Hendrickson, 2004), 248.

17. John Cassian, *The Conferences,* trans. Boniface Ramsey, Ancient Christian Writers 57 (New York: Newman, 1997), 8.5:377. I have slightly modified the translation.

18. Cassian, *Conferences,* 3.4:331.

19. Patrick Henry Reardon, *Christ in the Psalms* (Ben Lomond: Conciliar, 2000), 65.

## Chapter Eight: Slow Down, Quiet Down

1. Joyce Huggett, *The Joy of Listening to God: Hearing the Many Ways God Speaks to Us* (Downers Grove, IL: InterVarsity Press, 1986), 71–72.

2. Neil Postman, *Amusing Ourselves to Death: Public Discourse in the Age of Show Business* (New York: Penguin Books, 1986), 155–56.

3. C. S. Lewis, *The Screwtape Letters* (San Francisco: HarperSanFrancisco, 2001), 59.

4. Lewis, *Screwtape Letters,* 59–60.

5. Huggett, *Joy of Listening to God,* 171–72.

6. Huggett, *Joy of Listening to God,* 171.

7. Mary Pipher, *The Shelter of Each Other: Rebuilding Our Families* (New York: Ballantine Books, 1996), 90.

8. Richard J. Foster, *Celebration of Discipline: The Path to Spiritual Growth* (San Francisco: HarperOne, 2018), 15.

9. Lewis, *Screwtape Letters,* 120.

10. John Ortberg, *The Life You Always Wanted: Spiritual Disciplines for Ordinary People* (Grand Rapids, MI: Zondervan, 2002), 81.

11. Rosemary K. M. Sword and Philip Zimbardo, "Hurry Sickness: Is the Quest to Do All and Be All Costing Us Our Health," *The Time Cure* (blog), *Psychology Today*, February 9, 2013, https://www.psychology today.com/us/blog/the-time-cure/201302/hurry-sickness.

12. Sword and Zimbardo, "Hurry Sickness."

13. Ortberg, *Life You Always Wanted*, 76.

14. Juanita Rasmus, *Learning to Be: Finding Your Center After the Bottom Falls Out* (Downers Grove, IL: InterVarsity Press, 2020), 8.

15. Rasmus, *Learning to Be*, 122.

16. Rasmus, *Learning to Be*, 123.

17. I am indebted to Parker Palmer for describing the desert as a "learning space." That's exactly what it was. Parker J. Palmer, *To Know as We Are Known: Education as a Spiritual Journey* (San Francisco: HarperOne, 1993), 69.

18. Palmer, *To Know as We Are Known*, 69.

19. Basil quoted in Tito Colliander, *Way of the Ascetics: The Ancient Tradition of Discipline and Inner Growth* (Crestwood, NY: St Vladimir's Seminary Press, 1985), 28.

20. Thomas Merton, *The Wisdom of the Desert* (New York: New Directions Publishing, 1970), 3.

## Chapter Nine: Keep in Step with Jesus by Living More Simply

1. I ran across this insight in Richard J. Foster, *Study Guide for Celebration of Discipline* (San Francisco: HarperOne, 1983), loc. 644, Kindle.

2. John Ortberg, *The Life You Always Wanted* (Grand Rapids, MI: Zondervan, 1997, 2002), 168.

3. Richella Parham, *Mythical Me: Finding Freedom from Constant Comparison* (Downers Grove, IL: InterVarsity Press, 2019), 23.

4. Parham, *Mythical Me*, 28.

5. Foster, *Study Guide for Celebration of Discipline*, loc. 653.

6. Foster, *Study Guide for Celebration of Discipline*, loc. 653. My emphasis.

7. Antony DeMello, *One Minute Wisdom* (New York: Doubleday, 1988), 91; quoted in Belden Lane, *The Solace of Fierce Landscapes: Exploring Desert and Mountain Spirituality* (New York: Oxford Univ. Press, 1998), loc. 1228, Kindle.

8. The Williams quotation is found in Ortberg, *Life You Always Wanted*, 177.

9. Foster, *Study Guide for Celebration of Discipline*, loc. 644.

10. Ortberg, *Life You Always Wanted*, 168.

11. Richard J. Foster, *Celebration of Discipline: The Path to Spiritual Growth* (San Francisco: HarperOne, 2018), 130.

12. Foster, *Study Guide for Celebration of Discipline*, loc. 637.

13. Foster, *Celebration of Discipline*, 90.

14. Foster, *Celebration of Discipline*, 90.

15. Foster, *Celebration of Discipline*, 90–91.

16. Foster, *Celebration of Discipline*, 93.

## Chapter Ten: Confess What Is in Your Heart

1. Dietrich Bonhoeffer, *Life Together* (New York: Harper & Row, 1952), 118; quoted in Richard J. Foster, *Celebration of Discipline: The Path to Spiritual Growth* (San Francisco: HarperOne, 2018), 154.

2. Foster, *Celebration of Discipline*, 155.

3. John Chrysostom, "Sermon on Dying to Sin," in Richard J. Foster and James Bryan Smith, eds., *Devotional Classics*, rev. ed. (San Francisco: HarperSanFrancisco, 2005), 311.

4. "Whopping plank" comes from Stephen Sondheim's musical *Godspell*.

5. Owen Chadwick, ed., *Western Asceticism* (Philadelphia: Westminster Press, 1958), 102–3.

6. Chadwick, *Western Asceticism*, 68–69.

7.  Robert J. Wicks, *Crossing the Desert: Learning to Let Go, See Clearly, and Live Simply* (Notre Dame, IN: Sorin Books, 2007), 6–7.

8.  Wicks, *Crossing the Desert*, 7.

9.  Chadwick, *Western Asceticism*, 63. I have slightly modified the some-what stilted translation for readers unfamiliar with desert literature.

10. George Buttrick, Prayer, quoted in Foster and Smith, *Devotional Classics*, 88–89.

## Chapter Eleven: Count It All Joy

1.  Dallas Willard, *The Spirit of the Disciplines: Understanding How God Changes Lives* (San Francisco: Harper & Row, 1988), 81.

2.  Francis de Sales, *Introduction to the Devout Life*, excerpted in Richard J. Foster and James Bryan Smith, eds., *Devotional Classics*, rev. ed. (San Francisco: HarperSanFrancisco, 2005), 27.

3.  de Sales, *Introduction to the Devout Life*, excerpted in Foster and Smith, *Devotional Classics*, 27.

4.  de Sales, *Introduction to the Devout Life*, excerpted in Foster and Smith, *Devotional Classics*, 26–27.

5.  de Sales, *Introduction to the Devout Life*, excerpted in Foster and Smith, *Devotional Classics*, 26–27.

6.  de Sales, *Introduction to the Devout Life*, excerpted in Foster and Smith, *Devotional Classics*, 26–27.

7.  Thomas Merton, *Contemplative Prayer*, excerpted in Foster and Smith, *Devotional Classics*, 67.

8.  Merton, *Contemplative Prayer*, excerpted in Foster and Smith, *Devotional Classics*, 67.

9.  Merton, *Contemplative Prayer*, excerpted in Foster and Smith, *Devotional Classics*, 67–68.

10. Merton, *Contemplative Prayer*, excerpted in Foster and Smith, *Devotional Classics*, 68.

11. I write at length about Abba Antony and the desert dwellers in my book *Worshiping with the Church Fathers* (Downers Grove, IL: IVP Academic, 2009). Occasionally I am drawing on thoughts and material you can find there. Used with permission from IVP Academic.

12. Athanasius, *The Life of Antony and the Letter to Marcellinus*, trans. Robert C. Gregg (New York: Paulist Press, 1980), 51.

13. Athanasius, *Life of Antony*, 50.

14. Richard J. Foster, *Celebration of Discipline: The Path to Spiritual Growth*, rev. ed. (San Francisco: HarperOne, 2018), x–xi.

15. Cited in Victoria Barret, "A New Label for Kids Today: The Distracted Generation," *Forbes*, November 1, 2012.

16. Foster offers a gentle media fast over seven days in *Celebration of Discipline*, xi–xii.

17. Dallas Willard, *The Great Omission: Reclaiming Jesus's Essential Teachings on Discipleship* (San Francisco: HarperOne, 2006), 62.

18. You can find this slogan on the Renovaré website, renovare.org.

19. Henri Nouwen, excerpted in Foster and Smith, *Devotional Classics*, 80.

20. Nouwen, excerpted in Foster and Smith, *Devotional Classics*, 80.

21. Agnes Sanford, *The Healing Gifts of the Spirit* (San Francisco: HarperOne, 1984), 154.

22. Dallas Willard, *The Spirit of the Disciplines: Understanding How God Changes Lives* (San Francisco: Harper & Row, 1988), 81.

23. G. K. Chesterton, *Orthodoxy* (New York: Image Books, 1959), 58.

24. Chesterton, *Orthodoxy*, 58.

25. Chesterton, *Orthodoxy*, 58.

26. Dallas Willard, *The Divine Conspiracy: Rediscovering Our Hidden Life in God* (San Francisco: HarperSanFrancisco, 1998), 76.